FRIEND *and* FOE
in the U.S. Senate

Ross K. Baker

Copley Publishing Group
Acton, Massachusetts 01720

Copyright © 1999 by Copley Publishing Group.
Printed in the United States of America

ISBN 1-58390-002-0

Library of Congress Catalog Card Number: 98-073897.

Cover: Senators Kennedy and Hatch photographed by Maureen
Keating. Reprinted by permission of Maureen Keating.

Copley Publishing Group
138 Great Road
Acton, MA 01720
800.562.2147 • Fax: 978.263.9190
E-mail: publish@copleycustom.com

This book is dedicated to
Carole, Susannah,
and Sally

CONTENTS

Preface
and
Acknowledgments

Custom dictates that a book open with elaborate acknowledgments, made especially to those people who encouraged the author to surmount all sorts of obstacles to produce the literary or scholarly triumph which follows. I would like to break from that tradition and give recognition, first, to those people who tried to discourage me from this undertaking.

When, after a year as a senate staff member, I resolved that the subject of friendships among United States senators was worthy of investigation, I tried the idea on an old friend, Howard Simons, Managing Editor of the *Washington Post*. "Howard," I said, "I think I'd like to write a book about friendships in the U.S. Senate." He looked at me scornfully and said, "It will be the shortest book ever written."

Still undaunted several months later, I encountered James L. Sundquist of the Brookings Institution. Feeling that I would receive a better reception at the hands of a fellow political scientist, I said to him, "Jim, I think I'd like to write a book about friendship in the U.S. Senate." He looked at me skeptically and said, "The word 'friendship' does not occur in the literature of political science."

It is a mark of the value which I personally place on friendship that I have borne these two old friends no ill will. However, I now have my revenge: Contrary to Howard Simons's prediction, I have not written the shortest book on record, and—Jim Sundquist notwithstanding—I offer it as the work of a political scientist.

My original intention then, in writing this book had been to limit myself to looking into the friendship of U.S. senators. But the more I learned, the more I became convinced that the positive side of interpersonal relationships, while of great interest, was insufficient to give a complete picture of the human side of this American institution.

I found it hard to confine the twenty-five present and former senators interviewed to discussing their positive feelings about colleagues. Inevitably, allusions to unfavorable relationships crept into conversations, if for no other reason than to serve as a counterpoint to the friendly expressions. This led me to expand my list of questions to encompass these negative aspects.

At this point I realized that there were senators whose personal relationships with colleagues—both positive and negative—were nominal. There have always been "loners" in the Senate. The existence of mavericks has been well noted; some of these, such as Oregon's Wayne Morse, were independent-minded people, but Morse was not a social outsider by any stretch of the imagination. It was the senator standing aloof from any personal involvement with his colleagues that piqued my imagination. Do these emotional outsiders incur any political costs from the distance that they placed between themselves and the other members? Are they as unresponsive to the professional needs of their fellow-members as they were to their companionship?

An intriguing answer to this question was provided by a Southerner who had served on a committee with one of the Senate's most renowned loners, William Proxmire of Wisconsin. He told me he had approached the brilliant but cantankerous Proxmire to enlist his support in getting a measure reported out of committee. Proxmire's response to the bill—which was of great importance to the Southerner's state—was that he would not vote affirmatively to permit it to get to the Senate floor. Despite the entreaties from the Southerner about the personal value of the bill to him and his state, the Wisconsin senator remained obdurate, saying that it was simply not the sort of measure he could support. Then, just as the vote was about to be taken, Proxmire, in the words of the Southerner, "took a walk. 'Prox' just got up and walked out of the room. Sure, I didn't get his vote, but at that point it meant as much to me that he wasn't there to vote against it. From my point of view it was a friendly gesture, and I'll never forget it."

This account reveals a great deal not only about the nature of a notorious Senate loner but about the subtlety of interpersonal relationships and accommodation in the upper chamber. Friendship may be read into the grand gestures of good fellowship by outsiders—the warm handclasp and pat on the back—but for those inside the Senate the true *beau geste* is usually less spectacular, but not less significant for its muted quality. Whether Proxmire's decision to absent himself was a thoughtful personal gesture to a colleague or merely an effort to build up credits to be drawn on in the future is difficult to say; the line between the personal and the political in the Senate is not deeply etched. If this book has any consistent point to make it is that one.

The most abiding encouragement and support for this project came from Alan Rosenthal, Director of the Eagleton Institute of Politics at Rutgers University, who was my patron and host for the two years of interviewing, research, and writing that went into it. I sold him on the idea over a corned-beef and chopped-liver combination sandwich at the Broadway Delicatessen in East Brunswick, NJ, the locale for many subsequent discussions. He encouraged me to apply for an Eagleton Institute Faculty Associateship. I would like to think that the merits of the project accounted for my being awarded the associateship, but I have no illusions about the fact that Alan, a seasoned practitioner of old-style political payoffs, worked behind the scenes on my behalf. He is a crony in the most majestic sense of the word.

When Alan abandoned me by going off on sabbatical leave, the hand-holding was taken up by Jim Watson, Deputy Director of Eagleton. I also had the good fortune, in my second year at Eagleton, to share quarters with some truly wonderful people at the Center for the American Woman and Politics who certainly had better things to do than encourage someone writing about the most thoroughly male-dominated institution in America outside of the presidency and the Supreme Court. Nonetheless, Ruth Mandel, Director, and Marilyn Johnson, Deputy Director, encouraged me. It was my additional good fortune to benefit from Marilyn's canny sociological advice, especially regarding the chapter dealing with the Senate loner ·as leader.

Surpassed by no one in generosity was the Rutgers University Research Council. Fred Main, Director of the Research Council, kept me afloat in Metroliner tickets so that I could conduct the interviews. Gerald Pomper, Chairman of the Rutgers Department of Political Science, weighed in with some very special help for which I will always be grateful.

The job of typing the manuscript fell to some very able people who cheerfully struggled through the primitive early drafts and came up with the makings of a book. Foremost among these heroic personages was Edith Saks. Others who ably shouldered the burdens were Cynthia Schultz, Anine Gerity, and Christine Lenart. Bernice "Chickie" Charwin helped by doing battle for me with the IBM repairman. Castella Ransom and Janice Phillips fed me and discreetly looked the other way while I stole soft drinks from their kitchen. They are the guardians of "Wood Lawn," the splendid nineteenth-century mansion which is home for the Eagleton Institute. The opportunity to work in such delightful surroundings was an important source of inspiration.

The unsung heroes of this book must remain forever unsung, because their anonymity was the only price they demanded for helping me. At the top of the list are, of course, the twenty-five past and present members of the U.S. Senate who consented to be interviewed. I had resolved not to rely solely on current members, in the interests of tracing interpersonal relationships in the Senate through their recent history, not just their present expression. They leveled with me, as the interview material amply demonstrates. Their frankness in discussing friendships and feuds was a source of great satisfaction to me. They dodged few questions, and on occasion said some remarkably blunt things without being prompted. Their kindness and patience has convinced me that whatever prestige the Senate has enjoyed is in large measure due to its having been host to some very remarkable people.

Whatever may be alleged about the Senate staff constituting an "invisible government" on Capitol Hill, it is clear that the institution is blessed with the service of some greatly talented men and women. The ones who helped me know who they are. They bear their anonymity with great poise and dignity. That they go nameless here does not detract from my gratitude to them.

I will also protect my sources in the journalistic fraternity. The vast majority of the newspeople I called for help gave it willingly. (There were a few who never returned my calls; if my messages are still on their spindles I will be delighted to hear from them.) One who did respond willingly was Charles Peters, Editor of the *Washington Monthly*, who generously and constructively reviewed the manuscript.

I hope that those who read this book are not only those actively practicing, studying, and analyzing politics, but also the men and women who are served by the institution which is the subject of this book. When they visit Washington for their tour of Congress and are handed a Senate seating chart by the guides, they will see one hundred small rectangles with names on them. The objective of this book is to add flesh and blood to those abstract representations, for each one signifies a human being.

INTRODUCTION
TO THE 1999 EDITION

This is a book about the inner life of the United States Senate, an institution that lends itself readily to misinterpretation. The misinterpretation comes principally from durable but obsolete labels such as "The World's Greatest Deliberative Body" or "The Club": the former suggesting a place of soaring oratory and thoughtful deliberation; the latter evoking images of a close-knit fraternal group grounded in solidarity and comradery. In reality, Senate oratory is usually more somnolent than sonorous and, far from being fraternal, the Senate sometimes borders on the fratricidal. Because the two most common shorthand terms describe a place very different from the Senate as it actually is, I resolved, some twenty years ago, to apply a corrective.

One of the most influential and respected books of its time, *U.S. Senators and Their World* by Donald R. Matthews, described a Senate that was an institution in transition. The period in the life of the Senate observed and recorded by Matthews—1947 to 1957—was the tumultuous post World War II period of The Truman Doctrine, The Marshall Plan, the foundation of NATO, the unification of the armed services, the McCarthy troubles, Korea, and *Brown v. Board of Education*. But the events of the period defined the Senate less than they did the peculiar quality of the individuals who served.

Matthews' cut-off point, 1957, was a year before one the great electoral upheavals in Senate history. The election of 1958 saw an increase of 15 in the number of seats held by the Democrats. It was the largest gain in a single election in modern history. Only the elections of 1946 and 1980 approximated it.

The election that year was not simply a partisan phenomenon in which Republicans were replaced by Democrats—although it was surely that. It was a philosophical, generational, stylistic, and regional political earthquake.

Departing with the 85th Congress were conservative Republicans such as Frederick G. Payne of Maine, Edward J. Thye of Minnesota, and George Malone of Nevada, men born in the 19th Century or at the dawn of the 20th. One notable Republican casualty among younger Republicans was suffered, not on election day, but on May 2, 1957 when Joseph R. McCarthy died.

The replacements were far different: Edmund S. Muskie for Payne in Maine, Eugene J. McCarthy for Thye in Minnesota, Frank "Ted" Moss for Malone in Utah, and William Proxmire taking the McCarthy seat in Wisconsin in a special election. These were men of the 20th Century, shaped by the Great Depression and World War II.

With the onset of the Kennedy era, the Senate changed even more radically, with rising politicians emulating the young president's style of suave tough-mindedness. Cultivating the media began to provide more of a payoff than ingratiating oneself with colleagues or demonstrating the filial piety that younger senators were once expected to show their elders.

The core of Matthews' argument was that the life of the Senate was governed by a set of norms, and that adherence to them influenced a senator's success in the chamber. But even Matthews conceded that the deference that once obliged junior members to accept the tutelage of senior members was on its way out. There were to be no more apprentice senators. Every senator would enter the chamber a journeyman.

While Matthews' words were being digested by political science students, myself among them, other political scientists like Ralph Huitt were making the case that in the Senate, one style did not fit all, and that senators as cantankerous and independent as Wisconsin's Proxmire and Oregon's Wayne Morse could also be enormously effective.

Despite the changes in personnel, myths clung to the Senate with remarkable tenacity. William S. White's *Citadel*, the foremost argument for the Senate as a club, remained an influential portrait of the institution even though it became known that White was encouraged in this particular portrait of the Senate by Majority Leader Lyndon B.

Johnson, who wanted the world to think that the Senate was directed by an "inner club" of revered elders—men subject to his manipulations.

The Senate, as Lyndon Johnson wanted us to comprehend it, was not the Senate of his successor, the gentle and taciturn Mike Mansfield. The change in the Senate had little to do with Johnson the range boss being succeeded by the pastoral Mansfield. Old senators were being replaced by young senators. Those who had voted for American entry into World War II were giving way to those who had fought in that war. Even more significant, perhaps, was the fact that senators raised in the era of convention hall oratory were giving way to senators who were learning the lessons of television.

It is true that what we now call "the media" were always part of the senators' world. Influential journalists like Frank Kent, Henry L. Stoddard, Walter Lippmann, Joseph Krock, and Drew Pearson could glorify or tarnish a senator by what they wrote in a column. But senators were learning that they could establish their own channels to the public through television, without columnists as intermediaries. One measure of the growing awareness of the importance of the media was pointed out by Stephen Hess who found that in 1960 only 31 senators employed press secretaries. In 1984, 98 senators had press secretaries.[1]

When the media that were relevant to the careers of senators consisted of a state's most influential newspaper, a handful of national journals and newsmagazines, and three broadcast networks, senators could not always get their messages out if, indeed, they cared to do so. And even when Hess was conducting his study for *The Ultimate Insiders* in the early 1980s, he could conclude that, "The media's focus on a handful of senators is the same now as it was in 1953." and that "The typical senator is a supplicant to the television networks."[2]

Since Hess's study, cable television and its multitude of channels, such as CNN, MSNBC, the arrival of the Fox Network, and the proliferation of other media have changed the equation dramatically. If a senator wants to do so, he will be heard. That some do not choose to

[1] Stephen Hess, *Live from Capitol Hill* (Washington, DC: The Brookings Institution, 1991), p. 62.

[2] Stephen Hess, *The Ultimate Insiders* (Washington, DC: The Brookings Institution, 1986), pp. 91, 88.

be heard does not mean that access has been denied them. Senators that we see on television might be there by reason of their leadership positions or their policy expertise, or even their unusual style, but not solely on account of their seniority or membership in any "inner club."

· The proliferation of media and the growth of Senate staff have created a situation in which senatorial communication has become increasingly elliptical and indirect. Senators who wish to communicate with their colleagues can do it through the medium of television, and senator-to-senator conversation has been replaced by staff-to-staff consultation. One indication of the new impersonality of the Senate is that during the "Keating Five" case in 1987, many people found it difficult to believe that five U.S. senators would actually get together in a single office with federal regulators to ask them to give preferential treatment to a contributor.

Television is not merely a device by which senators communicate with one another, or a channel that brings a senator's views to his voters or the world; it is also the costly but indispensable ingredient for election and re-election. In any senate campaign, television will be the single most expensive item since all senators must campaign statewide and every state is a media market. Some senators, like those in New Jersey, must advertise in two or three media markets, which are among the most expensive in America. One journalist who covered the tense relations between the state's two senators in the early 1990s, characterized their media rivalry as "two fannies fighting for the same stool." Senators can see media coverage as a zero-sum game in which a TV camera aimed at one of a state's two senators, will necessarily subtract from the time it will spend trained on the other. Few things are surer than that no senator likes being eclipsed by another. When that happens, relationships turn chilly.

The costs of campaigning, and not just television, but direct mail, polling, and consultants of various kinds, impose on senators the obligation to raise $16,000 a week every week of their six-year term. Time on the phone soliciting money—a task most dread—diverts senators not only from their legislative chores but from time spent with colleagues.

These trends were beginning to be felt in 1975 when I first began looking into the interpersonal relations of U.S. senators. What

prompted me to get on the track of Senate friendships was the aston-
ishing frequency with which the terms "friend" and "friendship" were
used. It was used ceremonially in floor debate to soften the sting of cut-
and-thrust debate. Prefacing an acidulous remark with the unguent
phrase, "My distinguished colleague and good friend, the junior senator from ____," was a familiar part of the Senate's tradition of courtesy.
The terms also cropped up in the eulogies for dead colleagues. But if
all there was to friendship in the Senate was ritualism and formality, a
scholar did not need to be long detained studying it.

Equally discouraging was the fact that I could find very little evidence that senators sought the company of other senators outside the
walls of the Capitol. I found some tennis partners, a small dinner
group, and prayer groups, but little of the extramural social life of
legislators of an earlier day.

It gradually dawned on me, shortly after my interviews with senators and former senators began in 1978, that the word "friend" had
an elusive quality when spoken by a U.S. senator referring to a colleague. As most commonly used by senators it had none of the implications of intimacy, self-revelation, and sharing of confidences that
ordinary people might recognize. Senate friendship was, at one and
the same time, more superficial, instrumental, and provisional than
conventional friendship. But in the institutional context of the chamber itself, it was enormously important in light of the waning importance of norms.

While *Friend and Foe in the U.S. Senate* could not, conventionally,
be categorized as part of the rational choice school of political science
scholarship, it does share with that body of literature that came to be
known as "the new institutionalism," important reservations about
the sociological approach to congressional studies—of which
Matthews' book was an example. And while I did not come right out
and characterize senators as "utility maximizers," it seemed plausible
to me that self-interest loomed large in the calculations of senators.

My interviews with senators from 1977 to 1979 convinced me that
something other than a structure of norms was providing cohesion in
an increasingly individualistic Senate. A certain type of friendship
that I characterized as "institutional kinship" seemed to be the new
order in the Senate.

What makes *Friend and Foe in the U.S. Senate* reasonably comfortable in the company of works of the rational choice school is the fact that these peculiar Senate friendships are very much the product of individual calculations by individual senators who recognize that their political objectives cannot be achieved solely on their own. Individualists, to succeed, must pursue collective action. At the same time, however, senators chafed under a set of norms imposed by others and bridled at the limitations on their freedom of action that acceptance of those norms entailed.

Beginning in the later 1970s some ingenious work by a group of political scientists provided an elision between the literature of norms and what would come to be referred to as "the new institutionalism" by suggesting that those norms that members of Congress are most apt to abide by are "general benefit norms" that redound to the good of all members rather than "limited benefit norms" that give advantage to only a few.[3]

This trend toward "universalism" was also discerned in the manner in which Congress distributed benefits in the form of projects, grants, and subsidies. In particular, the early work of Barry Weingast and Kenneth Shepsle suggested the emergence of a new environment in which members of Congress seemed to be saying, "If I don't get something, no one else will either."

While the emergence of general benefit norms and distributive universalism signalled a more democratic Congress with fewer biases towards the most influential members, it was also associated with a less-cohesive more *laissez-faire* Congress.

The loosening of the allegiances of American citizens to the political parties was paralleled, albeit less dramatically, by an attenuation of the partisan attachments of members of Congress. De-emphasis of one's party label, especially by Democrats elected in the post-Watergate class of 1974—became, for some, an ingredient of political sur-

---

[3] See: Burdett A. Loomis, "Congressional Caucuses and the Politics of Representation," in Lawrence C. Dodd and Bruce I. Oppenheimer, eds., *Congress Reconsidered,* 2d ed. (Washington, DC: CQ Press, 1981), pp. 204–220 and Norman J. Ornstein, Robert L. Peabody, and David W. Rohde, "The Changing Senate: From the 1950s to the 1970s" in Lawrence C. Dodd and Bruce I. Oppenheimer, eds., *Congress Reconsidered* (Washington, DC: CQ Press, 1981), pp. 13–30.

vival. Democrats elected in districts with little Democratic party organization and meager Democratic bases, emphasized their ability to
deliver services rather than their identification with the party and its
national programs. This "personal vote," was simultaneously liberat-
ing for the member of Congress but also intimidating.[4] Neither seeking nor having available to them the resources of a political party,
members of Congress were on their own to sink or swim. This development also contributed to the rise of individualism in Congress.

It was my contention, in *Friend and Foe in the U.S. Senate* that a corrective to the "war of every man against every man" in the Senate
was a structure of bilateral and multilateral "friendships," the most
common of which I dubbed "institutional kinship."

Unlike institutional norms which are received standards, enforced
by the frowns of disapproval of senior members, institutional kinships derive from the experience of senators and are established by
living senators for the advantage and convenience of living senators.
They depend not on tradition but on current usage. Based upon a
track record of trust derived from shared experiences, these peculiar
friendships enable senators to save time in gathering information
and cues and reduce transaction costs in their dealings with colleagues. Life in the Senate is simply easier in the company of a few
trusted colleagues who can supply cues and information on issues
with which you are unfamiliar and, of even greater importance, to
give timely warning of impending threats.

If these Senate friendships are largely utilitarian and based upon self-
interest, they are not without an element of affect even in this resolutely
individualistic institution. They can, moreover, bring together senators
of contrasting political hues in mutually-advantageous consort.

Take the case of Senators John McCain, an Arizona Republican,
and Senator John F. Kerry, a Massachusetts Democrat. Both were
Navy veterans of the Vietnam War. McCain, a Navy pilot, was shot
down over North Vietnam in October, 1967. Imprisoned in the infa-
mous "Hanoi Hilton," he was not released until March, 1973 and dur-

---

[4] See: Thomas E. Mann, *Unsafe at Any Margin* (Washington, DC: American
Enterprise Institute, 1980), and Bruce E. Cain, Morris P. Fiorina, and John A.
Ferejohn, *The Personal Vote* (Cambridge, Mass.: Harvard University Press,
1987).

ing that period suffered torture, isolation, and illness. What made his imprisonment grimmer still was the fear that some of his own countrymen were giving aid and comfort to his North Vietnamese Captors. Among those countrymen, in McCain's view, was Navy Lieutenant John F. Kerry.

In April, 1971 Kerry had been part of an anti-Vietnam War demonstration in front of the U.S. Capitol. Kerry was seen throwing away his medals and ribbons in protest over the war. Word of Kerry's action somehow reached McCain in his prison cell and he and his fellow captives regarded the gesture as traitorous.

After McCain's release and convalescence, he won a seat in the House of Representatives as a Republican and, in 1984, was asked to come to Massachusetts to make a campaign appearance on behalf of a Republican Senate candidate named Ray Shamie. McCain accepted eagerly, knowing that Shamie's Democratic rival for the seat was former Navy lieutenant John Kerry, the man who had ostentatiously discarded his medals in front of the Capitol in 1971.   Kerry defeated the candidate backed by McCain in 1984, but in 1986, McCain was elected to the U.S. Senate. In 1991, the two were appointed to the Senate Select Committee on P.O.W./M.I.A. Affairs to look into the possibility that American prisoners were still being held against their will in Southeast Asia. The two senators, so different in personality and philosophy, and personally at odds, found themselves on the same side of an issue that both cared about passionately. Under attack from relatives of prisoners and men missing in action as well as the promoters of dubious "sightings" of Americans, McCain and Kerry, in the words of one of McCain's staff members, "covered each other's backs."[5]

Based on association with the P.O.W./M.I.A. issue and serving on the same committee, common experience drew the two together in what is a classic institutional kinship: "It would never be, 'I love you, man'" between them, especially given Kerry's reserve, but events would show that their bond ran deep and wide. 'I like him,' McCain told a reporter. 'We get along very well together. The thing about the

---

[5] James Carroll, "A Friendship that Ended the War," *The New Yorker*, October 21 and 28, 1996, p. 134.

Senate is you don't socialize with anybody, [but] when we travel together to Vietnam we talk.'"[6]

Important political consequence flow from this friendship for both men. Neither will now come into the state of the other (as McCain had done in 1984) and campaign against him. When Republican Governor William Weld challenged Kerry for the Senate seat in 1996, Republican McCain was asked whether he would be coming to Massachusetts on Weld's behalf. His response was categorical: "I simply would not do such a thing. I couldn't do that . . . I'm surprised you would ask . . .Going to campaign against John Kerry is just something I wouldn't consider."[7]

While such poignant moments do not abound in the United States Senate, there are enough of them to suggest that these relationships are not isolated phenomena. What makes them even more notable than their mere existence in the bare-knuckle world of politics and what suggests that there are serious political implications to be found, rather than just anecdotal charm, is what they contribute to institutional maintenance. It is demonstrable that many of these relationships cross party lines, and whatever they may do for individuals involved, they contribute in important ways to the cohesion of the U.S. Senate.

As in the McCain-Kerry case, some of these relationships vault impressively large ideological chasms. There is no better example than the close ties forged by liberal Democrat Ted Kennedy of Massachusetts and conservative Republican Orrin Hatch of Utah.

It is their joint service on the fractious Judiciary Committee that brought together these two unlikely friends. The relationship reached a peak in 1997 with the passage of the Kennedy-Hatch Bill, a $20 billion program to encourage the states to provide health insurance for the children of poor working families whose income is not so low as to qualify them for Medicaid. The money for the program came from an increase in the tax on cigarettes.

But joint sponsorship across partisan lines in the Senate is no sure-fire way of establishing a relationship based on institutional kinship.

---

[6] Op. cit., p. 134.

[7] Ibid.

Kennedy had also sponsored legislation with Republican Nancy L. Kassebaum of Kansas to protect workers from losing health benefits when they changed jobs and to prevent insurers from denying health benefits for pre-existing health problems, but the nature of the Kennedy-Hatch and Kennedy-Kassebaum relationships are different.

Kennedy-Kassebaum is a classic institutional kinship based upon long years of common service on the Senate Labor Committee. Kennedy-Hatch has a personal dimension that lifts it above the level of the Senate's most basic form of friendship. Kennedy and Hatch are allies.

The two collaborated on AIDS legislation, on rescinding parts of the 1986 immigration bill which forbade the hiring of illegal aliens because some legal immigrants were experiencing job discrimination. But beyond their cooperation on the two committees on which they serve, Labor and Judiciary, there is considerable personal fondness between the two, to the point where it was Hatch who publicly defended Kennedy when Kennedy came under attack for being drunk and disorderly in a Washington restaurant. The two are allies, but not in the sense that Kennedy is an ally of Democrat Chris Dodd of Connecticut who is philosophically-close to him. The Kennedy-Hatch alliance is more selective. What makes it an alliance, distinct from the more casual cooperation that took place between Kennedy and Kassebaum, is that it is sustained. The cooperation between the two has a long history and embraces more than a half-dozen pieces of major legislation. The affection that the two men feel for each other has survived such notorious clashes as the confirmation fights over the Supreme Court nominations of Robert Bork and Clarence Thomas. So, while their opposition to one another on a broad range of issues is taken for granted, their underlying alliance always seems to invite the attention, and also the disbelief, of those who doubt that such things can happen in a Senate that can sometimes appear hopelessly polarized.

Pure friendships are even more scarce in 1998 than in 1980. As Senator McCain observed, senators don't socialize very much. Yet there are friendships in the Senate in which the personal attraction seems as great as the political tie.

Perhaps it is the distinctiveness of politics in the Dakotas that breeds such close relationships among its senators. A reporter who covers the state delegations of a number of Plains states in Congress said of North Dakota's two Democratic senators, Kent Conrad and Byron Dorgan, "The two of them are probably the closest senators from the same state as any I've seen. With Dorgan and Conrad, you will occasionally find them on opposite sides of an issue, but if it happens, it's a big story for me because it's so rare."

I asked the reporter if she could recall any recent issue on which the two North Dakota Democrats were on opposite sides of an issue. There was a long pause and then a long, drawn out, "Nooooo."

"I've been covering those guys for four years," she said, "and I can't remember anything. And not just on North Dakota issues are they together. It's any issue. They are like clones of each other."

The Dorgan-Conrad bond is one that goes back many years and also includes the state's single House member, Earl Pomeroy. When Dorgan first ran for the House in 1974, Kent Conrad was his campaign manager and Pomeroy was their driver. Currently, Conrad's wife, Lucy Calautti is Dorgan's chief of staff in the Senate and serves as political strategist for both senators.[8]

The two senators are allies, beyond doubt, and would seem to be close personally, but it is actually Dorgan and Senate Minority Leader Thomas Daschle who are even closer. Daschle named Dorgan his assistant floor leader in 1994. The degree of political agreement among Daschle, Dorgan, and Conrad is so high that it would be surprising if they did not get along so well in personal terms.

So while the senate friendships in which personal liking plays a major role are not numerous, they do exist.

It may be a reflection on American politics, or at least on the world of the Senate, that the foes outnumber the personal friends. They may outnumber them by an even more impressive margin than outsiders would estimate because of the very highly-developed senatorial ability to conceal hostile relationships.

When these hostilities burst to the surface, the display is quite spectacular. In February, 1993, the long-standing feud between Oregon's two Republican senators Bob Packwood and Mark Hatfield erupted publicly after Packwood was accused of making improper

---

8 "Lucy Calautti, Low Profile Power on the Hill," *The Hill*, Wednesday, March 8, 1995, p. 17.

sexual advances over a period of years to 23 women. Hatfield who viewed Packwood, in the words of their late colleague, Senator Joseph S. Clark, as "an unscrupulous son-of-a-bitch" gave no aid and comfort to his fellow Oregonian. Hatfield praised the courage of the 23 women in coming forward with their accusations. Previously, Packwood had likened his own troubles to the accusations of fund-raising improprieties against Hatfield that were made public in 1990. Hatfield was clearly angered by Packwood's attempt to equate the two sets of allegations and left little doubt in his public statements that the two situations were not comparable.[9]

Going public with senatorial feuds was not restricted to Oregon's senators. While not referring by name to his South Dakota Republican colleague Larry Pressler who was up for re-election in 1990, Democrat Tom Daschle referred to South Dakota's "empty seat" in the Senate and, in urging a vote for Pressler's opponent, said that, "A Senate seat is a terrible thing to waste."

It was front-page news in *The Star-Ledger*, New Jersey's most widely-read newspaper, when the state's two Democratic senators went public with their grievances against one another. Senators are skilled at concealing their hostility towards colleagues. A Maine political journalist, commenting on the icy relationships between the then Republican senator William Cohen [now Secretary of Defense] and fellow-Republican Olympia Snowe, observed that "Cohen and Snowe are very, very focused on their public images . . .They're not going to skirmish in public over nothing. Behind the scenes, sure!"

Such decorum does not apply in New Jersey where, on a plane trip from Washington to Newark Democrats Frank Lautenberg and Robert Torricelli found themselves seated in the same row. A lobbyist, seated between them, asked them if he should move so that the two senators could sit next to each other. They declined the offer. The incident was evidence of the total breakdown in communications between the two offices and the fact that members of the state's House delegation have found themselves having to attend two separate meetings on the same subject because neither senator will consent to a joint appearance.[10]

---

[9] "Hatfield Gives No Succor to Colleague Packwood," *Roll Call*, Thursday, February 18, 1993, p. 11.

The kind of hostility found in the Lautenberg-Torricelli relationship is rare in that it has surfaced and become a matter of public discussion. That other senators are better at concealing animus should not be seen as evidence that hard-feelings among such notoriously-competitive politicians is unusual.

Congress is an institution that has attempted to enforce a basic level of collegiality through the use of debate rules that require members who speak on the floor of the chamber to address all remarks to their colleagues indirectly. Senators' remarks begin with the words "Mr. President" and those of House members with "Mr. Speaker" so as to have pointed remarks glance off a third party and hit their target somewhat more gently. But control of hostility is not the same as avoiding conflict, because conflict is embedded in any political system in which people are free to hold opposing views. One would see little overt conflict in the Iraqi parliament or any of the decorative legislative bodies that dictators create. But even in the freewheeling congressional politics on Capitol Hill there are differences between the levels of conflict in the House and in the Senate.

The Senate, unlike the House, is a consensus-seeking body. It has to be. In the House, an absolute majority is 218: one-half plus one of the entire membership of 435 voting members. In the Senate, 51 votes gets you nowhere on most issues because of the filibuster. The weapon of unlimited debate vests in each senator a veto over the legislative process that can only be overcome if 60 colleagues agree to vote for cloture to end the filibuster. Much normal business in the Senate is also done by unanimous consent which is literally what it says it is: every last senator agreeing. Because it is rare to have 60 seats held by either party, a partisan goal of achieving a filibuster-proof membership is illusory. But even if one party achieved the 60 seats, senators cannot be counted on to vote the party line. There is, in fact, no threshold that would guarantee a filibuster-proof Senate on every controversial vote.

Despite the great upheavals in the world since the first publication of *Friend and Foe in the U.S.Senate* two decades ago, the Senate and its basic dynamics have changed little. Periodic alarms that warn

---

[10] Robert Cohen, "Will the Senator Yield to His Colleague? Uh, No." *The Sunday Star-Ledger*, Sunday, February 15, 1998, p. 1.

us that the Senate is becoming like the House usually turn out to be false. Complaints from senators themselves, that partisanship threatens to overcome the enforced civility of the institution, are usually overdrawn. Sometimes, outsiders have a better sense of the durability of the Senate than the senators themselves.

What makes the Senate the institution that it is is the dominant role of the individual senator. It is an institution subject to laws but preeminently of men, and women. What transpires among these 100 people and how they do their jobs cannot easily be codified because of the elusive quality of human nature. To attempt that would be an act of arrogance, doomed to fail. My goal is more modest: understanding and insight.

A FRIEND IN POWER

A veteran congressman returns to his office in the Capitol from a White House meeting with President Carter on a crucial energy bill. The fate of this important piece of legislation hangs in the balance; the forces arrayed against the president's measure are almost equal to those supporting it. The congressman speaks about the meeting and assesses the chances of passage of the bill:

> The president was enormously impressive in the meeting. He had all the facts at his fingertips. We asked him questions and he fielded every one himself. He didn't refer a single question from us to his aides or to Schlesinger [the Secretary of Energy]. Even the most obscure question he could answer with the most meticulous detail—how the bill would impact on Western Europe, everything!

> You ask what chance the bill has and I have to tell you, I just don't know. He's the brightest president I've ever known, maybe even one of the brightest men. Trouble is, for all his intellect, he doesn't have a single friend on the Hill. Whatever he achieves up here will have to come on the basis of the excellence of what he sends up here. There's no emotional commitment to the guy.

A Washington lawyer who has seen presidents come and go muses on President Carter's relations with Congress:

> At the depth of Lyndon Johnson's unpopularity with the public over the Vietnam War, when his popularity was down to 30 percent, there were a dozen senators who would still walk across hot coals for him—John Pastore, Clint Anderson, guys like that. They were his friends. They forgave him things

because of their personal feelings about him. With Jimmy Carter there's none of that. There's no residue of good feeling, no carry-over from one issue to the next; he's got to fight each issue as if nothing's gone before. When Congress passes an administration bill you can be damn sure it's not because of cronyism. This President has no cronies.

Retiring Congressman Otis Pike speaks to a television reporter about President Carter's vow to lay down the law to congressional Democrats opposing his programs and the threat by one of his aides to formulate an "enemies list" of those in his party habitually critical of the president. He uses the occasion to discuss the chief executive's human qualities.

I think he's a little distant. He is—he is hard to get close to, or feel warm with; but I'm not sure that congressmen ought to feel warm with the President of the United States. I don't have any objection to the concept that the President of the United States is not a crony with the congressmen. I—I think maybe that's a good idea. . . .

I don't see [an enemies list] developing [but] I'll tell you this: I think it would be much more useful to the President if he had a "friends list."[1]

This view is seconded by a high official in the president's own administration.

The president does not have an easy personal relationship with many people on Capitol Hill. He has that Southern manner. He smiles and makes polite conversation but he does not draw people into intimate relationships. He's a very private person underneath all that politeness.[2]

Vice-President Mondale, a man who was comfortable in the Senate and who relished the opportunities it offered for easy informality

---

[1] Interview by Phil Jones with Congressman Otis Pike, CBS "Morning News," August 31, 1978.

[2] Hedrick Smith, "Problems of a Problem Solver," *New York Times Magazine,* January 8, 1978, p. 33.

with colleagues, would steal off late in a hectic day to put his feet up on the office coffee table of his friend, Wisconsin senator Gaylord Nelson, and swap tales about the foibles of the "world's greatest deliberative body." Now he reflects on the formal and controlled world to which fate has consigned him:

> In the Senate, you have friends; in the executive, you interface. There's a wonderful thing about the legislative branch that is missed too much in the executive branch; if someone is pompous or posturing, your colleagues can hardly wait to deflate you. There's no way, if you've got friends, that you can avoid getting blasted if you're making a fool of yourself. I think there's a lot of strength in that. In the executive branch, they tend to be very serious, very dignified, very pro- grammed, nineteen points on every argument. It almost gets to be too much.[3]

What interpretation is to be placed on the uses of the terms "friend" and "friendship" by these people in political life? We may assume that the congressman lamenting the president's lack of con- sistent supporters in Congress implies that he lacks political allies. In the case of the Washington lawyer quoted above there is the sugges- tion that something more than votes, something more approaching personal loyalty, is referred to. For Congressman Pike there is an explicit verdict on personal qualities contained in the term "friend." In much the same fashion the quoted official speaks of the president's reserved personal qualities; he sees him as something of a loner. Vice- President Mondale's testimony on friendship speaks of a quality that is at the same time personal and political.

There is a ritual use of the term in the elaborate and deferential salutations that serve as preludes for speeches by senators. There is the arrant flattery which suffuses the encomiums of Egyptian Presi- dent Anwar Sadat when he speaks of "my friend Jimmy Carter" in the same terms he used for "my good friend Henry [Kissinger]" The word can be used as an epithet, as when military officers speak about

[3] Martin Tolchin, "The Mondales: Making the Most of Being Number 2," *New York Times Magazine*, February 28, 1978, p. 54.

the intentions of "our friends the Russians." The word is used ostentatiously, almost promiscuously, in politics.

By contrast, one rarely hears the term "enemy" used in political life even with regard to those whose malicious intent is manifest. In the wars of words that prevail between ideological foes in their hostile camps, the enmity that prevails is dealt with by euphemism and circumlocution. The enemy is "the other side." John F. Kennedy, in his inaugural address, directed an appeal to "those nations who would make themselves our adversary." Richard Nixon in 1969 used almost precisely the same phrase. In the depths of the cold war Harry Truman could bring himself to allude only to "a regime with contrary aims." Eisenhower alone among modern Presidents used the almost ineffable words "foe" and "enemy."

Our concern herein is not merely the rhetorical use of terms like "friend" and "foe" in politics but is the role of friendship and hostility in the interpersonal relationships prevailing among politicians. We will examine these relationships of harmony or enmity in one American political institution, the United States Senate, devoting much attention to the nature of senatorial friendship. The foregoing passages virtually mandate an effort at refining this concept. The varieties of friendship which will be presented are not concepts which are forcibly imposed on reality; they flow quite readily from the testimonies of twenty-five people who are or have been senators. While no equal effort will be made to break senatorial enmity down into its constituent parts, considerable attention will be paid to the sources of senatorial conflict.

We will first be exploring the conditions which give rise to senatorial friendship, evaluating the properties of each of its forms, and examining what sets one kind of senate friendship apart from another. We will look at those human and institutional properties of senatorial strife and examine its effects in the same manner as we do the payoffs of senatorial friendship. Although an extensive consideration of personality is beyond the purview of this book, one particular senate type will receive some attention. That type is the "loner," the senator who has developed no close ties with his colleagues, the apart. The paradoxical frequency with which loners are elected to leadership positions in the Senate will be part of this exploration.

It should be borne in mind that although the Senate is the focus of our interest, much of what is said here is applicable to other political worlds and in some instances to our private worlds as well.

This question whether congressional relationships differ in kind from those prevailing among ordinary citizens is an important one. Are friendship and hostility in public life totally occluded by issues, interests, and ideology? Do love or revenge play any important role in matters of state? Most important, and also most elusive, is the question whether personal friendship and hostility really matter here, whether issues and interests so effectively dominate political decisions that personal preferences and aversions are held in abeyance in the interest of senators' overriding constituencies—both geographical and functional.

It may be argued with considerable validity that the U.S. Senate is typical neither of American political institutions nor even of American legislatures. The Senate is a very special place. Senators can be said to hold the penultimate political positions in the federal system. They stand out as individuals to an extent not enjoyed or endured by members of the House. They stand at the threshold of American political supremacy, the presidency. Sixteen have crossed that threshold. The Senate has given more of its members to the Presidency than either the House of Representatives or any of the state houses. It can justly be looked upon as the nursery of presidents. Senators in this sense are not typical.

United States senators, moreover, are not just "plain folks." They live in a world in which they are media cynosures, favor brokers, and representatives of national issues and constituencies. To be a U.S. senator, Henry Adams wrote, was to "occupy one of the dogmatic stations of life." Being at the very heart of the "Washington Establishment," senators often appear as two-dimensional cardboard figures festooned with labels reading "liberal," or "Southerner," or "oil-state spokesman." We often expect them to act accordingly and perform as ideological abstractions, playing their roles in a theatre of politics in which good does battle with evil.

Senators, however, are not born; they are made. Few of them spring directly from private life into the upper chamber. Before they are senators they are lawyers, or state legislators, or governors. They are products—albeit less emphatically so nowadays—of state political parties. Their primary political impressions are generally not formed in the Senate. Those who have served on state or local legislative bodies have performed their duties in institutions which, though not wholly unlike the Senate, do vary somewhat in their political ground rules from those in the federal body. In most states, the governor is a far more commanding figure vis-à-vis the state legislature than is the president in regard to the Senate. The state legislators, on the whole, are less professional—certainly less "full-time" in their schedules. They function without senators' elaborate retinues of staff; the attention lavished upon them as individuals does not dimly approximate that in which senators bask. Even senators' counterparts in the U.S. House of Representatives, with whom they somewhat uneasily share Washington center-stage, are eclipsed by senatorial grandeur.

Yet for all these differences, the legislative process among the various levels of government is very much a constant: Bills are introduced, hearings held, interests expressed, speeches made, and votes taken. We would expect the nature of interpersonal relationships everywhere to be not radically dissimilar from those in the Senate; since many senators received their political baptism in the state legislatures, the forms of etiquette practiced there are part of the baggage that follows them onwards and upwards. If senators as individuals are not typical of American legislators, the Senate is, however, part of a national legislative network with common processes and dynamics.

The Senate, moreover, is but one part of a larger American political universe greater than even the legislative sphere. This general context is the avenue which will be used to approach the complexities of senatorial friendship.

Distinctions are typically made between "political friendship" and "personal friendship" as if the one were governed wholly by political agreement of necessity and the other exclusively by one individual's liking for another. Friendship in the day-to-day practice of the political world is far most subtle and complex. If the United States Senate is at all representative of American political institutions, the evidence of twenty-five individuals who are or have been members of that body suggests strongly that such an either-or characterization, whatever its simplicity, does not accurately describe the essence of most of these relationships. Friendships among U.S. senators are at one and the same time political *and* personal; what varies is which of the two qualities is dominant and defines the nature of the friendship. Elected by the voters—not selected by the members—senators find themselves thrown together with colleagues not of their choosing. Before long, however, they will probably find within the membership colleagues to whom they would have been attracted elsewhere: They may find that an agreement on fundamental political values or a habit of voting the same way holds the key to more personal ties. By contrast, they may discover an ideological opposite, expected to offer little in the way of human attractiveness, to be that most pleasant of surprises, the noble adversary.

Friendship among senators takes two general forms: friendships in which professional or political qualities are dominant while personal attraction, though not insignificant, is not the most prominent feature, and friendships of a more personal variety in which sociability, emotional commitment, and exchange of personal confidences assume a role at least as important as political or professional ties. The first general form of friendship—which, in the interests of simplicity, we will refer to as "political friendship"—subsumes two specific varieties: *institutional kinship* and *alliance*. The "personal friendships" encompass three specific varieties: *mentor-protégé* relationships, *social friendship* (both intramural and extramural) and *pure friendship*. Despite their division into political and personal types, all of these relationships contain both political and personal elements. There is no impermeable barrier between the two; it is rather a case of which property is dominant.

Institutional kinship relations arise out of professional pride, collegiality, and a satisfying business relationship. Fondness is not necessarily absent, but the emotional content of this relationship is limited. This form of friendship presupposes no agreement on political values. The *alliance* is the product of more or less consistent political agreement, but it is more than simply a pair or group voting together on most issues. Consistent political cooperation, over time, tends to yield to alliance members important personal bonds and feelings of human, as well as political, solidarity. Crossing the line between political and personal friendships, *mentor-protégé* friendships defy the usual forms of human friendship in that they embrace people of different generations; they are relationships of great mutual solicitude and assistance. *Social friendship* among senators reflects a basically personal attraction founded upon compatible social styles and shared interest in sports, games, and other forms of recreation. Political agreement and professional standards are often irrelevant to this form of friendship. The premium in this relationship is on sociability, companionship, and leisure-time association. Despite the emphasis in this form of friendship on personal rather than political or professional qualities, it rarely involves emotional commitments. *Pure friendships* likewise involve such an emotional commitment. Affection for a colleague as a person and concern for his welfare and problems is the most salient feature of the relationship. In practice, such relationships of pure friendship are enjoyed by senators who share the same political values, but the emotional ties develop a life of their own independent of the harmony of their views. This emotional attachment enables the relationship to survive all but the most serious disagreements over policy. The rarest of all the forms of senate friendship, it involves under certain circumstances the sharing of personal confidences and personal problems.

These five forms of friendship reflect ascending degrees of personal intimacy, the least intimate and most business-related being institutional kinship and the most intimate being pure friendship, in which sentiment, while usually based upon common philosophical values, assumes a dominant role.

Institutional kinship is a friendship based upon the *esprit de corps* that comes from having been elected to a prestigious institution and the accommodations that are so valuable in achieving success there. Politicians pursue elective office voluntarily, and the attractions of such a post would seem to outweigh the discomfort suffered in achieving it. In their attitude toward the institutions or groups in which they find themselves, politicians would necessarily feel differently from, for example, army recruits or mental patients, whose membership is dictated by circumstance rather than choice. Considerable prestige and gratification must necessarily attach, in the mind of the politician, to the winning of elective office, especially when lofty.

The very rigors of the electoral process seem to deepen the attachment of the politician to the attained office, making it all the more cherished. This effect has been noted by social psychologists concerned with questions of group dynamics and group cohesion. Their research indicates that the more formidable the obstacles to membership in a group, the more highly valued that membership is likely to be.[4] What is not entirely clear, however, is whether the fondness felt by the novice is directed towards the prestige and status attached to becoming a member of a highly select organization or towards the individuals making up the organization. It is logical to assume that people run for elective office for far different reasons from those which impel them to seek membership in a country club or fraternal order. The primary purpose of a city council or the U.S. House of Representatives is not, after all, good fellowship and conviviality. These may be byproducts of membership in such bodies, and there may even be some politicians for whom these considerations become important, but the raison d'être of public office is clearly not the development of personal attachments. At the same time, members of a legislative body, no matter how individualistic it may be, cannot achieve their objectives alone; no legislator can afford to be a social isolate. Whatever he may think of his colleagues personally, his success and fate are in some way linked to theirs. Institutional kinship at the most basic level is a positive and collegial disposition towards fellow members and a willingness to demonstrate it. The following passage indicates how this form of political friendship expresses itself in the House.

> When the buzzers sound for the opening call of the House, the corridors begin to seethe, people emerge from everywhere. . . . You feel good. You feel friendly toward everyone. It's like the first day of school; it seems brand new and hopeful. When you shake hands, you mean it. You may not know the man very well. But he, too, is back from the "district." . . .

[4] Elliot Aronson and Judson Mills, "The Effect of Severity of Initiation on Looking for a Group," *Journal of Abnormal and Social Psychology*, Vol. 59, pp. 177–81, (1959) reprinted in Dorwin Cartwright and Alvin Zander (eds.), *Group Dynamics* (New York: Harper and Row, 1960), pp. 95–103.

The emotions are real. The affection is a heartfelt display. It is the camaraderie of the shared experience. . . . They have returned from the indifferent cruelties of the political wars.[5]

Reveling in the fellowship of political survivors, the returning members are "saddened by the failure of friends to understand, as much as they were outraged by the indignities suffered from their opponents. Elections are unrelenting and painful. The public image of the thick-skinned politico is an inaccurate stereotype which conceals the private feelings."[6]

It is difficult to dispute the very obvious evidence of institutional pride and ritualistic bonhomie that prevails in certain political settings. Skeptics, however, are inclined to stress the ambiguities of these expressions and suggest that such outpourings of public affection mask a considerably more ambivalent relationship among politicians. This effect is observable in the U.S. Senate.

Possessed of the prima donna's disdain for peers, compelled by their profession to fight one another on issues, they have measured each other as enemies. But they are conscious, too, that they are brothers, that ambition makes them endure the same indignities, wage the same lonely struggle for career survival. And so they compensate for the mutual hostility inherent in their situation with the kind of exaggerated cordiality that is evident as they enter the doorways together.[7]

Observers are universally impressed by the great amount of physical contact occurring on the floor of the Senate, prompting a staff aide to comment, "You look down from the gallery sometimes and get the feeling that you wandered into a homosexual steambath. There's a lot of that touchy-feely that goes on among those guys."

A Midwestern Democrat known as one of the most aggressively physical greeters in the Senate once caused great discomfort by his effusiveness. He had gone back to his state for a party reception; at

[5] Clem Miller, *Member of the House* (New York: Scribner's, 1962), p. 80.

[6] Ibid.

[7] James Boyd, "Legislate? Who Me?: A Day in the Life of a Senator," *Washington Monthly*, February, 1969, p. 44.

the reception he spied one of the state officials in the crowd. The official flinched in horror as the senator approached him, holding up his hand to ward off what he knew was coming. The senator connected with a bone-jarring slap on the back of the official, who collapsed on the floor in agony, looking up at the senator with tears of pain in his eyes. "I tried to warn you," he groaned; "I just got out of the hospital after six weeks in traction for a slipped disc!" The chastening effect of this incident on the senator must have been only momentary, for he continues the practice with undiminished enthusiasm.

There are real incentives in the Senate to be well-liked, popular, and a good buddy to your colleagues. Most politicians, after all, are extroverts, well-skilled in glad-handing, and masterful in their effusiveness. Popularity, moreover, is seen by many as an essential ingredient in political success—both in elections and in legislative chambers.

The processes of induction into Congress stress the importance of good colleague relationships.

> Making friends with his colleagues is a most important activity indeed, and [the freshman congressman] should develop friendly relationships with committee and House staff and agency personnel as well. . . .
>
> Because so much of a legislator's time is spent in close association with colleagues, and because their cooperation is so often required if he is to succeed, freshmen members are especially cautioned about intragroup relationships."[8]

The elected representative, then, cannot expect to restrict his good feeling solely to the institution itself. He must deal with his colleagues as individuals and keep his interpersonal relationships in some semblance of good order.

Institutional kinship, then, in the broadest sense is the expression of pride at being part of a select institution—a pride which is accentuated by the ordeals of initiation common to all. But it is quite clearly more than simple esprit de corps; it is a relationship whose

---

[8] Charles L. Clapp, *The Congressman, His Work As He Sees It* (Washington, DC: The Brookings Institution, 1963), pp. 12–13.

origins are found in the interdependence of senators. This relationship is important not only in spite of, but because of, the individualistic quality of the Senate. Loyalty in this mode of political friendship is clearly owed to the institution in terms of its maintenance and legally prescribed goals, but it is not restricted to dedication to an institutional abstraction. It is a recognition of human mutuality and interdependence in the service of political survival. What it implies for the individual is, in the words of William S. White, "A gift if not for friendship at least for amicable association with other minds and with the interests of others."[9] Failure to adhere to these modest standards of institutional kinship does not subject the member to punishment from the group; sanctions, if they are applied, are individual rather than collective.

Beneath the external trappings of institutional kinship—the jovial expressions of pride and solidarity which are so much a part of the public face of a legislative body—is a shared community of experience and fate which amounts to an interpersonal pact of mutual assistance for those who share in it. Clinton Anderson of New Mexico, one of the most influential senators of recent years, in reflecting upon the human qualities of those with whom he had served saw the elements of institutional kinship summed up in a single man.

> [Clyde] Hoey [D.–N.C.] was a man of superb integrity, who would not have traded a vote improperly under any circumstances. Yet, he shared the Senate's sense of camaraderie, which meant that he would always help a colleague, no matter what difference he might have with him ideologically.[10]

Institutional kinship, founded not upon abstract standards but on practical experience, usually involves a period of mutual exploration and testing. Robert A. Taft as Senate Majority Leader and Lyndon B. Johnson as Minority Leader

> not only got along well in performing their official duties but enjoyed a warm personal relationship as well. This was born after they assumed the Senate leadership of their respective

[9] William S. White, *Citadel* (New York: Harper and Bros., 1956), p. 117.

[10] Clinton P. Anderson, *Outsider in the Senate* (New York: World Publishing Co., 1970), p. 97.

parties. Prior to that time they had really not known each other at all.

Each approached the other warily during the early days of the 1953 session, but the feeling-out period did not last long. . . .

Their mutual regard had its genesis, no doubt, in the respect each felt toward the other as a man. Neither even entertained the slightest doubt about the other's integrity. Both literally loved the Senate. Each valued a worthy opponent and neither of them had any use for the kind of aimless, time-wasting chitchat that Johnson jeered at as "just visiting" and Taft forthrightly scorned as "nonsense."[11]

It has been noted that "the role of the Senate in the political system has changed over the last twenty years in such a way as to decrease the impact of norms internal to the Senate on the behavior and status of Senators."[12] Junior senators no longer quaver before the displeasure of their senior colleagues, passively accept membership on committees irrelevant to their own needs and those of their constituents, or cower voicelessly in the back benches. However, institutional kinship still provides the cohesion for an increasingly individualistic institution. To say that the time-killing, witless drudgery and humiliating exercises of deference are no more does not mean that the Senate is now composed of a hundred atoms with nothing to bind them. For the mutual respect, empathy, and consideration which are the ingredients of institutional kinship are not mere ornaments; they are the essentials of an enduring and continuous institution, and, although love and ardor may not characterize the relations of senators united by its bonds, this form of political friendship is the principal counterweight to centrifugal tendencies which would otherwise tear the Senate asunder. The explosion of special interests and the exponential rise in groups seeking legislative remedies and benefits have indeed fostered a competitiveness and indi-

[11] Booth Mooney, *The Lyndon Johnson Story* (New York: Farrar, Straus, and Cudahy, 1956), pp. 109–110.

[12] "Goodbye to the Inner Club," *The Washington Monthly*, August 1969, pp. 30–34.

vidualism among legislators that now makes institutional cohesion more and more tenuous; but the slender threads of common experience, fellowship, trust, and mutuality—the components of institutional kinship—serve to provide an important, perhaps indispensable, force for cohesion. They evolve not from any overarching set of norms but derive from the practical experience of human interaction. They reflect not an ideal conception of the "good senator" or an institution-wide standard applicable to all members, but are rather an expression of individual determinations of the professional worthiness of one's colleagues and the good qualities of their character.

The readiness of some senators to define friendship in terms consistent with those of institutional kinship is illustrated by an incident described by a staff aide to a Democratic senator. She had established an easygoing and relaxed relationship with her boss, and one day, while they were having lunch together, tried to draw him out on his feelings towards his colleagues. As she relates the incident,

> I asked him who his best friend was in the Senate. He thought for a minute and said, "I have a great deal of respect for Frank Church." I told him that I was thinking more in terms of who he liked rather than who he respected. He got sort of a puzzled look on his face and said, "Like I just told you, Frank Church."

The alliance type of political friendship is less common than institutional kinship, and, unlike the latter, is dependent upon a more or less enduring congruence of political principles or goals. The personal affection found in this form of friendship is principally a product of consistent political cooperation. It does not stand up well under the strain of repeated and serious divergence of positions, but periodic defections for good cause do not destroy it.

Alliances develop most commonly among senators who are ideologically compatible; but in some policy areas where lines are not drawn along philosophical axes, it is possible for alliances to be established for special kinds of legislation. Common partisanship also facilitates the establishment of alliances. To the extent that parties do to some degree reflect a coherent set of political principles, partisanship is linked to ideology.[13] Consistent support of the same positions, advocacy of the same issues, adherence to the same set of political principles, or simple allegiance to the same party can move senators in the direction of an alliance. These factors, however, tend to be objective conditions; there are subjective components to the alliance as well. Consultation, collaboration, and the communication of intentions form part of this equation. A measure of personal commitment, if not affection, can develop over the course of sustained political cooperation.

Such alliances span partisan differences somewhat more readily than ideological ones, although in some situations even philosophical differences can be bridged for alliance purposes. The *bipartisan alliance* is a simple reflection of political realities characteristic of a legislative setting. As one former aide to a liberal Democrat in the Senate put it, "You need friends on the other side of the aisle." Studies on the disposition of legislators to follow the party line suggest that partisan cohesion often depends upon the issue involved, leading one student of Congress to observe, "Whatever the final conclusions regarding the role of party in the decisions made by congressmen . . . it is obvious that the impact of party cannot be studied without attention to the policy content." This same commentator suggests that partisanship is not an important factor on questions of international involvement, is moderately strong on social welfare and agricultural questions, and is exceedingly strong on questions of government management.[14] In the Senate especially, where there are votes on treaties and cloture motions requiring considerably more than a bare majority of votes, bipartisan support is mandatory even if one party holds considerably more seats than the other.

---

[13] One useful test of the congruence of party and ideology appeared in 1964 when *Congressional Quarterly* computed the difference between the votes of congressional Democrats and Republicans on a range of votes which was said to reflect preferences for a larger or smaller role for government in national affairs. The results for both houses of congress showed that 70 percent of Democrats supported a more expansive federal role, while only 33 percent of Republicans did. (*Congressional Quarterly Weekly Report*, Vol. 22 (1964), p. 2549.)

[14] Aage R. Clausen, *How Congressmen Decide: A Policy Focus* (New York: St. Martin's Press, 1973), pp. 95–96.

The *transideological alliance* is often found where state or regional interests are concerned. A liberal Democratic Senator from the West has described his relations with the other Senator from his state—a conservative Republican in terms of these exigencies—thus:

> We became political friends and I respected [him]. He seemed to respect me and we found that if we could come to an agreement on a matter relating to the management of natural resources [in our state], or a dam, a water development project, a natural recreation area, or a wilderness, that then we could quickly secure Senate agreement, and we broke what had been a very serious impasse that had lasted for years [in our state], where development of resources had come to a standstill because it became such a partisan fight and everything became a kind of stalemate.

> It was the public power interests against the private utilities where the dams and water development projects were concerned, and the Democrats [were] against the Republicans, and we decided that if [our state's] interests were to be effectively represented this impasse had to be broken, and the two of us could when we discovered that the two of us—though we were not always in agreement—were not so far in disagreement on many matters that compromise was impossible. When we discovered that, we began to work together and we broke the impasse and [our state] immensely benefited from that working relationship.

Where state interests were concerned, the relationship between the liberal Democrat and the conservative Republican assumed a cooperative pattern.

> We began to cooperate where we could and we rather liked the results. Furthermore, I found that he was a man that I could trust implicitly. He was also a man whose word was absolutely reliable once he gave it. There was never any fear that he'd change his position, and there was never any backbiting, never any surreptitious leaks that could be politically embarrassing to me. . . . He was a man of good character and independent, very independent, and he had the courage of his convictions, so that's a man you can work with.

The political value of forging with a colleague an alliance spanning both party and ideology is particularly great in the legislative world because of the effect noted by John Kingdon that "a given argument or piece of information from a perfectly predictable source is less noticed than the same argument or piece of information coming from an unexpected source. [Accordingly,] when Richard Poff [R.–Va.] argued against a provision [in a House bill] which would have placed the Office of Economic Opportunity's legal aid program directly under a governor's control, for instance, it had more effect among Republicans than if Emmanuel Celler (D.–N.Y.) had been making the same case, because Poff was well known as a conservative. When Edith Green [D.–Ore.] argued a bill punishing universities, it had more effect than if, say, John Bracemas [D.–Ind.] had been making the same argument, because of her previous record of supporting education causes with which Southerners and Republicans were more in accord."[15]

The very shock value of this transideological type of alliance suggests its relative rarity and its association with particular kinds of issues. Nonetheless, whenever such issues of a particular nature arise, partisan and ideological traces can be kicked over. The canny legislative leader who knows his colleagues well can identify those who can serve as "umbrellas" and "whose support would make it possible for four or five others to vote the right way."[16] An alliance of this kind, like the instrument to which it is likened, is most useful in stormy weather. It can be invoked with good effect when the need arises. It is, however, restricted to peculiar issues or situations. In its commonest form the alliance is a working relationship based on mutuality of political values or interests but never entirely fixed or permanent. The greater the degree of philosophical or policy agreement, the more constant it will be. The bipartisan and transideological varieties are the most limited, temporary, and specific to issues, but are often very decisive when votes are close. Highly instrumen-

---

15 John W. Kingdon, *Congressmen's Voting Decisions* (New York: Harper and Row, 1973), p. 80.

16 Doris Kearns, *Lyndon Johnson and the American Dream* (New York: New American Library/Signet Books, 1976), p. 128.

tal in political terms, the various modes of the alliance reflect sober and calculated political judgment rather than deep fondness or social and personal bonds of the type prevailing outside the political arena. Of course, the addition of these more personal factors adds durability to them.

Agreement on political fundamentals or fidelity to the same set of issues is not an important part of an institutional kinship relationship. In an alliance, however, it is at the core of the association. Among institutional-kinship friends cooperation tends to be sporadic and is usually in the realm of procedural support; in an alliance collaboration is more consistent and related to substantive matters. Sometimes an alliance is a composite both of the regional and ideological attributes of its members. In the early 1950s three liberal Republicans from New England—George Aiken of Vermont, Margaret Chase Smith of Maine, and Charles Tobey of New Hampshire— were bound in such an alliance of ideological agreement and warm personal regard. At the same time, an alliance of two powerful, oil-state Democrats, Lyndon Johnson of Texas and Robert Kerr of Oklahoma, was moving to establish control of the then minority party, along with such other partisan and regional cohorts as Clinton Anderson of New Mexico and Carl Hayden of Arizona. This alliance was further reinforced by the fact that these senators were among the most influential individuals on the Democratic side of the aisle.

Occasionally alliances are established which appear incomprehensible to outsiders. Such an alliance existed between Lyndon Johnson and Hubert Humphrey.

> Their special relationship was kept out of the press because the only reporter who understood it was Johnson's friend Bill White. Although Humphrey continued to spout his extreme liberalism, when Johnson needed his help or his vote, he made himself available. In return, said his aide, Johnson "rewarded Humphrey often with powerful help for special projects or liberal legislation causes."[17]

Less conspiratorial and more ennobling was their relationship from the perspective of another one of Johnson's aides, Harry McPherson,

---

[17] Alfred Steinberg, *Sam Johnson's Boy* (New York: Macmillan Co., 1968), p. 345.

who found the two closer politically and personally than institutional-kinship friends would be, but not so intimate as to cast their relationship into the realm of personal friendship.

> With Lyndon Johnson, Humphrey's relationship was extremely complex. At bottom there was mutual affection and respect. They wanted, or believed they wanted, the same things.[18]

There is more to this type of alliance than similar voting records or compatible philosophies. It is not at all unusual in the Senate for members who share virtually every political characteristic to be unable to abide each other. A liberal who struggled relentlessly to secure a seat on the Committee on Foreign Relations, where he could have lent his strength to the foreign-policy views of its chairman, J. William Fulbright, found that his presence on the committee caused Fulbright considerable discomfort.

> When I finally got to Foreign Relations after much pain and suffering, I found Bill Fulbright, with whom I agree on most things but who very definitely came out of the state of Arkansas. He wasn't too pleased to help out renegade liberals from the northeast.

Even some of those whose political characteristics are congruent to the point of representing the same state on behalf of the same party and, indeed, the same wing of that party turn out to be not only non-allies but even deadly enemies. For example, the Wednesday Club of liberal Senate Republicans found itself the cockpit of the epic feud between Oregon's two liberal Republican senators, Mark O. Hatfield and Robert Packwood. Hatfield told the membership of the Wednesday Club, in effect, that they had to choose between Packwood and himself. A member of the group recalls Hatfield saying,

> "You have to make a choice, boys, I'm sorry." Finally they called him on it and it didn't require a choice, but for a long time Packwood was not in the Wednesday Club. Politically, they agreed on practically everything, but Hatfield regarded Packwood as an unscrupulous son-of-a-bitch. I don't know

---

[18] Harry McPherson, *A Political Education* (Boston: Little, Brown & Co., 1972), p. 38.

what Packwood's view was on the other side, because I didn't have occasion to talk with him. I don't think their relationship has basically improved, but at least they speak to each other now.

Personal friendship is the rarest of the friendships that occur between politicians, just as it is the rarest of relationships among human beings in general. As in the case of the alliance, an essential agreement on political fundamentals seems to be a major element in personal friendship, but unlike the alliance there is a depth of feeling that develops independently of political agreement. Allies may agree on important aspects of philosophy or policy, but with personal friendship there must also be personal regard. It represents a bond of men more than of measures.

There are dangers inherent in all forms of personal friendship. In American politics, unlike almost any other sphere of human activity, there is a dark side to this type of friendship: the spectre of cronyism. In the contemporary political setting, in which rectitude is put forth as a stark and absolute political virtue, the disposition to favor a friend assumes an ominous and corrupt coloration. One veteran Washington lawyer, reflecting on the consequences of the current preoccupation with public virtue, has observed, "Officials are less and less inclined to do favors for friends. It would be very foolish to do favors that cannot be justified on anything but personal friendship."[19]

Personal friendship has often led politicians into political trouble. In recent memory there is the spectacle of President Carter, elected in large measure by dint of his devotion to probity, clinging tenaciously to his friend and budget director Bert Lance in the face of demands for his resignation over business indiscretions, and, more remotely, President Eisenhower spending three months of agony and indecision over whether to ask for the resignation of Sherman Adams, a political advisor who accepted gifts, and defending his retention of Adams at a press conference because, as he said, "I need him."[20]

[19] *New York Times*, December 24, 1977, p. 22.

[20] For a poignant account of Eisenhower's painful decision in the Adams affair, see Emmet John Hughes, *The Ordeal of Power* (New York: Atheneum, 1975), pp. 266–269.

Harry Truman as president found his long-term friendship with his military aide Harry Vaughan an embarrassment when his old friend was accused of accepting a freezer from a lobbyist. But Truman stuck by him tenaciously at considerable political cost.[21] Lyndon Johnson confronted the same choice between friendship and political survival when, scarcely a month before the 1964 presidential election, his oldest and closest assistant, Walter Jenkins, was arrested one block from the White House for sexual misconduct. Once the incident became public, Johnson acted quickly, but not without anguish. "[He] was torn between two conflicting forces: friendship and the fact that the election was less than three weeks away. . . . Johnson resolved the conflict between friendship and election by coming down on the side of election." He accepted Jenkins' resignation. [22]

Some American politicians simply have no personal friends. They may have seen the pitfalls in personal friendship and kept people at arm's length. Others are simply insular and remote men needing no emotional sustenance or human contact beyond what their families provide. James K. Polk, one of the most assiduous diarists among American presidents, is an example of a political leader who was almost innocent of any close personal ties. "Cave Johnson [his Postmaster-General] seems to have been the only man with whom he ever approached any kind of relaxed intimacy. Even in this relationship, to judge from the two men's correspondence, all the jocularity and personal references proceeded from Johnson, who appeared to sense a warmth in Polk that was never expressed openly."[23] Polk's own accounts in his journal of his limited social activities reflect a joyless and perfunctory quality in these contacts, even with those with whom he was said to have been close.

> Wednesday, 1st April, 1846—Mrs. Polk and myself paid a visit this evening at seven o'clock to Mr. Johnson, the Postmaster-

---

21 Margaret Truman, *Harry S. Truman* (New York: William Morrow, 1972), pp. 421–425.

22 Roland Evans and Robert Novak, *Lyndon B. Johnson: The Exercise of Power* (New York: New American Library, 1966), p. 480.

23 Charles Grier Sellers, Jr., *James K. Polk, Jacksonian* (Princeton: Princeton University Press, 1957), p. 276.

General, and sat an hour with the family. It is the first visit of
the kind which I have made since I have been President, except
to call on Mrs. Madison and on Mr. Attorney-General Mason
when he was sick last summer, and to dine with Mr. Bancroft
the past winter. My time has been wholly occupied in my
office, in the discharge of my public duties. My confinement to
my office has been constant and unceasing, and my labours
very great.[24]

While not wholly friendless, Richard Nixon's closest personal friends
were two men wholly divorced from any association with political
life. Never on close personal terms with the conservatives in the
Republican party, and regarded with caution by the liberals, he had
no natural political group to turn to for intimates. His closest friends
were a millionaire real estate broker from Florida, Charles "Bebe"
Rebozo, and the wealthy inventor of the aerosol valve, Robert Abplanalp.

An example of the opposite tendency is Warren G. Harding, who
commingled personal friendships and the political world to a remarkable and self-defeating degree. He appointed to high posts in his
administration a half-dozen of his poker-playing cronies, some of
whom were later convicted of crimes.

Personal friendship in politics, then, is not an unalloyed boon. It
is, moreover, often rare in a profession in which the term "friend" is
used so ritualistically. In my interviews with U.S. senators, I posed
the question: "Over the years that you spent in the Senate, who
would you say were your closest friends?" The general nature of the
responses fell into two categories: senators who mentioned only one
or two names, and senators who mentioned more than a dozen. In
the latter category there were some senators who denominated fully
one-quarter of the Senate as "friends." Of course, by my question I
meant personal friends—a distinction which I later clarified to the
people interviewed. It seems clear that the very frequency with
which the term "friend" is now used has hopelessly confounded and
debased its meaning. Where it was once sufficient in senatorial salutations on the floor to refer to "my distinguished colleague, the Junior

[24] James K. Polk, *Polk: The Diary of a President,* Allan Nevins (ed.), (New York:
Capricorn Books, 1968), p. 69.

Senator from Iowa," it is now very common to hear a senator intone "my distinguished colleague and good friend." The parliamentary use of the term cannot be an operational definition of personal friendship; it may be evidence of simple civility and the senatorial aversion to the personal pronoun—or even an expression of institutional kinship—but it is not in itself a measure of personal friendship. What, then, are the attributes and varieties of personal friendship in the Senate?

One variety of personal friendship is the mentor-protégé friendship. It typically spans generations, which is rather remarkable considering that personal friendships generally spring up between people of roughly the same age. Usually generational differences are a barrier. I once inquired of a Western Democrat in the Senate about his relations with his senior colleague at the time of his election. (The senior senator from the state was a right-wing Republican.) "Was ideology a barrier in your relationship?" I asked. "No, it really wasn't; it was more the age differential than the ideology. We were really products of different generations . . . there was a tremendous generation gap between us."

Mentor-protégé friendships operate in defiance of this general tendency. Mentor and protégé commonly have their roots in the same state or region and are members of the same party or wing of the party. A well-known example of this variety of personal friendship is the relationship that existed between Walter F. Mondale and Hubert H. Humphrey. Even before Mondale took the Minnesota Senate seat vacated by Humphrey on becoming Vice-President in 1964, he was very much a Humphrey protégé. Their acquaintance had been established when Humphrey was mayor of Minneapolis. It matured through close association in the Minnesota Democratic-Farmer Labor party, a state party organization of unusual cohesiveness during this period. Their association developed into personal friendship when Mondale entered the Senate, but was subjected to severe strains during the 1968 presidential election: Mondale was one of two Humphrey campaign managers, chosen after the bitterly fratricidal Democratic National Convention in Chicago; Humphrey's dogged loyalty to outgoing President Lyndon Johnson and his steadfast refusal to repudiate the American role in the Vietnam War caused great conflict for Mondale. By instinct and principle against he war, he struggled behind the scenes to win Humphrey's soul away from Johnson, but never aired his differences with Humphrey publicly.

Like all protégés, Mondale chafed under Humphrey's paternalism. When Humphrey returned to the Senate as Minnesota's junior senator, Mondale was again lost in the shadow of the older man who was by then more an institution than a mere senator. Publicly they celebrated their close friendship; privately they competed. Mondale often expressed frustration—though never on the record—at being upstaged by Humphrey.

Yet for all the private annoyances, the Mondale-Humphrey friendship was a warm one. The intimacy of this friendship, however, should not be exaggerated. Hubert Humphrey was not Walter Mondale's best friend, although Mondale's political debt to the older man was great. In recent years he came more abreast of Humphrey—his elevation to the Vice-Presidency in 1976 signalled that he had become a force in his own right—but the fact of Humphrey's patronage has been part of Mondale's political baggage and a burden that he did not always bear cheerfully.

American political history abounds with examples of mentor-protégé friendships. Jefferson was mentor to Madison and Monroe. Andrew Jackson's protégé Martin Van Buren succeeded him in the White House; their personal relationship was always a close one. Henry Clay had considered John Tyler a protégé; the sole consolation —if it can be called that—which he experienced after losing the Whig Party nomination to William Henry Harrison in 1840 was the fact that Tyler was placed on the ticket as Vice-Presidential candidate. But the fond feelings of Clay for Tyler were abruptly shattered shortly after Harrison's death when the new president vetoed Clay's bill to charter a national bank. The Tyler cabinet resigned at this almost en masse, but a personal toll was added to Tyler's political costs with the rupture of this friendship.

In more recent times the various "father-son" relationships of Lyndon B. Johnson might be considered examples of the mentor-protégé relationship. Johnson's three most prominently mentioned political fathers were Franklin Roosevelt, Sam Rayburn, and Richard Russell. Johnson's characterizations of these friendships must be treated with some skepticism, for he used friendship in the manner of a skilled surgeon using a scalpel. With his superb knack for buttering up elderly bachelor or childless politicians, advancing himself as a surrogate son and heir-presumptive, his view of friendship was usually highly instrumental and in the service of his political ambitions. The very frequency of his statements that an older politician "was like a Daddy to me" tends to cast doubt on the profundity of some of these relationships.

Johnson did have a keen understanding of the emotional needs of the powerful but lonely old men who dominated the Congress in the 1940s and 1950s.

> Recognizing that the older men in the Senate were often troubled by a half-conscious sense that their performance was deteriorating with age, Johnson made a special point of helping them with their committee work, briefing them on the issues, and assisting them on the floor. These were men who had once been at the center of things, who had experienced the power to control events. "Now," as Johnson had put it, "they feared humiliation, they craved attention. And when they found it, it was like a spring in the desert; their gratitude couldn't adequately express itself with anything less than total support and dependence on me."[25]

Because of a number of forces, both within and without the Senate, the mentor-protégé relationship is fast disappearing. The strong state parties and local organizations which produced "Daley men" or "Hague men" no longer exist. National causes which once provided a convenient political shorthand for politicians—"silverites" or "New Dealers" or "Progressives"—are no longer applied. Great men after whom lesser men might style themselves—"La Follette Republicans" or "Jacksonians"—no longer cast broad political shadows. Powerful House Speakers and Senate floor leaders to whom disciples gravitated have been replaced by men who deal more in service than in leadership. Each senator is now a political force in his own right. Perhaps most important is the fact that no senator or congressman wants to be known as someone else's protégé. If one were to set up a category of "Carter Democrats" it would contain one occupant—Jimmy Carter.

---

[25] Doris Kearns, op. cit., p. 126.

Still, if the mentor-protégé mode of personal friendship has declined in importance, other friendship bonds of a personal nature have persisted. In legislative bodies generally and in Congress in particular, there is a tendency for people with similar interests to gravitate to one another and forge friendships that are both professional and social. They like being with one another; they "party" together, entertain each other in their homes, and share recreational time. However, the senators I have interviewed, virtually without exception, confessed that they spent little time in social activities outside the Senate. The most common reason for this was simple lack of time; but, while some said they would like to have the chance to get to know their colleagues better in a social setting, others admitted that they would just as soon spend their time away from the Senate in the company of non-senators, preferably non-politicians. Nonetheless, there is a social network among congenial legislators that finds its expression in both the political and social realms. There are senators, for example, who play tennis together and attend karate classes and dinners with colleagues. Pure sociability, rather than alliance-building or simple institutional kinship, is the motive for this variety of personal friendship—but political dividends can be reaped. It is the type of friendship that would spring up between business associates wishing to carry their relationship beyond the confines of the office but not necessarily to extend it to the revelation of innermost secrets. It is pure sociability, yet it does not embrace all colleagues; it is much more selective.

Social friendships among people in public life are sometimes bipartisan and can even span rather imposing ideological gaps because their raison d'être is as much social as it is political. In some cases the ideological chasm bridged by these social friendships is astounding. In late 1977, for example, it was reported that Congressman Paul McCloskey, Jr.(R.–Cal.), who had campaigned against President Nixon in the 1972 Republican primary and introduced an impeachment motion against Nixon in 1970, had purchased a vacation home in New Mexico with John D. Ehrlichman, one of Nixon's closest associates and a prominent figure in the Watergate scandal. It turns out that the two men had attended Stanford University Law

School together, participated together in the Stanford Law School debate team, and had remained friends over the years.[26]

Hubert Humphrey, in his first Senate career (before becoming Vice-President) had an unusual social friend in conservative Democrat A. Willis Robertson. While not an ally in a substantive sense, Humphrey did find the elderly Virginia Democrat helpful on procedural matters. Their social relationship did not extend beyond the Senate, but these men of vastly differing political philosophies found that political cooperation could flow from the easygoing social rapport they had established. Humphrey's description of his relationship with Robertson points up the political value of what was a typical social friendship.

> Senator Willis Robertson of Virginia was one of the stalwart opponents of the civil rights bill. He was always good for an hour speech, but it was a strain on him at his advanced age. Occasionally, to make it easier for him, I would interrupt to ask questions. He would smile and respond, acknowledging without words my gesture. Afterward, we might share his Virginia sour-mash whiskey.
>
> It might seem strange to help and socialize with an opponent in such a crucial legislative battle. In Senate terms, it was not. On those rare occasions when a liberal colleague had slipped the traces and we were shy a body on a quorum call, I'd find Willis and he would come to the Senate floor, never letting me down when I needed him.[27]

Attendance at the same college or law school, especially the elite ones, serves as a basis for firm social ties for those in politics. Social class also seems to play something of a role in the choice of friends. The only two senators in my group of interviewees who might be called socialites identified each other as best social friends. However, the number of senators who might be considered socially prominent is small, consisting, in the 96th Congress, of perhaps six men of substantial inherited wealth and acknowledged status in "high society."

[26] *New York Times*, November 12, 1977.

[27] Hubert H. Humphrey, *The Education of a Public Man* (Garden City, NY: Doubleday & Co., 1976), p. 478.

There is one type of association, particularly prominent in the House of Representatives, that has an important social component—the sociolegislative group.[28] But for the fact that these groups have an express political purpose, they might well be included in a discussion of social friendship because their business is often transacted over meals or drinks. The sociability content of these groups varies, but business, as opposed to strict conviviality, is the guiding principle.

Dating back at least as far as the turn of the century, when the Tantalus Club was founded for the purpose of coordinating political strategy among freshmen Republicans in the House, the sociolegislative group has been an enduring feature in the lower chamber. House Speaker Nicholas Longworth presided over outings of the Stateman's Sunday Morning Marching Club in the early twentieth century, and New York Congressmen Fiorello LaGuardia and John Boylan established a bipartisan club known as the LaGuardia-Boylan Spaghetti Association in the 1920s and early 1930s. But bipartisanship in the sociolegislative groups is no longer the norm. The best known of the current crop are the Chowder and Marching Club, the SOS Club, and the Acorns. These are typically Republican fraternities and a feature of the House only; they have no counterpart in the Senate, with the exception of the more loosely structured Wednesday Club of liberal Republican senators where ideology, not liking, is the foundation.[29]

These groups should most properly be considered alliances. They resemble the non-social Democratic Study Group and Black Caucus (both in the House) more than they do other informal groups having little or no legislative purpose. Although in recruitment social compatibility does play a role, status, circumstance, and convergence of political objectives play a greater one. The Chowder and Marching Club, for example, was started by a group of Republican congressmen who had fought in World War II. Its purpose was the defeat of a veterans' benefit bill which the members considered extravagant. The various "class associations" in the House of members first

[28] This term is used by Donald R. Matthews and James A. Stimson in their *Yeas and Nays: Normal Decision-Making in the House of Representatives* (New York: John Wiley & Sons, 1975), p. 99.

[29] For an extended discussion of House clubs see Neil MacNeil, *Forge of Democracy* (New York: David McKay, 1963), pp. 295–296.

elected in the same year is obviously organized more by status than by affinity; the social aspects of these class associations are minimal. In the Senate, however, such organizations of political cohorts have been victims of the individualism now rampant.

Closer to the heart of the purely social connection are the various "watering holes" which have existed over the years in both Senate and House. Some are open to all comers; others are gatherings for either Democrats or Republicans. The most famous of these, House Speaker Sam Rayburn's "Board of Education" was strictly by invitation only. To be requested to "strike a blow for liberty"—the euphemism for having a drink with Rayburn and his buddies—was a signal to a politician or journalist of admission to the charmed circle of Rayburn's intimates. The Board of Education, also referred to as "Rayburn College," had originally been established by Rayburn's mentor and former Speaker John Nance Garner of Texas, who had used the Board to coordinate strategy with his Republican opposite number, Congressman Nicholas Longworth; Rayburn continued the tradition. It was at a Board gathering in the small room on the first floor of the Capitol adjacent to the Senate members' private dining room that Vice-President Harry Truman was sitting on April 12, 1945. "As the Speaker mixed the bourbon with just the right amount of water, he casually told [Truman] that Steve Early, the White House press secretary had left a message, asking that [Truman] return the call immediately."[30] The call was to inform Truman that President Roosevelt had died at Warm Springs, Georgia and that Truman was now President.

Various accounts conflict over just what the balance was between business and sociability at Rayburn's Board of Education or earlier the Garner-Longworth Board. Truman in his own memoirs says nothing about bourbon and water and earnestly asserts, "I went to the office of House Speaker Sam Rayburn . . . to get an agreement between the Speaker and the Vice-President on certain legislation and discuss the domestic and world situation generally."[31] Arthur Krock, who was present that day at the Board meeting, casts doubt

[30] Margaret Truman, op. cit., p. 208.

[31] Harry S. Truman, *Memoirs of Harry S. Truman*, 2 vols. (New York: Doubleday, 195), Vol. 1, p. 4.

on Truman's assertion that serious business was being conducted when the White House call was placed. "It was in the midst of the jollity," Krock writes, "that Truman was summoned. . . ."[32] Returning after a year to Rayburn's office to mark the first anniversary of Roosevelt's death, Krock recalled that most of the time was spent by Rayburn and Chief Justice Fred Vinson swapping political stories.[33]

Although sociability was fairly constant in Rayburn's Board of Education, in House Minority Leader Charles Halleck's "Clinic," and in Senate Minority Leader Everett Dirksen's own watering hole, politics was never far below the surface. Even though the hosts were sparing and discriminating in their invitations and a substantial measure of selection was involved, the members were bound together by serious political purpose; important matters of business were transacted, albeit in a relaxed and chatty atmosphere. Decisions and strategies were planned; despite the social coloration, the underlying logic for Rayburn and others was the building and maintenance of legislative coalitions. Accordingly, these clubs belong most appropriately in the category of alliances.

A social friendship can spring up as the result of encounters in one of the many places in the Senate complex where Senators alone congregate. It can remain a relationship of luncheon companions and business associates gathering for cocktails in one of the hideaway offices, or it can extend beyond Senate walls and involve the exchange of home visits and dinner parties. Accordingly, social friendships can be both intramural and extramural. Shop talk, of course, intrudes as it would at the lunches or cocktail parties of any group of congenial business associates. Perhaps the best test of its rather pure sociability is that it is nonstrategic and proceeds at a light, airy, and somewhat superficial level, both politically and emotionally. While the alliance is a coming together of politicians for cooperative political purposes of a more or less regular character, the social friendship is the more or less regular coming together of politicians for purposes of conviviality or recreation. Such friendship, while not

---

[32] Arthur Krock, *The Consent of the Governed and Other Deceits* (Boston: Little, Brown & Co., 1971), p. 191.

[33] Ibid.

without political advantages and consequences, can sometimes have an apolitical etiquette, especially in its extramural form; the injection of political persuasion, arm-twisting, or earnest politicking into these relationships may on occasion create resentment.[34]

To summarize: Institutional kinships are relationships based on trust and dependability but are limited in terms of deep human commitment; their effects are most decisive in terms of institutional stability and individual political needs. An alliance is politically intensive without deep personal involvement. The relations between a mentor and his protégé are by no means asymmetrical or one-sided; patronage and assistance usually do call forth loyalty and devotion, but there are inescapably instrumental qualities of a political nature lurking in these associations. They may mature into something greater, but in practice they are often sullied by at least some ulterior motivation. Social friendship, although personal, puts its premium on a form of sociability that involves no serious emotional demands.

Although many if not most observers deny that pure friendship can exist among competitive people doomed by their own ambitions to live in a world of favor-seeking, backslapping, and trading of positions and associations, it does in fact exist. It is rare and often difficult to detect, given the frequency with which the word "friend" is superficially bandied about in American politics. It is rare partly because we cynically equate it with cronyism, and want to assure ourselves that all public decisions are rational and untainted by emotion. It is rare because politicians are wary people; they are constantly on display and surround themselves by an elaborate array of defenses. It is rare because pure friendship involves self-revelation and the confiding of the very thoughts and problems that would make a politician vulnerable. It is rare; but it does exist. And let us remember that to say it is rare among politicians is not to say it is common outside politics.

---

[34] Sociologist Georg Simmel postulated an unwritten rule of social protocol that states, in effect, that people tend to avoid contaminating purely social occasions with serious talk. People at play find the introduction of weighty matters an intrusion unless the social setting is merely a pretext for business. See "The Sociology of Sociability," *American Journal of Sociology*, vol. 55, no. 2 (Sept. 1949), pp. 254–261.

As in the case of social friendship, common background characteristics among politicians often provide the foundation for pure
friendship, although shared political values can play an important
role. Sometimes it is difficult to separate the most salient element in
a personal bond of pure friendship among politicians. For example, a
relationship of unusual intimacy is said to have existed in the Senate
in recent years among certain liberal Democratic senators who are
Roman Catholics—more specifically, Irish Catholics. It is said that
Majority Leader Mike Mansfield (Mont.), Sen. Edward M. Kennedy
(Mass.), and Sen. Philip Hart (Mich.) were warm personal friends.
Hart, whose last years were blighted by cancer served as the pivot for
a broader group of Catholic senators that included Democrats
Edmund S. Muskie (Me.) and Eugene McCarthy (Minn.). Whatever
may be said of Philip Hart's accomplishments as a senator, it seems
clear that he was a man who was virtually without enemies. A Senate staff member has described Muskie and Hart as "homebodies"
whose idea of a night on the town was "eating chow mein at the
Moon Palace restaurant." He also described the tearful parting of
Mansfield and Hart when the former Majority Leader was leaving to
take up his new post as U.S. Ambassador to Japan; Mansfield knew
that it was unlikely that he would ever again see Hart alive. Hart
brought forth a degree of affection even from fellow politicians who
do not wear their emotions on their sleeves. Eugene McCarthy,
despite some differences with Hart over the latter's hesitation in joining the anti-Vietnam War movement, was probably closer to Hart
than to any other politician. McCarthy, in his eulogy to Hart,
expressed a view of him that was shared by many people: "He was
not only pleasing to God; he also met the sometimes more difficult
test of being pleasing to man."[35] It would be difficult to dismiss the
point that the circle of senators around Hart was drawn there by reasons of common party or political principle, but it seems clear that
those similarities alone did not account for the degree of intimacy
that prevailed. Occasionally, something as simple as the presence of
a rare human being in a political group can serve as the focus of an
association of great intimacy.

[35] Eugene McCarthy, "Philip Hart," *New Republic*, January 15, 1977, p. 13.

Such universally beloved men in politics are unusual. It is difficult in a long and active political career to avoid making at least some enemies. Tough political battles in which stakes are high almost necessarily create enmities of both a political and personal nature. It has been asserted that those who have avoided making enemies cannot have attained very much of a consequential nature.[36] In the U.S. Senate one often hears the observation that the best-liked members are typically those whose names do not frequently appear on successful bills; they simply are not sufficiently ruthless to lean heavily on their colleagues. But if this is true of the best-liked, it is also true of the least-liked as well.

For a politician the establishment of a pure friendship involves a degree of risk, for in this variety of political friendship there is a likelihood of self-revelation, the exposure of innermost thoughts, the exchange of confidences, and the laying bare of personal problems. The pure friend is entrusted with information which, if revealed, could prove the political undoing of a comrade. It is not a relationship to be embarked on lightly or one that develops easily. Thus many politicians feel safer restricting their closest relationships to those outside the political realm. Yet only another politician can truly understand the agonies and pressures of public life.

Given the disposition of politicians to be cautious and wary, and given the notorious examples of politicians being betrayed or disappointed by personal friends who were also political associates, it is not surprising that many seek to simply separate personal friendship from politics as much as practicable. This does not mean they seek friends from among those with no interest in politics, but rather that they discourage their friends from becoming officeholders, or officeholders friends. It relieves the politician of having a built-in supplicant for favors, allowing a purer form of friendship uncontaminated by ulterior motives.

Richard Nixon and his three businessman friends, Rebozo, Abplanalp, and Elmer Bobst, are examples of this type of association.

---

[36] Roger Hilsman, *To Move a Nation* (Garden City, NY: Doubleday, 1967), p. 581. Hilsman is quite blunt: "No one moves a nation without opposition—a public figure without enemies is a political eunuch."

A current example of pure friendship in politics can be found in the experience of Jimmy Carter. His two closest personal friends, Bert Lance and Charles Kirbo, chose different paths after the 1976 presidential election. Lance came to Washington and almost immediately blundered into a political minefield over his business practices as a banker in Georgia. Despite Carter's spirited defense of Lance, Carter was forced to accept his resignation rather than suffer politically from a protracted battle to keep him. Charles Kirbo, on the other hand, elected to stay in Georgia and not to join the administration. He is still drawn on for advice by Carter, but has thus far chosen to avoid official entanglements. His influence, however, is only slightly less consequential for his being in Atlanta. Another current example is afforded by Walter Mondale's closest personal friend, Duluth businessman Frank Befra. He is Mondale's fishing buddy; but the friendship is far from apolitical, since the Vice-President is said to seek political advice from him. Befra may fall into that class of individuals who might be styled as "professional friends of politicians"; he is also a hunting buddy of Nebraska Democratic Sen. J. James Exon. Such a role was played in the 1950s by George E. Allen, the "friend of Presidents."

For many other politicians the divorce between politics and pure friendship is virtually absolute. Typical of this class of politicians is the senator who said, "I have friends, really personal friends that I feel strongly about, who are neighbors in [the Washington suburbs]. They are people we have come to know on weekends and we enjoy being with, and we have a cabin in [the mountains] and we have a set of friends up there. They are people with no connection with the Senate and, indeed, no connection with politics as such."

The closest personal friend of a powerful Senate Democrat is a Washington lawyer who serves as the senator's attorney. A partner of this lawyer observed that although the senator sees his associate as his closest friend, few deeply personal exchanges ever take place between the two men.

> They spend a great deal of time talking about his private finances, if you call that personal. He complains a great deal about his home . . . and gripes . . . about how much it costs him to maintain it and his home in Washington. I doubt whether

his marriage ever comes up in those conversations or his children. I'd say it's pretty much his money problems.

For Kansas Republican Robert Dole there were also no close personal friends either in the Senate or at home. "There is no way to keep friendships going on a working basis," he confided to a reporter. "Anyone you see, well, it's all job-related." Even his family life has suffered from the peculiar inversion of values that the political life imposes. "You tend to feel those close to you would understand and strangers won't, I guess. You give your life to strangers—maybe it should be the other way around."[37]

Many who have observed the impact of friendship in American politics and found the topic worthy of comment have come very close to denying that such a thing as friendship among politicians actually exists, or else feel that it occurs in such an attenuated and instrumental form that it does not really rise to the dignity of the term as commonly recognized by ordinary people. The reasons for the inhospitality of political life to deep personal attachment often reflect unflatteringly on American politics in the most general sense.

> In England, loyalty—or at least an appearance of loyalty—to colleagues and to party doctrine is the key to success: in America success comes to the man who knows exactly when to jettison a principle or a friendship in order to board a bandwagon.[38]

The vulnerability of friendship to political expediency is not only recognized and understood by American politicians but often even condoned. In a recent Democratic primary campaign for the U.S. Senate in New Jersey this tendency to subordinate friendship to self-interest—and to gain acceptance for such an act—was demonstrated forcefully. On April 10, 1978, Democratic Congressman James Florio announced in Trenton his support for Bill Bradley for the Senate nomination. But one of Bradley's opponents in the primary was state senator Alexander J. Menza, who had the previous year taken the

---

[37] Myra MacPherson, *The Power Lovers* (New York: G.P. Putnam's Sons, 1975), pp. 228, 231.

[38] R. H. S. Crossman, *The Charm of Politics* (New York: Harper & Bros., 1958), p. 12.

bold step of endorsing Florio's bid for the Democratic nomination for governor against the incumbent Democratic governor, Brendan Byrne. Florio explained this apparent act of ingratitude by reporting that a poll taken in his district showed that Bradley, not Menza or the other candidate, would be the most likely winner. "Alex Menza is a good friend," Florio asserted, "but I'm making a determination on the objective consideration of who I think can win." Of Florio, who had forsaken him in the interests of "objective considerations," Menza observed philosophically, "Jim has to do what he has to do. Politics makes strange bedfellows."[39]

There are other perils than political expediency to friendship in American politics. One commentator observes that the politician is "distrustful even of an audience of friends because he knows that every sentence from his mouth may be taken someday by itself and used to harm him. . . ."[40] Private matters confided to a friend by a politician can be revealed and produce damaging consequences. The adversary nature of elective politics, moreover, seems to call forth the need to impugn the qualities of an opponent. It is very difficult to restrict such attacks to the political level; there is always a temptation to resort to *ad hominem* assaults on an electoral opponent, and politicians have had to adapt themselves to deal with this. It is an unusual relationship between political rivals that can survive this buffeting with cordiality intact. A thick skin or a short memory would seem to be required equipment.

To become inured to such personal attacks "reduces the shock and helps a politician to react with more calm than a layman would, just as an athlete is not depressed or offended by bumps he takes from other players in the course of the game."[41] The armored exterior of the politician, however, produces a less sensitive person who is resistant to being touched deeply. This view holds that—like the surgeon, the policeman, and the combat infantryman—the politician must steel himself, be wary of people, and avoid identifying too closely

---

[39] David Wald, "Florio Endorses Bradley; Bontempo Backs Menza," *Star-Ledger* (Newark, N.J.), april 11, 1978, p. 4.

[40] Stimson Bullitt, *To Be a Politician*, rev. ed. (New Haven: Yale University Press, 1977), p. 12.

[41] Ibid.

with those who may turn on him or be taken from him suddenly and without warning. The combined effects of political expediency and human cupidity and inconstancy are corrosive and dictate to the politician that "he must guard against deep personal involvements because election campaigns demand nonchalance about personal attack and often require him to abandon past associates in order to form new coalitions."[42]

Even for those who celebrate the virtues of personal attachments in politics, there is an apologetic and pathetic quality to their defenses of friendship. Hubert Humphrey's verdict on the value of friends to a politician assumed this tone:

Cronies and retainers who slavishly surround a powerful man, sycophants chorusing his praise, may be disgusting and worthy of derision by outsiders. They may even be galling to the man himself. But in the highly competitive, all-or-nothing world of politics, where it seems there are always more people shooting at you than helping, loyalty, above all else, seems important. Poker-playing friends of Harry Truman, bridge-playing friends of Dwight Eisenhower, even a beer-guzzling buddy of an alderman, provide the protective environment for a political man to be himself, to relax, and enjoy the normal diversions of life. Without them, the isolation of even a lowly office becomes intolerable."[43]

In the ensuing chapters the individual varieties of political friendship will be discussed in the context of the U.S. Senate. Chapter 2 will examine institutional kinship. Chapter 3 is devoted to alliances, with special attention paid to the relationships between senators from the same state. Chapter 4 will describe the overall social ambience of Senate life and examine informal groups within the Senate. Chapter 5 will examine the extramural social lives of senators. Chapter 6 will be devoted to the closest personal bonds among senators—the mentor-protégé bond and pure friendship—and will deal with the ques-

---

[42] Herbert Jacob, "Initial Recruitment of Elected Officials in the U.S.—A Model," *Journal of Politics*, vol. 24, no. 4 (November, 1962), p. 709.

[43] Hubert H. Humphrey, op. cit., p. 79.

tion of extra-Senate friendships, in which senators choose their most intimate associates from those outside the Senate.

In Chapter 7, the focus of the study will shift to those senators who hold themselves aloof from personal ties to their colleagues, the loners. It will also consider the question of the nexus between leadership and "lonership" in the Senate. Chapter 8 will consider the obverse side of friendship among senators: hostility and enmity. The Senate has been the locale for a number of bitter and enduring personal feuds and the effects of these embittered relationships will be addressed. The final chapter will be given over to comparison of Senate friendship with that in other spheres of life and to an effort to place it in the broader context of friendship in political life in general. What are perhaps the ultimate questions surrounding senatorial and other friendships will also be addressed: whether friendship really does, and should, matter in politics. For the congeniality of friendship and politics is not only a descriptive and analytical question, but an ethical and normative one as well.

Little Groups of Friends

In Anthony Trollope's novel *The Prime Minister* a sinister and socially ambitious young man, Ferdinand Lopez, marries the daughter of a prominent attorney and proceeds to fleece her of her inheritance (to pay off his bad debts), speculate recklessly, and blackmail the Prime Minister. His excesses come to the attention of the Progress Club, an exclusive London group of which Lopez is a member. One evening, the membership takes up the question of whether Lopez should be expelled for his beastly behavior.

> Among the members of the club there was a much-divided opinion whether he should be expelled or not. There was a strong party who declared that his conduct socially, morally, and politically had been so bad that nothing short of expulsion would meet the case. But there were others who said that no act had been proved against him which the club ought to notice. He had, no doubt, shown himself to be a blackguard, a man without a spark of honor or honesty. But then—as they said who thought his position in the club to be unassailable—what has the club to do with that? "If you turn out all the blackguards and all the dishonourable men, where will the club be?" was a question asked with a great deal of vigour by one middle-aged gentleman who was supposed to know the club-world very thoroughly. He had committed no offense which the law could recognize and punish, nor had he sinned against the club rules. "He is not required to be a man of honour by any regulation of which I am aware," said the middle- · aged gentleman.

Discussion—both popular and scholarly—of the forces which shape the behavior of senators has traditionally drawn an analogy between the U.S. Senate and such an elite social club. Both, it has been asserted, maintain control over the conduct of their members less by a rigorous official code of conduct than by an informal set of norms. Much of the understanding governing the behavior of senators towards one another has been a firm belief in the operation of these norms. Simply stated, a norm is

> a standard shared by the members of a social group to which the members are expected to conform, and conformity to which is enforced by positive and negative sanctions.[1]

The existence of norms and their less-formal companions, "folkways" (see below), have been well-noted in the legislative sphere, and their values and effects have been set forth in detail:

> Any organization must develop norms of behavior that contribute to its achieving organizational goals. Such norms provide the stability and predictability necessary for the institution's maintenance and goal achievement. . . .

> Legislative norms may be classified in terms of the primary functions they perform. Some contribute to the chamber's goal achievement in terms of decision-making or representation; others contribute to maintaining the existing system by regulating the level of conflict . . . . [2]

The experimental evidence which suggests that the force of group norms on an individual is so commanding is reinforced by the conviction that these pressures are universal. Stated most directly,

> One of the basic assumptions of group dynamics has been that general laws concerning group life can be discovered which will hold for such apparently different groups as a juvenile gang, the executive board of the YMCA, a jury, and a railroad maintenance crew.[3]

---

[1] Julius Gould and William L. Kolb (eds.), *A Dictionary of the Social Sciences* (New York: Free Press, 1964), p. 472.

[2] David J. Vogler, *The Politics of Congress* (2nd edition) (Boston: Allyn and Bacon, 1977), pp. 226–227.

[3] Dorwin Cartwright and Alvin Zander (eds.), *Group Dynamics* (New York: Harper and Row, 1960), p. 38.

Without denying the universality of certain types of norms among types of groups, is there reason to believe that what holds for a rifle company in combat, patients in a mental institution, and a group of inmates in a penitentiary will also hold for the U.S. Senate? Many of the social-psychological findings on the operation of norms emanate from experiments performed on groups quite unlike the U.S. Senate. In addition to being uniquely insusceptible to experimental manipulation, the Senate has certain characteristics not shared by most groups which have been the subject of investigation. First, senators choose to be in the Senate; they are not drafted, committed, or sentenced to their incumbency. Second, they have external, individual sources of support in the constituencies which elected them and to which they are principally responsible; although internal standards, rules, and statuses may influence their conduct within the Senate, the more extreme forms of group sanction can rarely be applied to them. Third, there is a considerably greater degree of nonconformity tolerated in the Senate than in most other enduring groups.

The most respected analysis of the rules that govern the interpersonal relationships of U.S. senators is found in the work of Donald R. Matthews, who stated in 1960 that there had evolved in the Senate standards of conduct which Matthews described as "folkways."[4] These standards, which are in effect norms, are "highly functional to the Senate social system, since they provide motivation for the performance of vital duties and essential modes of behavior which, otherwise, would go unrewarded."[5] Norms, or folkways, as Matthews described them, were the collective property of the Senate and set standards to which all senators were expected to conform.

Senators were expected to endure a period of tutelage or "apprenticeship" when they first arrived. They were expected to be deferential and silent until they passed muster as full-fledged members. They were expected to be dutiful, accept their share of the burdens of legislative work, and not spend a great deal of time calling attention to their plans or accomplishments. They were expected to specialize in the work of their committees, however trivial, and not aspire to be

[4] *U.S. Senators and Their World* (New York: Vintage Books, 1960).

[5] Ibid., p. 116.

generalists. There was an expectation that political disagreements would not color personal relationships, that senators would sympathize with and assist colleagues where possible with the assumption that such help would be requited, and that members would wear Senate membership as a badge of pride and not quickly be off in hot pursuit of higher office, using their new status as senators to foster that ambition.

The passage of time and change of circumstances have not been kind to these institutional standards of conduct and interpersonal deportment. New senators are now off and running when they arrive. Many are prepared on the day of their induction with a fistful of floor speeches, and can barely be restrained from charging off to their first press conference. The media attention lavished upon freshman Democrat Dennis DeConcini of Arizona during the Panama Canal debates in 1978 would have been unimaginable twenty years previously; no one would have cared then about the views of a low seniority senator. Fears of venturing outside the subject matter of one's committees seem to have receded to a point where senators experience no great inhibitions about declaiming on almost any subject. The so-called "Johnson rule" which eventuated into every senator receiving a major committee assignment with one subcommittee chairmanship has flattened the Senate hierarchical pyramid and dispersed power more broadly. While pride in being a senator has not diminished—the positions themselves are avidly sought and tenaciously cherished—the use of the Senate as a springboard to the White House has, if anything, increased.

Recent reappraisals of the status of Senate norms make the case that these standards of behavior are not moribund or obsolescent but, rather, have merely been altered and adapted to comport with other changes taking place in the Senate. Norms, it is said,

> do not appear in Congress by magic. Rather, they stem from institutional process and interaction. By the same token, they are not immutable. They change when personnel, times, and the issues confronting Congress change. The single most important source of change in norms is turnover in personnel.[6]

[6] Randall B. Ripley, *Congress, Process and Policy* (New York: W. W. Norton & Co., 1975), p. 61.

The norms which are said to have weathered the storm of increasing Senate individualism are those which confer general benefits on all members. Those norms which redound to the advantages of a few members, most notably apprenticeship, are held to have been extinguished by change.[7]

Senators continue to be diligent in performing the legislative tasks falling to them. Despite the wider range of members' pronouncements, the committee system continues to operate as a device for the division and specialization of labor and the development of expertise. And, for the most part, political disagreements still do not seem to contaminate personal feelings. The venerable practice of "logrolling," or mutual aid on legislation, has also survived and—despite the presidential aspirations lurking in the bosoms of most senators and the relentless self-promotion and headline-grabbing (once regarded with revulsion and now eliciting only mild grumbling)—there is still considerable pride in being a senator.

These old attitudes and practices prevail, without question. But what are the consequences of violating these norms? Does the consistent flouting of these standards, which does occur, call forth some collective response? Presumably, norms are the property of the collectivity, are institution-wide, and influence the behavior of all senators, or at least a preponderant number. Norms, however, are not like some disembodied spirits haunting the floor and cloakroom of the Senate, waiting to possess new members. They are not part of the Senate chamber's ornamentation, like the Minton tiles on the floor or the Brumidi frescoes on the walls. Norms which guided the behavior of Robert Taft and Styles Bridges do not necessarily constrain Howard Metzenbaum and John Durkin.

One reasonable test for the strength and vitality of norms and folkways is the degree to which violations incur penalties for the violator. If norms and folkways are operating with some authority, one would expect to find sanctions delimiting the outermost limits of acceptable behavior. It is important to remember, however, that the

---

[7] David W. Rohde, Norman J. Ornstein, and Roert L. Peabody, "Political Change and Legislative Norms in the United States Senate," paper presented at the annual meeting of the American Political Science Association, Chicago, September 1974, p. 3.

Senate has never placed a very firm construction on the definition of deviant behavior in its members. The Senate, as Ralph Huitt points out, "is not disposed to impose sanctions on any behavior but the most outrageous." The point is important. A group may be expected to punish deviant behavior, and the Senate has proved in the past that it could and would do so with dreadful finality. Calculated and continued flouting of the dignity and good order of the Senate, easier to recognize than define, is deviance which compels sanctions. . . . But the Senate is of all official bodies . . . perhaps the most tolerant of individualistic, even eccentric behavior."[8]

The Senate of 1954 could not have avoided censuring Joseph McCarthy for his rampages. All the elements were in place: misbehavior of the most egregious kind; a recognized group of leaders prepared to stipulate where the line of censurable behavior should be drawn; a reasonable degree of institutional cohesion, a high level of agreement on what is or is not a good senator, and a disposition to enforce those norms. But leaving aside the extremity of McCarthy's transgressions, the resounding quality of the Senate's repudiation of the Wisconsin Republican (the vote to condemn was 67–22) was at least in part a reflection of the nature of the Senate in those years.

The Senate has shown a disposition at certain times in its history to levy sanctions on members whose misconduct was less extreme than that of McCarthy, but with a severity that fell short of condemnation. In an institution whose members are not given to acting out of petulance, the number of occasions in which collective disapproval is officially registered are rare. If little personal or political cost is involved in a vote, senators may refrain from supporting the bills or amendments of an unpopular member, but such occasions are uncommon. Senators have in the past been willing to discipline a deviant short of censure or expulsion. They show little enthusiasm for even this today.

Even in those areas of senatorial conduct in which actual violations of law are concerned, senators have no stomach for sitting in judgement on their colleagues. An assignment to the Senate Ethics

---

[8] Ralph K. Huitt, "The Outsider in the Senate: An Alternative Role," in Ralph K. Huitt and Robert L. Peabody (eds.), *Congress: Two Decades of Analysis* (New York: Harper and Row, 1969), pp. 160–161.

Committee is considered an unpleasant burden at best and more typically a distasteful imposition. Senators struggle to be free of this assignment. Connecticut Democrat Abraham Ribicoff, for one, found his role in the investigation of alleged campaign-fund improprieties by Georgia Democrat Herman Talmadge particularly awkward. Ribicoff pointed out that he had sat next to Talmadge on the Finance Committee for years, they had served together on the Joint Committee on Taxation, and he considered Talmadge a friend and practically a "seat mate"; he could not conceal his eagerness to be rid of committee service.[9]

Even the inquiry into improprieties in the income-disclosure forms of former Senator Edward Brooke (R.–Mass.), a rather unpopular senator, provided little satisfaction for the members. Given the reluctance of senators to assist in the adjudication and enforcement of formal standards of conduct, doubt exists as to their readiness to act collectively against those who transgress their informal codes of behavior. There may be broad agreement among senators on what constitutes ideal or unacceptable conduct, but when violations occur who is it that wields the sanctions central to any system of institutional norms? In an individualistic Senate—and there is no reason to think that the contemporary Senate is anything but resolutely individualistic—is there sufficient cohesion to enforce standards? If enforcement of institutional norms is not provided by the institution, who then will be the custodians and executors of these norms? Collective rebuking of errant senators may once have been the sanctioning mechanism in the Senate. It is difficult to conceive now of such an occurrence in a Senate where coming to grips with allegations of outright illegality is shunned or sidestepped.

The individualistic and competitive quality of the modern Senate and the inclination of senators to build extra-Senate constituencies argues strongly that the overarching norms and folkways binding on all and backed up by sanctions have lost their vitality altogether or exist in such a pallid and attenuated form that their injunctive and inhibiting power operates only sporadically. This is not to say that another Joseph McCarthy bent upon laying waste his senatorial ene-

[9] Interview on CBS "Morning News," March 20, 1979.

mies would not be brought to book, but rather that the arraignment would be more difficult and consensus more difficult to achieve.

The moribund state of institutional norms in today's Senate reflects the fundamental incompatibility of a prescribed code of conduct to which all are required to adhere with an institution so deficient in cohesion and so much at odds on overall direction. The time may again come when comprehensive norms and folkways as an expression of a Senate-wide agreement will manifest themselves, but in the absence of senators powerful and prestigious enough to assert and invigilate over them, without sanctions to enforce conformity to them, it is difficult to argue with conviction that they continue to retain much vitality.

Norms, or at least understandings which govern interpersonal behavior, persist in the Senate, but where they reside, for whom they are relevant, and by whose hands they are enforced must be reappraised. If norms are seen as the property of the institution and the subject of collective sanctioning, their vitality and even their existence are open to question. If, however, norms are seen as understandings which influence the relationships of small groups, even pairs, of members, their lease on life becomes less tenuous. These relationships are based upon a process of experience and testing; what emerges from this process is a more or less enduring form of friendship which I have designated institutional kinship. The norms governing the relationships are not institution-wide but are coterminous with the group of Senators associated with them. These friendships have institutional consequences, constituting as they do a web of interpersonal and professional ties. They are particularly important for the Senate at a time of great individualism, while being in a very important sense an expression of that very individualism.

An individualistic Senate—indeed today an almost anarchic one—requires a laissez-faire system of standards to govern relationships among its members. If, as has been suggested earlier, consensual norms and cogent sanctions are on the wane, it can be argued that the Senate is verging on a system in which each senator is his own judge of acceptable behavior in a colleague. It may be that there is considerable agreement on what constitutes a good colleague, but it would be left to the individual senator to make that determination; it is not mandated by the raised eyebrow of an elder, the collective

disapprobation of committee chairmen, or the strictures of a powerful floor leader. To some degree, even in an individualistic Senate, the
single member is not wholly free to choose those with whom he will
associate and whom he will shun. He will necessarily see more of
those with whom he shares partisanship or committee membership,
but beyond that he is free to pick and choose those with whom he
will establish close working relationships. His disapproval of a colleague, likewise, will be a product of his own best judgment. The role
he essays for himself will reflect his own strategies and objectives.
There are no institutional liabilities attached to being an outsider in
the modern Senate. The same would apply to the loner, the maverick,
or even perhaps the demagogue. To say that the full force of Senate-
wide norms has been spent, then, does not mean that a toll in interpersonal relationships will not be exacted for personal or
professional shortcomings.

What appears to have taken up the slack created by enfeebled
general norms and folkways (which now seem little more than folk-
lore) is a structure of private understandings among individual senators—not mandated from above and not eternal—which serve as
the bonding agents which allow the institution to endure. These have
always existed in the Senate, but they become particularly important
when other and more comprehensive sources of cohesion are deficient, as they are now. This network of relationships is that of institutional kinship.

What sets the ground rules of institutional kinship apart from
those for institution-wide norms is the ability of each senator to
define for himself those qualities he prizes in a colleague, rather than
have them defined for him by collective agreement on what constitutes the "good Senator" or "Senate type." Each senator is thus free
to set his own standards and enforce them unilaterally. It is a form of
pact which stipulates that adherence will produce mutual benefits
and breaches will bring about common grief.

The structure of institutional kinship is not coextensive with the
membership of the Senate. These are relationships which embrace
some senators and not others. They are based on a set of personal
understandings which are closely related to the needs, objectives,
and career goals of the individuals involved.

When senators were asked what qualities they prized most highly in a colleague, certain adjectives occurred more frequently than others. These qualities were dependability and reliability, trustworthiness (sometimes expressed as "integrity" or "honesty"), and intelligence. Also mentioned prominently, but somewhat less frequently, were dedication, hard work, and courage. A premium was clearly placed by these senators on traits that could redound to their own political benefit, or at least not cause them to be cast into jeopardy. The quality of being a person of one's word, of not going back on an agreement, of not making another senator appear foolish, of not gulling a colleague or leading him on—these were the traits most valued. A sense of humor was mentioned by only one senator as a valued trait. Inconstancy, unreliability, laziness, and undependability were cited as the least-esteemed qualities. The term used most frequently to describe the possessors of the most desirable traits was "respect"; that word best encapsulates the relationship of institutional kinship. The adjectives used above are not redolent of adoration, devotion, or even, particularly, of warmth, but in this commonest of Senate friendships respect may be sufficient unto itself.

These tests which senators apply to their colleagues reflect the fact that although the Senate is highly individualistic, there is a recognition of interdependency. A senator acknowledges that he cannot achieve his objectives without the help of others. In most instances this dependence on others is mandated by the specialization of the Senate, although in other areas he has discretion in his choice of workmates.

A congenial nature and a personality which invites cordial relationships are important ingredients, but there pragmatic rather than sentimental forces at work in the forging of this class of friendship. Indeed, these instrumental elements can be seen to outweigh those based on sentiment. To be "well-liked" in the Senate is a designation with a very specific and precise meaning: It is not the gift of being a boon companion; it is not even having a sunny disposition or having a good sense of humor. Indeed some of the "best-liked" senators of recent years have been remote, even dour, personalities—Taft, Stennis, McClellan, Robert Byrd. These are men whom even the most uncritical observer would not characterize as "charming," yet all have been described as "well-liked."

Partisanship and ideology play a relatively minor role in institutional kinships. Indeed, some of its most forceful expressions occur in the interaction of senators with points of view that normally conflict. Two liberal Democratic Senators illustrated below one of the aspects of institutional kinship in operation by citing their relationships with Sen. Russell Long—a colleague with whom they were not often in political accord. This aspect is the disposition of a colleague to be politically empathetic.

One of these Democrats, a Westerner, stressed the fact that

> Long was very candid. You would ask him a question [on a bill on which he was an expert] and he'd probably say, "You don't want to vote for this," because he'd already evaluated my ideological thinking, which is different from his in many instances. Now he didn't need to gratuitously tell me that, but he'll tell me and give me the answer. That is what he does, but he'll throw in, "No, you won't want to be for this one."

Another liberal Democrat, an Easterner, attributed the same tendency to Long.

> [Russell Long] had a wide, broad knowledge of all bills pertaining to finance and taxation. He was also a very astute politician who had been in Congress for a long time and was familiar with the different areas of the country, and it would not be inconsistent with my memory of Russell Long to have him sponsoring a bill—pushing a bill—that would favor, say, the gas and oil interests that he really cared about. But he knew that I represented a consumer state and I can hear him today saying, "You don't want to vote for that, representing [a consumer state]." There's no way in the world I would have voted with Russell Long, in spite of my friendship with him and admiration for him, on an oil or gas measure. I'd vote the straight consumer point of view every time and he'd vote straight industry and we'd laugh about it. But a very basic difference of approach to this type of legislation between him and myself in no way affected our personal relationship.

The last comment of this senator points to another characteristic of institutional kinship—that of restraint, the ability to contain differences at the level of policy and avoid having them impair personal relations. This may be a quality of politicians in general, but it is a well-recognized feature of the Senate.

> In the inner life of the Senate there exists among the members live-and-let-live attitude toward each other that transcends specific disagreements on political matters. Personal friend-ships and alliances within the Senate are not dependent on such criteria. The senators mutually recognize the primary natural law of political survival."[10]

An example of the fusion of empathy and restraint was provided by former Sen. Joseph S. Clark. In 1956, Clark, the liberal Democratic mayor of Philadelphia, was campaigning for the Senate seat of Republican James Duff. One of Clark's campaign vows was to vote against James Eastland for chairman of the Judiciary Committee when the Senate Democrats would organize in January 1957. Clark made Eastland and his chairmanship of the committee (which had jurisdiction over civil rights legislation) a major issue in his appeals to black and liberal voters. Clark defeated Duff in November 1956, but after the first flush of victory had passed he began to be con-cerned about his own effectiveness as a senator, given that he had attacked one of the Senate's barons.

Clark telephoned Hubert Humphrey to ask his advice on how to deal with Eastland once he arrived at the Senate. The two men agreed to meet for lunch in New York to discuss Clark's strategy towards Eastland. At the lunch, Clark expressed concern to Humphrey and predicted trouble for himself, since his attacks on Eastland's fitness for the chairmanship had been widely publicized. Humphrey sug-gested to Clark that he arrange an appointment with Eastland upon arriving in Washington, in order to mollify the Mississippian. Clark agreed. When he appeared at Eastland's office armed with an array of explanations, Clark began by attempting to explain his campaign statements, whereupon Eastland waved his omnipresent cigar at Clark and said, "Hell, Joe, don't worry. I know what it takes to get

---

[10] Neil MacNeil, *Dirksen: Portrait of a Public Man* (New York and Cleveland: World Publishing Co., 1970), p. 137

elected in Pennsylvania." While Eastland made no political convert of Clark by his magnanimity, their relationship began on a more harmonious note.

Diligence, unlike restraint and empathy, sounds little like an ingredient of friendship, but in light of the unique construction placed upon the term in the Senate the simple willingness of a colleague to do his homework and be a reliable informant on issues should be seen as an element of institutional kinship. By itself, of course, it might be considered so devoid of affect that it should be excluded, but there is a strongly instrumental and pragmatic cast to this variety of Senate friendship. Hard work was so prominently mentioned among those qualities esteemed by senators that it is difficult to exclude it. Viewed in the context of the other traits—as part of the complex of qualities—it helps to solidify the bonds of institutional kinship. As one Midwestern Democrat put it,

> If I go to the floor and really don't know an issue, I know who does know it and who I trust and respect. You learn that. There are a number of people I wouldn't bother going to. They're a little sloppy or, you know, they may have a strong bias and not give you both sides. . . . You learn who's really qualified, who's really prepared, who really has evaluated the situation. . . . You soon find out who among your colleagues are really reliable, have studied something in depth and have a good, balanced view of things. . . .

The same standard was set by a New England Republican, formerly in the Senate, who observed with characteristic terseness, "I like people whether they're in the Senate or anywhere else who tend to the business of the day." This ex-Senator went on to sum up the peculiar amalgam of pragmatic and emotional elements that go into making up institutional kinship.

> If I can depend on anyone, they're worthwhile friends. —— served in the Senate (from my state). He was quite weak, but his word was always good and this is what he was known for around the Senate. They'd say, "Talk with ——. What he tells you, you can depend on." This was very true.

For those Senators who share in institutional-kinship relations with their colleagues, friendship is defined in terms of four understandings.

1. *Empathy*—the understanding that a colleague will be disposed to put himself in another's place and visualize and appreciate the constraints under which he operates

2. *Integrity*—the understanding that a colleague will be as good as his word and keep his promises

3. *Diligence*—the understanding that a colleague will discharge his assignments and responsibilities and not jeopardize another by providing slipshod or unreliable information

4. *Restraint*—the understanding that differences will be contained at the level of policy and not degenerate into personal animus

As the functional replacement for debilitated comprehensive norms and folkways now lacking reinforcing sanctions, how does institutional kinship work?

For the senators governed by its understandings it provides incentives for cooperation even though they may be separated by partisan or ideological differences. It enables them to exchange information and identify reliable sources of expertise on the basis of actual experience, rather than simply on the basis of position. It helps senators avoid dealing with each other as abstractions or bearers of political labels and enables them to establish human contact. It provides a network of relationships which, in the aggregate, provide important cohesion at a time of great dispersion of power. It provides dependable sources of support for the achievement of legislative objectives. It reduces the chances for the debilitating personal feuds which detract from legislative effectiveness. It constitutes an economical device for structuring relationships in terms of the actual political needs of the individual senator.

Most specifically, it ensures that, at the very least, information on bills with which a senator is unfamiliar will not only be given but interpreted in a politically useful manner; that the expert on a measure will not slant or distort information in his own interests. It implies not a long-term commitment to cooperation but merely legislative indulgence on a case-by-case basis.

It also encourages the reliable giving of cues and voting hints irrespective of the positions of each party involved. In a study of the elements influencing the votes of members of the House, roughly one-third of the sampled congressmen indicated that friends served as sources of information. "Friendship" was not defined in that study, but an illustrative quotation from it suggests that it approximates our concept of institutional kinship.

> Your personal chats with your colleagues who are on that committee I think are very important. In other words, *if you have a friend on that committee, who you respect as a man of integrity, seriousness, and intellectual honesty,* you ask him and he's almost honor bound to give you a straight analysis of it. I find I rely quite a bit on people I know and think a lot of on [a] committee that has a bill up for debate."[11]

The tendency on the part of the congressman quoted above to see friendship in terms of "respect, integrity, seriousness, and intellectual honesty" and not in terms of devotion, sociability, or even partisanship and ideological compatibility invites the suggestion that something akin to institutional kinship is involved. Mere specialization is not this congressman's test for a cue-giver; if that were true, almost anyone on the committee could be looked to for cues. The friend providing the cues may very well be identical to the cue-taker in terms of party, region, political philosophy, or similarity of constituency, but there is no evidence that this is a pattern.

Personal friends—social and "pure"—may also provide cues, as may allies and mentors, but the frequency of institutional-kinship relationships as compared to the other varieties of senatorial friendship suggests that its overall impact is greater. A member need not have any higher or more intimate form of friendship with a colleague than institutional kinship to solicit—and expect—reliable information and cues on measures outside his realm of expertise. This bond

---

[11] Donald R. Matthews and James A. Stimson, *Yeas and Nays: Normal Decision-Making in the House of Representatives* (New York: John Wiley & Sons), p. 84. (Emphasis added.)

dictates that a member can turn to one expert rather than another for advice with the understanding that it will be informed and accurate, not misleading or self-serving, and consonant with the political imperatives of the solicitor.

· It is certainly appropriate here to raise the question whether these relationships rise to the dignity of the term "friendship." Could not the term "institutional kinship" be replaced just as well by the words "good working relationships" or "mutual respect"? It is true that as friendship is conventionally defined, terms like diligence, integrity, restraint, and even empathy have a rather bloodless quality to them. Those outside the Senate or outside politics might well feel squeamish about accepting these somewhat formal nouns as the ingredients of friendship. They do not evoke the emotional commitment which we normally associate with friendship. Yet there are reasons to accept them as legitimate indices of a particular, and peculiar, form of friendship.

I do not suggest that institutional kinship as a mode of friendship has any applicability outside the world of legislative politics. The terminology of friendship may not be as universal or commonly understood as we think. Supreme Court justices refer to their colleagues as "brethren." Communist party membership brings with it the term "comrade"—a word which in its primary sense is not at all political. Fraternities and black neighborhoods in America are populated by "brothers" and sororities, feminist groups, and convents by "sisters." The emotional content of these appellations may be suspect, but they are accepted by the groups for which they are appropriate. In the Senate, "friend" has an exasperatingly variable meaning, but at least one definition can be found in the notion of institutional kinship.

Institutional kinship can be considered a modality of senatorial friendship because that is what senators say it is. As difficult as it is for outsiders to accept the idea that people who agree on almost nothing in the substantive conduct of their business can style each other as "friends," one is inescapably compelled to give it credence. Illogical as it is to suppose that sour and taciturn old men who communicate with grunts and scowls can be designated friends by youthful and outgoing colleagues, there is a logic that dictates accepting the supposition. For in a profession such as politics, in which superficiality of contact is the norm while intimacy and self-revelation are the exceptions, in a legislative world in which stakes are high and judgements must be made on cold calculations of self-interest, and in a Senate world in which competitiveness and individualism have achieved their apotheosis, some form of human relationship consistent with both political necessity and the human need for comity and support must arise if the institution is to survive and personal goals are to be achieved.

The emotional commitment inherent in institutional kinship is not great, but neither is it insignificant. We cannot dismiss it as a form of friendship simply because our own standards of friendship are more exacting. In an institution in which simple empathy with a colleague's subjection to pressure is deemed a friendly act, in which a word kept, a job well-done, or a feud averted are perceived as friendly gestures, the imposition of an inflexible definition of friendship would be unwarranted. That such friendship is more directed to the tasks at hand than to matters of the heart does not cause the definition to fail; for all its pragmatic and instrumental aspects it has the stuff of human feeling as well.

We are disposed to be skeptical of expressions of praise in an institution in which encomiums are lavished on colleagues so ostentatiously and ritualistically; there is, indeed, much praise-mongering in the U.S. Senate. No well-staffed Senate office is without a writer who can, when the occasion arises, provide a tribute or eulogy for his boss to deliver on the floor or insert in the *Congressional Record*. The sincerity and authenticity of much of this formalistic ritual is certainly open to challenge; Senate tributes to colleagues are normally evidence of nothing more than the most elemental civility. There are occasions, however, when the phrases and idioms used cause us to wonder just how hollow these rituals really are, as the following instances show.

The winter of 1977–78 was a particularly grim one for the U.S. Senate. Bitter conference committee disputes with the House on deregulation of natural gas and abortion payments under Medicare were exhausting and frustrating. Facing the Senate was the Panama Canal Treaty debate and ratification vote. Relations between the Senate and the White House were shaky, and an election year was in the offing. Into this gloomy political context, death was to intrude taking from the Senate three of its senior members. On November 27, John

L. McClellan, the Arkansas Democrat and chairman of the Committee on Appropriations, died at his home in Little Rock. On January 12, Lee Metcalf (D.–Mont.), an eighteen-year veteran of the Senate and expert on public utilities, died in Helena. The following evening, Hubert H. Humphrey, the senior Democratic senator from Minnesota, former Vice-President, presidential candidate, and the country's most prominent liberal politician, died at his home at Waverly, Minnesota after a long struggle with cancer.

This triple bereavement provided the occasion for an outpouring of grief unparalleled even in a Senate not given to restraint in these matters. More remarkable even than the number of tributes delivered—and virtually every senator eulogized at least one of the departed colleagues—was the prominence of the words "friend" and "friendship" in the tributes. The excerpts from the eulogies given here illustrate their tone.

Of Lee Metcalf it was said:

> One of the saddest things about serving in the U.S. Senate is that because of the nature of the institution you often become close friends with someone only to have that friendship interrupted by retirements, electoral defeats, or death. We have lost just such a friend in Lee Metcalf. (Walter D. Huddleston [D.–Ky.])

> I would like to pay tribute to our friend and colleague, Lee Metcalf, whose death last week saddened and shocked all of us. (William Hathaway [D.–Me.])

> I will miss Senator Metcalf—both as a friend and a colleague. (William Roth [R.–Del.])

> Lee Metcalf was my friend. While we differed in political philosophy on many occasions, my respect for him never diminished. (James O. Eastland [D.–Miss.])

Of John McClellan it was said:

> I suppose that the friendships which normally develop between members of any state delegation to Congress are special ones. (Dale Bumpers [D.–Ark.])

> He was my colleague and friend and I will miss him very much. (Abraham Ribicoff [D.–Conn.])

I will miss him as a valued friend. (Clifford Hansen [R.–Wyo.])

I will miss him as a colleague and a friend. (Edward M. Kennedy [D.–Mass.]

Of Hubert Humphrey it was said:

He will be sorely missed by all of us who served with him and grew to cherish his friendship. . . . (Richard Schweiker [R.–Pa.])

With his death the nation has lost one of its most distinguished citizens, the Senate has lost a legislator of great talent, and I have lost a friend. (John Stennis [D.–Miss.])

As a friend and colleague, Senator Humphrey will be sorely missed. (Joseph Biden [D.–Del.])

I shall miss Hubert Humphrey greatly. We did not always agree, but he was always my friend. (James Allen [D.–Ala.])[12]

These tributes are but a few of those delivered on the Senate floor or inserted into the *Congressional Record*. It would have been painfully redundant to have included them all, but those cited are representative; in their invocation of friendship with the deceased senators they reflect the tone of all. Several features of this Senate ritual are worthy of note. First, although all three of the deceased senators were Democrats, three more personally and philosophically different men could hardly be imagined. McClellan, a remote and insular person whose life had been deeply touched by tragedy, was one of the old-line Southern committee chairmen and also a very conservative Democrat. Metcalf was an easygoing and unaggressive senator who suffered from a drinking problem. He was very much a peripheral figure in the Senate, although certainly one who was well liked. Humphrey was a monumental figure in American politics, a skilled parliamentarian, and a liberal of great dynamism. Both Humphrey and Metcalf—but especially Humphrey—were capable of attracting friends by their manner and nature. It is, however, difficult to believe that John McClellan's capacity for friendship matched those of Met-

12 These eulogies have been excerpted from *Congressional Record*, 95th congress, 1st session, November 29, 1977, pp. S19171 ff. (the McClellan tributes) and *Congressional Record*, 95th Congress, 2nd session, January 24, 1978, pp. 301 ff (the Humphrey and Metcalf tributes).

calf and Humphrey. Indeed, shortly before his death one of McClellan's colleagues reported that McClellan had told him that in his thirty-five years in the Senate he had never been inside the office of a fellow senator. Yet in all three tributes, the word "friendship" figured prominently.

Another noteworthy characteristic of these eulogies is that the accolades to friendship were bestowed with little heed to partisan or ideological boundaries. It does not surprise us to hear the liberal Democrat Birch Bayh (D.–Ind.) referring to Hubert Humphrey as "a dear friend"; [13] but we are brought up short when James O. Eastland (D.–Miss.), whose positions on virtually every aspect of national policy were passionately and diametrically opposed to those of Humphrey, quotes Faulkner in praise of Humphrey's "love and honor and pity and pride and compassion and sacrifice." These qualities, he says, "best describe the life of our friend from Minnesota."[14]

For the outsider disposed to view the Senate through the crystalline prism of ideology, Bayh's words seem heartfelt and those of Eastland hypocritical. How surprised we are to learn then that Eastland's words were not simply deposited at the desk for inclusion in the *Record*, but actually delivered on the floor of the Senate—this by a man for whom formal statements in the chamber were so unusual as to approximate total eclipses of the sun in their rarity. How is it possible that the living embodiment of everything that Humphrey struggled against could arise and call Humphrey beloved?

Times and people change, of course, but even in more fractious times this tribute, or one like it, could well have been delivered in the Senate. To the outside world, inclined as it is to see the upper chamber solely as a stage where pageants of policy and principle are put on by players made up to represent public points of view, human qualities seem little more than backdrop or histrionic contrivance. Like Hamlet pronouncing upon the staged emotions of the players, we wonder what in the senator

> *Could force his soul so to his own conceit*
> *That from her working all his visage warned,*

---

[13] *Congressional Record*, 95th Congress, 1st session, January 24, 1978, p. S331.

[14] *Congressional Record*, 95th Congress, 1st session, January 24, 1978, p. S350.

Tears in his eyes, distraction in his aspect,
A broken voice, and his whole function suiting
With forms to his conceit? And all for nothing!
For Hecuba!
What's Hecuba to him, or he to Hecuba,
That he should weep for her? . . .

But we must allow for the rhetorical license of politicians and concede them the measure of sincerity which permits this unique form of friendship. That we have more rigorous standards does not preclude them from defining it in a manner that to them is sensible and comprehensible.

CHAPTER THREE

THE ALLIANCE

In Richard Rovere's portrait of Joseph R. McCarthy, *Senator Joe McCarthy*, there occurs a passage which reveals much about both the controversial junior senator from Wisconsin and the Senate as a human institution. Rovere relates the efforts made to stave off the condemnation of McCarthy in the summer of 1954. A compromise had reportedly been worked out between McCarthy's lawyer, Edward Bennett Williams, and President Eisenhower. McCarthy, according to this account, would have been given the chance to withdraw his remarks accusing the Watkins Committee—set up to investigate McCarthy's activities—of being "an unwitting handmaiden" of communism and to promise to reform his ways; in return for this apology and pledge, the White House would have requested that the resolution of condemnation be withdrawn. For Republicans leaning toward censure but fearful of McCarthy's strength with the electorate, such a face-saving gesture would have been welcome. McCarthy, however, turned down the proferred compromise because

> he knew it would hurt his two great supporters in the Senate, William Jenner, of Indiana, and Herman Welker, of Idaho, who believed in his mission far more than he did. Jenner and Welker had worked night and day not simply to avoid censure but to gain vindication for McCarthy, and McCarthy gave the emissaries of compromise the explanation that he could not accept it because his friends would feel let down.[1]

Although it does seem difficult to believe that such motives would have animated McCarthy, Rovere suggests that they were consistent with the personality of a man who would browbeat a witness

[1] Richard Rovere, *Senator Joe McCarthy* (New York: Harcourt, Brace, 1959), pp. 56–57.

and then offer to shake his hand. His concern over the feelings of Jenner and Welker can be explained in terms of McCarthy's complicated and capricious character, but it may also reflect a sentiment, less idiosyncratic and more broadly senatorial in nature, which holds that senators on occasion care very much about abruptly parting company with those with whom they have been closely associated. Individualistic as senators are, the rule "Every man for himself" does sometimes yield to a feeling of solidarity towards those whose causes have been one's own.

Rovere describes Welker and Jenner as McCarthy's "friends." The evidence suggests that both liked the Wisconsin Republican; their attachment to the principles he purported to espouse may have been more pronounced than that to the man himself, but the friendship which prevailed among these senators was far more intimate than the casual association of institutional kinship. It fell short, however, of the more personal forms of friendship. In fact, they were allies. The Senate alliance, of which this relationship was evidently an example, serves as the bridge between the more explicitly instrumental institutional kinship—with its emphasis on qualities deemed essentially "senatorial"—and the personal relationships of companionship, sociability, and confidence found in the more intimate varieties of Senate friendship.

In defending the alliance and distinguishing it from other forms of association among senators, a useful analogy can be made to relationships in the business world. Businessmen, especially those in large corporations, have as little direct influence over who their associates will be as do senators over who will sit with them in the chamber. Even in the more intimate setting of the Senate committee, considerations of party, region, and expertise play a far greater role than the compatibility of personalities in the determination of committee assignments. The businessman, too, discovers that his coworkers are chosen by the personnel department on the basis of their value to the corporation rather than compatibility with particular individuals. Yet both the business executive and the senator in their separate worlds have a measure of discretion in terms of those with whom they do not absolutely have to associate. The process of sorting out those with whom contact and interaction are mandatory and those with whom association is optional (but can be justified both in business and human terms) typically evolves over time. This choice may not result in the development of a profound and intimate attachment, but may be as simple a decision as, "He's the kind of person I enjoy working with."

In complex organizations with high levels of specialization where the division of tasks produces considerable compartmentalization, there is a strong tendency for the individual to know best those with whom he works most continuously, whose particular tasks he shares. A senator who has major assignments to the Agriculture Committee and the Armed Services Committee will have at least the opportunity to become more familiar with those committee colleagues than with others. In recent years, moreover, individual senators have been more successful in getting themselves assigned to committees of their choice, rather than being arbitrarily placed by the leadership, so a measure of self-selection does now take place; a member very likely finds that he is on a committee with colleagues whose substantive interests he shares. Similarly, the corporate executive presenting himself as a specialist in marketing, advertising, or personnel and the academic as an historian, classicist, or mathematician will find themselves in a milieu with people of similar interests. The processes of self-selection and specialization in complex institutions are mutually reinforcing.

It is possible to overstress the parallels between large institutions such as corporations and universities and a relatively small institution like the senate. Senators are subject to specialization, but they are not truly compartmentalized; they are far more familiar with all the other senators than are corporate division chiefs with management personnel or professors in a large university with other professors. Size alone is not necessarily the decisive element in this greater familiarity with colleagues that senators have. For one thing, each senator is a public figure in his own right, something of a celebrity whose reputation is in the public domain to an extent not necessarily true of corporate executives, professors, or even high-ranking military officers. Even a freshman senator will usually bring to the Senate a wide measure of recognition attained in the House, in state politics, or in other spheres of public life.

The other factor unique to the Senate is the fact that it acts as a body, albeit mostly upon the recommendations of committees. Most corporate and academic decision making is not institution-wide;

there are few occasions on which entire universities or all of corporate management come together. Boards of directors do meet regularly with corporate presidents and university presidents meet with trustees, but the dictates of hierarchy and specialization in these institutions decree that most often sales managers, for example, interact with other sales personnel and members of a philosophy department with other philosophers. Some reaching out across jurisdictional and disciplinary boundaries does take place in both the business world and universities but the reasons for this are circumstantial and intermittent rather than formal and regular. There is no equivalent in these other institutions to the Senate in session, the quorum call, or the roll-call vote.

Yet despite the fact that the relatively compact Senate—composed of members with high visibility acting collectively—is an institution in which personal and professional contact are not random, a Senator does not work with all colleagues with the same degree of regularity, continuity, or intimacy. Senate Alliances reflect this reality.

It would not be difficult to postulate an enduring commitment to the same set of political principles among individual senators by simply noting that they tend to vote together more often than not or even virtually all the time. But that a pair or group of senators is part of a discernible coalition or alignment on roll-call votes could lead us to infer certain things about the personal side of their relationships which may simply not be true. This is not to say that consistent patterns of voting agreement reveal nothing about personal relationships, but rather that they do not tell the whole story—or perhaps the right story—about the extent to which consistent support for the same measures can give rise to feelings of commitment and personal regard. The extent to which a senator sees himself as being allied with others not so much by circumstance as by choice may explain actions which would be unintelligible if only the ostensive criteria are used.

An analysis undertaken more than twenty-five years ago—which possibly reflects the coalitions of a bygone era—identified a number of voting blocs in the Senate, the members of which voted together on a number of issues over a sustained period; it concluded that underlying these coalitions were interpersonal relationships of great complexity which

> reflected interaction and association. That is, the members of
> blocs such as these not only were in some measure aware of

their common responses when the roll was called, but presumably also were in contact with one another prior to such votes and on a more or less continuing basis. The nature of this contact almost certainly is informal and relatively unorganized, though it may be far from simple, but its reality in the life of the legislative party seems unquestionable.[2]

In the alliance, then, we look not so much at the uniformity of voting records among senators—although that might provide a clue to the existence of this form of friendship—but more to evidence that members actually perceive themselves as involved in cooperative endeavors which cannot always be deduced from even the highest levels of agreement on recorded votes.

Few senators vote together more consistently than George McGovern and Thomas Eagleton. Both are Democrats; both liberals; both represent Midwestern farm states. Yet their mutual antipathy is well known; it dates back to 1972 when McGovern dropped Eagleton from the Democratic ticket as the Vice-Presidential candidate. Birch Bayh and Vance Hartke shared not only partisanship and ideology but the distinction of representing Indiana in the Senate. Yet the two men could barely abide one another. The historical list of senators who shared every politically relevant attribute but regarded each other as rivals or even enemies is a long one embracing some of the Senate's most illustrious names.

Alliances, especially those which exist over a long period of time, are of course subject to modification as issues, individuals, and the Senate itself change. A long-term alliance, typically based on both political agreement and personal regard, may give way to indifference or even enmity when the issue which once united the senators is redefined or is no longer important. Changing political conditions may compel an erstwhile alliance member to forsake his partners in the interest of political survival. Personal ambition for higher office may cause a senator to bolt from an alliance which might be regarded as politically disadvantageous. Or alliance members may fall to quarreling over just who is the senior partner. Despite these forces contributing to the fragility of alliances in a body so relentlessly

---

[2] David Truman, *The Congressional Party* (New York: John Wiley & Sons, 1959), pp. 90–91.

individualistic, such associations have existed and continue to exist, albeit sometimes in an attenuated form. The depth of commitment will vary from partner to partner; the temptation to break ranks is a constant peril, and all recognize the disruptive effect of political expediency. But what distinguishes the alliance from a loosely affiliated group of senators who just happen to vote the same way is the existence of certain expectations of a type directed to allies and not to more casual associates. There are expectations of consultation here and expectations that an ally will not lightly and frivolously break ranks with those to whom he is tied by links preeminently political but, most important, tinged with the coloration of human attachment.

The alliance as an association of senators based on agreement on an issue or complex of issues and solidified by the development of personal ties can be seen as a permanent feature of the U.S. Senate. In the years before the Civil War, the question of the status of slavery was the one on which the most decisive battle-lines were drawn, yet the complexion of the opinions in Congress in the group conventionally described as "anti-slavery" ran from the pallid and temporizing "popular sovereignty" of Sen. Stephen Douglas of Illinois to the deep-dyed abolitionism of Sen. William Seward of New York (of the "irrepressible conflict" speech). Much closer to the latter than to the former in their attitudes on this question were Sen. Charles Sumner, a Free-Soil party man from Massachusetts, and William Pitt Fessenden, a Whig from Maine fiercely opposed to Douglas's Kansas-Nebraska Bill, which was designed to remove the old northern limit on slavery established by the 1820 compromise.

Fessenden's election to the Senate had sent a thrill of hope through Sumner.

> [Fessenden] came in the midst of that terrible debate on the Kansas and Nebraska Bill by which the country was convulsed to its center, and his arrival had the effect of a reinforcement on the field of battle. . . . There he stood. Not a Senator loving freedom . . . did not feel on that day that a champion had come.[3]

---

[3] Quoted in Charles A. Jellison, *Fessenden of Maine* (Syracuse: Syracuse University Press, 1962), p. 74.

After two years together in the Senate there was "no member of the Senate with the possible exception of Jacob Collamer of Vermont, for whom Fessenden had a stronger personal regard than he had for Charles Sumner. They were close then—'my dear Sumner' and 'my dear Fessenden'—and it was not an uncommon sight to see them walking arm-in-arm into the Senate chamber."[4] After Sumner was beaten senseless on the floor of the Senate by Rep. Preston Brooks of South Carolina for his "Rape of Kansas" speech, Fessenden wrote to his wounded ally, saying,

> I miss you very much, my dear Sumner, and so do we all, looking forward impatiently to the time when we can have the aid of your great powers. But let not your own impatient ardor disappoint us. Be sure that your physical vigor is well restored before plunging again into this whirlpool of abominations.[5]

Close agreement among politicians on important public questions often causes them to deemphasize personal differences or even deny that they exist. On matters of great controversy, when a politician needs all the allies he can get, he cannot grant himself the luxury of indulging in likes and dislikes. However, when the clamp of political exigency which holds politicians together finally is loosened, the abrasive play of conflicting personalities may become more pronounced. By the second year of the Civil War, the anti-slavery forces were no longer a beleaguered minority in Congress. Most Southern congressmen had departed to join the Confederacy and the Republicans were in the ascendancy in the North. The old imperatives for subordinating personality to policy were no longer so compelling.

With the onset of the war, Sumner and Fessenden fell to quarreling. In 1862 Fessenden was musing, "If I could cut the throats of about half a dozen Republican senators . . . Sumner would be the first victim, as by far the greatest fool of the lot."[6] Although their paths were diverging over matters relating to the war and slavery, their growing personal animus spilled over to other matters as well; after a particularly bitter clash on the floor of the Senate chamber in 1864

---

[4] Ibid., p. 93.

[5] Ibid.

[6] Quoted in ibid., p. 177.

over a bank bill, Fessenden confided in a letter to his son, "I would gladly let the dirty dog [Sumner] alone if I could, but to bear his insolence, and suffer his malignity to have full swing would only be to destroy myself."[7]

The feud carried on for several more years, but there was a reconciliation of sorts in 1868 when Fessenden spoke approvingly of Sumner as a choice for secretary of state in Grant's cabinet; there were even a few kind remarks exchanged on the floor the following year, but the two men had diverged so radically since the time in the 1850s when they served as part of the small corporal's guard of Free-Soil senators that any hope of reconstructing the alliance would have been impossible.

With New York's Seward, with whom he served in the Senate for ten years, Sumner unquestionably had an early alliance. In Sumner's own words, he saw in his relationship with Seward "those congenial sentiments on things higher than party [which produced] a peculiar bond of friendship."[8] Although united by principle and "congenial sentiments, " the Seward-Sumner alliance collapsed on the eve of the war when Seward supported the Crittendon Compromise, the last-ditch effort to save the Union which involved, among other things, a proposal for a constitutional amendment barring Congress from interfering with slavery in any state. Sumner regarded Seward's defection not only as political apostasy but as a personal betrayal as well.

> Sumner became frantic with anxiety. He could not sleep nights; his health was impaired. . . . He could not be diverted from his concern over Seward's defection.[9]

By the time Henry Adams had the opportunity to observe and evaluate the relationship between the two senators, it had deteriorated to the point where Adams could remark, "The two men would have disliked each other by instinct had they lived in different planets."[10]

---

[7] Ibid., p. 178.

[8] David Donald, *Charles Sumner and the Coming of the Civil War* (New York: Alfred A. Knopf, 1960), p. 208.

[9] Ibid., p. 273.

The case of Charles Sumner may reveal more about the peculiarities of his own temperament than about the dynamics of Senate alliances, but it may also suggest more generally that a too-rigid adherence to principles on the part of an alliance partner tends to undercut one of the essential properties of the alliance—a willingness to accommodate a partner with favors when there is little or no political cost. One of the few tangible obligations owed each other by alliance partners is the rendering of such low-risk favors as joining as co-sponsor on an ally's bill when such co-sponsorship would entail no betrayal of long-held principles, or favoring an ally with a vote on a matter of great importance to him but of little direct significance to one's self or constituency. To do more than that is not expected; to decline to render a politically risky favor incurs no penalties in the healthy alliance. This Sumner was unwilling to do at one stage of his otherwise close alliance with Seward, and the event was a warning signal that it was headed for trouble.

Late in 1854 when Seward was up for reelection and anxious to demonstrate to his New York constituency that he could "deliver" for them, he sponsored a subsidy for the Collins Steamship Company and approached Sumner for his support. Sumner replied that he found the subsidy unwarranted in terms of its economic value. Seward then appealed to Sumner to vote for the bill as a personal favor. Sumner responded that he had not been sent to the Senate to get Seward reelected. Seward was furious and shouted, "Sumner, you're a damned fool!" Ultimately Sumner did vote for the bill, but felt constrained to explain his vote in a floor speech. The incident caused a temporary breach in their relationship, and for several months the two men did not exchange a word.[11]

Perhaps the most impressive alliance the Senate has ever seen, in terms of duration, cohesion, and political significance, was that of a group of conservative Republican senators which existed more or less continuously from the early 1880s to the middle of the first decade of the twentieth century. Although modified by death, defeat,

[10] Henry Adams, *The Education of Henry Adams* (New York: Random House, Modern Library, 1931), p. 102.

[11] David Donald, op. cit., p. 270–271.

and occasional defection, it was sustained by an enduring core of conservative economic and social principles and a substantial amount of personal commitment.

The source of continuity in this alliance was Nelson W. Aldrich, a Rhode Island Republican who served in the Senate from 1881 until 1911. His original alliance partners were Sen. Orville H. Platt (R.–Conn.) and Sen. William B. Allison (R.–Iowa). United by party and ideology, their friendship was cemented by their common membership on the Senate Finance Committee. This assignment gave the three a strategic position from which to determine the course of tariff policy—which in the last two decades of the nineteenth century was one of the most important national economic issues. In 1885 the original three were joined by a fourth political comrade, John Coit Spooner, a Wisconsin Republican and corporation lawyer who was considered one of the best legal minds in the Senate. Spooner went on the Judiciary Committee, serving there as a point of contact and cooperation with his allies on the other key committees. By the time Spooner arrived in the Senate, Aldrich was chairman of the Committee on Rules as well as being a dominant figure on Finance. Allison, in addition to being chairman of the Republican caucus, was also chairman of the Appropriations Committee. Platt served on the Finance and Judiciary Committees and as chairman of the Committee on Patents. This group of conservative Republicans constituted a tight-knit group which came to be known, simply, as "The Four."

> It were a difficult—perhaps an impossible—task to trace out all of the ramifications of the interplay of these four men upon one another. That there was something common to them all, that it was distinctive, powerful, and constant, goes without saying. They could not else have formed the close fraternity they did. . . .
>
> They compose a genuine cabal, perhaps the only one in the history of the Senate. While they hold together—just nine years— they are at the very heart of the Republican policy.[12]

---

[12] Nathaniel Wright Stephenson, *Nelson W. Aldrich* (New York: Charles Scribner's Sons, 1930), p. 135.

The marvelously complementary qualities of the Four were noted by freshman senator Albert Beveridge of Indiana who saw Aldrich as the manager, Allison as the "conciliator and adjuster," Spooner as floor leader and debater, and Platt as "designer and builder."[13] The transcendent conviction of the Four of the rightness of high protective tariffs and the gold standard caused these senators to stick together "as close and affectionately as a stamp sticks to a love letter. . . . [They] stood shoulder to shoulder, not as party men but as representatives of the creditor classes, of the part of the country where creditor classes were in the saddle."[14] Where the issue shifted away from monetary and tariff questions to matters of foreign policy, the adhesive of class and economic solidarity gave way somewhat, but not enough to cause an irreparable breach.

However, the question of the annexation of Hawaii threatened to drive a wedge between the Four. "Three days after Dewey's exploit [at Manila Bay], a joint resolution for the annexation of the Hawaiian Republic was introduced in the House of Representatives and was passed on June 15 [1898], by an overwhelming vote."[15] Spooner had gone on record as opposing annexation. The four stood together against the war with Spain, but Allison, Platt, and Aldrich now favored the annexation of the islands. However, the Four had anticipated that the issue of Hawaii would come up.

> So close and intimate was their fraternity that they were able to form an accord. Mr. Spooner would go on record as opposing the annexation but he would not vote against it.[16]

When the vote was taken in the Senate, Spooner was paired, but announced that he would have voted against the annexation.

The personal regard shared by these men and their mutual inclination, when they disagreed, to do so amicably was a hallmark of

[13] Dorothy Ganfield Fowler, *John Coit Spooner, Defender of Presidents* (New York: University Publishers, 1961), p. 213.

[14] Matthew Josephson, *The Politicos, 1865–1896* (New York: Harcourt, Brace & Co., 1938), p. 537.

[15] Dorothy Ganfield Fowler, op. cit., p. 234.

[16] Nathaniel Wright Stephenson, op. cit., p. 161.

their alliance. But the broad national social and political scene which had served as backdrop for this enduring pageant of political friendship began to shift at the turn of the century. The clamor for change was being heard with great alarm by conservatives; nowhere was the clamor more intense than in the farm areas of the Midwest. It spelled potential trouble for Allison in Iowa. For Spooner in Wisconsin it expressed itself in the 1906 elections with the election of Robert La Follette to the Senate. The split between creditor East and debtor West was beginning to find Aldrich and Platt on one side of certain issues and Spooner and Allison on the other.

In 1901–1902 the regional cleavage in the ranks of the Four was manifested on two occasions: one was a bill subsidizing steamship lines, which Platt and Aldrich supported and Spooner and Allison opposed, and the other a measure on freight rates which split the Four on the same axis. Nonetheless they continued to maintain close personal ties, and reinforced the political bonds through extensive social contact that summer in the Arlington Hotel which served as the locale for what Aldrich's biographer called "a continuous senatorial house party." Although conviviality may have been the subterfuge for these gatherings at Platt's apartment, the objective was "thrashing over the next step in some legislative programme."[17]

Premonitions of changes in the offing that would alter profoundly the political basis of their association seemed to make the Four cling to each other more tenaciously in the more personal aspects of their relationship. The political vulnerabilities of all of them in their home states in the face of a crescendo of progressivism began, however, to widen splits to the point where pure sentiment alone could no longer bridge them.

Before things could evolve further, however, infirmity and death intervened. Platt died in 1905. Spooner resigned from the Senate in 1907, and Allison, who had been ailing during most of that year, died in 1908. The finality of death and departure ended an alliance that might have ended sooner without the intense personal ties which prevailed among its members. One indication of this was the recollection by Allison's junior colleague from Iowa, Jonathan Dolliver, of

[17] Ibid., p. 204.

one of his last conversations with the older man. Although a "lieu-tenant " rather than a principal of the Four, Dolliver was at one point on the verge of jumping on the bandwagon of progressivism. The old Republican leader pleaded thus with his protégé:

> Jonathan, don't do it; don't do it now; wait until I am gone. I know [the conservatism of the old Senate] is wrong. It has grown up gradually here in the last quarter of a century. I have gone along with it. These men are my associates. I have only a little while left, and I haven't got the strength to break away.[18]

An almost perfect congruence of political principles, class inter-ests, and formal partisan allegiances accounted, in large measure, for the durability of this alliance of Senate conservatives. Yet one is inescapably drawn to the conclusion that in the absence of the affec-tion that these men actually had for one another, their association would have dissolved far earlier. Indeed, if Allison's plea to Dolliver can be taken at its face value, the emotional attachment had virtually taken on a life of its own. Despite the regional clashes which found Spooner and Aldrich on opposite sides of issues after the turn of the century, Aldrich would lament, after the Wisconsin senator's depar-ture, "If Spooner were only here."[19]

At its height, the Four exerted a political influence far out of pro-portion to its collective votes. As chairmen and party leaders of the Senate at the apogee of its influence, they dominated not only the upper chamber (and occasionally the House) but even the White House as well. Even had they been bitter enemies they would have had to have had periodic contact with one another, but their mutual fondness made these professional contacts pleasurable rather than simply obligatory.

However, although they extended their relationship into the social realm, sociability per se did not define the nature of their rela-tionship. The Four had selected one another from a Senate comprised of many others whose philosophies, political allegiances, and leader-

---

[18] Robert M. La Follette, *La Follette's Autobiography* (Madison, Wis.: The Robert M. La Follette Co., 1913), pp. 433–434.

[19] Nathaniel Wright Stephenson, op. cit., p. 320.

ship roles might have entitled them to membership in the Four but who achieved only junior partnerships, "lieutenancies," or temporary affiliations. The Four complemented each other in both political and personal terms: Aldrich, the skillful, single-minded strategist, unshakable in his convictions; Spooner, the legal technician and fearsome debater; Platt, reserved and shrewd but responsible—the legislative sentinel of the Four; and Allison, even-tempered, sensible, and always the conciliator. The spirit of the times, the nature of the Senate, and the qualities of the men all came together to produce an alliance of unusual durability and unsurpassed power.

The political coming of age of the Progressive movement found its expression in the election to the Senate of a number of men as dedicated to reform as the Four was to the status quo. Like that of the Republican old guard, whose dominance extended over a period of two decades, the golden age of the Progressives spanned many years of Senate history. Its onset was signaled by the election of Robert M. La Follette, Sr. and his arrival in the Senate in 1906. Its formal disappearance can probably be put at the time of the departure from the upper chamber of Burton Wheeler in 1947. In its forty year tenure in the Senate, the Progressive bloc was composed of greater and lesser figures, of evanescent men and those whose imprint on the institution was lasting. It spanned generations—embracing the elder and younger La Follettes of Wisconsin and William Borah of Idaho, who took his seat in 1907, and Burton Wheeler of Montana, who did not arrive until 1923. Indeed, this group of Western senators was less a bloc than it was a more or less continuous ideological presence, fighting the trusts, battling for publicly owned power, defending the farmers and ranchers, and campaigning for direct citizen participation in the political process. These general tendencies, however, were qualified by the relentless independence of these men, whose maverick qualities were so pronounced as to call into question whether they ever constituted anything more than a vague political alignment.

For one thing, their partisan identities were astoundingly dissimilar. Indeed, the word "party" did not occupy a prominent place in the vocabularies of most of them, except as an epithet. La Follette the elder was a Republican, although of a decidedly exotic sort for 1906. His son was a Progressive-Republican from 1925 until 1935, but from that year until 1947 simply a Progressive. Borah was a Republican, as were Albert Cummins of Iowa and Hiram Johnson of California. Thomas Walsh of Montana was a Democrat, as was his home-state colleague Burton Wheeler. George Norris of Nebraska was a Republican from 1913 until 1937 and an Independent Republican from 1937 to 1943. Aside from the somewhat loose-jointed set of principles which they expounded with some regularity, their regional affiliation seemed to form the most authentic basis for their cohesion. The Senate group of Progressives was innocent of any Eastern members.

The most concrete expression of their existence as a coalition in the Senate was a label applied to them by one of their most persistent antagonists, Sen. George Higgins Moses of New Hampshire. In a speech to a convention of manufacturers in 1929, Moses made caustic reference to these Westerners as the "Sons of the Wild Jackasses." This hostile appellation was the most tangible bond shared by these men. That their only identifying tag was hung upon them by an adversary and not by themselves suggests that their cohesion was perceived more acutely by those outside the group than those within. It was unquestionably an alignment, probably a coalition, but somewhat less surely an alliance, if judged by the cohesive standard of the Four. But this was a new era in the Senate, and the Western Progressives were men impatient for reform and less apt to be governed by sentiment.

The dimension of sociability, if not wholly lacking in the "Sons of the Wild Jackasses," was certainly not an identifying characteristic. Not only would it be difficult to imagine the "Sons" disporting themselves at a Washington watering-hole in the manner of the Four, but there is reason to conclude that there was not even much regular consultation of a serious political nature. As newspaperman Ray Tucker described them in 1932.

> The popular notion that they always act in concert and pre-meditation is erroneous. In only two forays—-the attack upon the nomination of Judge [John J.] Parker [as Associate Justice of the Supreme Court in 1930] and upon the Hawley-Smoot [tariff] bill—have they met beforehand to map out a definite plan, and to parcel out various duties among themselves.[20]

---

[20] Ray Tucker and Frederick R. Barkley, *Sons of the Wild Jackasses* (Boston: L. C. Page & Co., 1932), p. 17.

In their unfettered independence these Progressives can be seen as the precursors of the modern individualistic Senate. In casting off the dead hand of tradition they also swept away much of the camaraderie of the old Senate. They were men with a serious political purpose, and in the coziness of the old associations they saw the stifling cloak of reaction. In repudiating the politics of the Four, they rejected much of their intimacy as well. They were the issue-oriented politicians par excellence.

> Theirs [was] not a compromising spirit, and this lack of a give-and-take philosophy, with their want of a sense of humor may [have been] their cardinal fault and weakness, although it . . . often proved to be their strength.[21]

Comparisons drawn between La Follette and two of the other charter members of the "Wild Jackasses" suggest that their personalities were not so much complementary as contrasting. The elder La Follette, Norris, and Borah formed a triptych. (Aldrich, Platt, Spooner, and Allison together were more like a mosaic.) The elder La Follette was intense, intransigent, flamboyant, and single-minded. Norris was subdued, gentle, and retiring, although his principles were held no less dearly. Borah was at home in the world of ideas, in contrast to La Follette, a man of action. Both Norris and Borah were capable of maintaining decent personal relationships with those with whom they differed politically. La Follette's ardor got in the way of this, making reconciliation in the aftermath of battles almost impossible. But it was not only the conservatives that La Follette alienated; it was a substantial segment of the radicals as well.[22]

The extent to which the Progressive senators cohered politically seems to vary with the period or issue under discussion. When their numbers were limited, as in the early years of the twentieth century, there seems to have been a cohesion born of this compactness. The elder La Follette, in his autobiography, tells of the first meeting of the Progressive contingent in the Senate in 1907, when he called in Cum-

---

[21] Ibid., p. 18.

[22] Claudius O. Johnson, *Borah of Idaho* (New York: Longmans, Green & Co., 1936), p. 168, and Richard L. Neuberger and Stephen B. Kahn, *Integrity: The Life of George W. Norris* (New York: Vanguard Press, 1937), p. 54.

mins, Borah, and a one-term Senate Progressive, Joseph M. Dixon of
Montana, to discuss the Naval Appropriations Bills for the purpose
of "concerted action on legislation"; they parcelled out the work,
"determined on the items in the bill that should be opposed . . .
shared them among us and . . . went to work."[23] As the Progressives'
numbers increased, their collaboration and agreement became more
sporadic. At the onset of the Wilson administration, for example, La
Follette supported the Underwood tariff—which provided for lower
duties—but Norris and Borah opposed it. Later, in 1917, La Follette
and Norris attempted to block Wilson's Armed-Ship Bill; Borah
joined with the majority of the Senate in support of this bill. When La
Follette, Norris, Cummins, and twelve other senators filibustered
against it, Borah stood his ground in favor of the measure but never
chided the other progressives. When the vote on the declaration of
war came several months later, Norris and La Follette voted against
the resolution; Borah voted for it.

But it was not so much that the Progressives were eternally at
odds with each other as it was that they tended to operate *parallel* to
each other. As it was observed in the late 1930s by Richard Neuberger
and Stephen Kahn,

> they fight as individuals. Their energy is spent on a dozen
> fronts. They seldom unite. Borah battles for isolationism; Nor-
> ris demands public ownership of hydroelectric power; [L. J.]
> Frazier [of North Dakota] insists upon relief for farm mort-
> gagors. Together, agreed on a common course, these men
> might accomplish much. Scattered and dispersed, they are
> helpless against the cohesion of a conservative majority.[24]

In anticipating the contemporary Senate, the alliance of the Progressives was not so much a repudiation of the old form of association
which held together the conservatives as it was an adaptation of it to
suit the objectives and temperaments of politicians pledged to
change. Serene and comfortable relationships are much more compatible with the upholding of the status quo, it seems, than with the
turmoil of change. The general aura which surrounded the Senate in

---

[23] Robert M. La Follette, op. cit., p. 395.

[24] Richard L. Neuberger and Stephen B. Kahn, op. cit., pp. 378–379.

the salad days of the Four had been dissipated by the dynamic reformism introduced into national politics by Theodore Roosevelt and Woodrow Wilson. But the Progressive senators, for all of their individualistic and even uncoordinated forays on behalf of a multitude of reforms, were not indifferent to each other as human beings. Their overall philosophical agreement was matched by a substantial enough degree of personal attachment to qualify their faction as an alliance during the period of their greatest influence in the Senate.

So long as economic conservatism and a resolutely pro-big business attitude prevailed in the White House—as it did under Harding, Coolidge, and Hoover—the Senate Progressives were able to retain their distinctiveness. This contrast between the Senate group and the presidency diminished with the onset of Franklin D. Roosevelt's New Deal. It was not that the Progressives furled their banners and marched passively to the beat of the New Deal drummer, but rather that their role as voices in the wilderness now tended to be drowned out by a more resounding one. Roosevelt secured a substantial degree of support from this group which had provided the political counterpoint to the three Republican presidents, but there were some notes of discord. Arthur Capper, a Kansas Republican who had been aligned with the Progressives, turned out to be Roosevelt's most consistent supporter; Borah was the least reliable. Of seventeen New Deal measures which came before the Senate between 1933 and 1935, Capper supported all, while Borah supported eleven and opposed six.[25]

Although committed to a general set of political principles, the members of the Progressive alliance were divided not only by partisan identities but also by their definitions of the importance of partisanship. What united them most decisively was their economic regionalism on such questions as tariff reform; the peculiar problems of the farmers and ranchers of the Mountain states and the Far West presented probably the most reliable measure of the cohesion of this alliance. Their isolationism—another political trait shared by most of the members—was a product of both their own convictions and the traditional aversions of voters of their regions to foreign entanglements. The eventual decline of their alliance was not so much the

---

[25] Claudius O. Johnson, op. cit., p. 484.

product of the redefinition of issues as it was of the fact that the presidency had become a far more estimable vehicle for expressing them. Their recognition of this can be found in the fact that over the course of the alliance, the elder La Follette, Johnson, Wheeler, Norris, and Borah had made either tentative or formal bids for the presidency or vice-presidency. Unlike the Four, who preferred to control events though the occupation of strategic posts in the Senate, the Progressives set their sights on the White House. The Four had been at the very core of Senate power. They were the insiders who made all of the important decisions, and the retention of this power depended to a significant degree on cohesion within the influential group. There was, then, a very practical incentive for the friendship that prevailed. Party discipline had also increased during this period and the shared political faith of the Four served to solidify their bond.

The Progressives, by contrast, were most active during a period of Senate individualism. Unencumbered by leadership positions and unchastened by party loyalty to any significant degree, the Senate Progressives were united only by a vague set of political principles and a considerably more palpable regional commitment. Their independent natures and individual efforts to become custodians of particular reformist issues made for a less cohesive personal bond than that among the Four, but a measure of genuine affection did develop among them—friendship which pointed more to the alliances of the distant future than to those of the immediate past.

The alliances that have been considered thus far have been based upon a number of properties. A more or less common set of political principles and ideological orientations have played a role in all. Partisanship has tended to play a less significant part in these relationships. Regional attachments were important in the alliances of the anti-slavery senators and the progressives. These attachments, if anything, were at cross-purposes with the alliance cohesion in the case of the Four where common social backgrounds were factors (as they also were in the Fessenden-Sumner alliance). The Progressives, in addition to their general agreement on reformist principles, shared many background characteristics; the group as a whole was decidedly more backwoods than Back Bay. The fellowship of leadership was important in the relations of the Four and of less consequence in the cohesion of the Progressives. Of the factors which have been examined in all cases in terms of their ability to produce a measure of personal attachment, three—ideology, party, and region—seem to loom largest as sources of political friendship. It might be possible then to predict that in relationships where these three elements are present senators holding these attributes in common would likely be allies.

An example of an almost-perfect matching of political and geographical identities which produced a lengthy, if feud-ridden, relationship was that of Senators Mark Hanna and Joseph Foraker of Ohio. Ten years apart in age, they hailed from opposite ends of the Buckeye state—Foraker from Cincinnati and Hanna from Cleveland. Their friendship was established at the 1884 Republican National Convention, where both supported the nomination of "favorite son" Sen. John Sherman, who was defeated as the party's standard-bearer by James G. Blaine. After the close of the convention, Hanna wrote to Foraker,

> Among the few pleasures I found at the Convention was meeting and working with you. I hope soon to have the pleasure of renewing the acquaintance under more peaceful and comfortable circumstances . . . I hear nothing but praise for you on all sides, all of which I heartily endorse and will hope to be considered among sincere friends.[26]

And a few days later he wrote,

> I assure you, my dear fellow, it will not be my fault if our acquaintance does not ripen, for I shall certainly *go for you* whenever you are within reach.[27]

The ripening of the Hanna-Foraker friendship did not survive the next Republican National Convention, held in Chicago. Both were publicly committed again to the nomination of John Sherman, but Hanna came to suspect the genuineness of Foraker's commitment to

[26] Herbert Croly, *Marcus Alonzo Hanna* (New York: Macmillan Co., 1919), p. 125.

[27] Ibid.

their fellow-Ohioan's candidacy. Foraker claimed to be offended by Hanna's purchase of the votes of black Southern delegates. Though the two men had shared adjacent suites at the convention hotel, Foraker, after his arraignment of Hanna for the delegate-buying, checked out of his adjoining rooms and moved to another floor of the hotel. An exchange of letters followed the convention—as hostile in tone as the 1884 communications had been cordial. There ensued a formal schism in the Republican party of Ohio that was to persist for two decades. Yet, although the personal bitterness between Hanna and Foraker continued unabated over a period of twenty years and often descended to pettiness and meanness—all the more uncomfortable when both men entered the Senate chamber and were forced into contact with one another—there was restraint to their animus; it was never permitted to interfere with the dominance that the Republican Party had achieved in Ohio. The political stakes were simply too high to permit personal grievance to become politically damaging.

Yet as parties have declined in importance and senators have increasingly built up personal, rather than party, organizations, and have even sought to avoid being too strongly identified with a party label, some of the inhibitions against political fratricide have been weakened. The surest current inhibition to unbounded enmity between two senators from the same state and same party is that such feuding impairs their ability to deliver benefits to their state, and hence diminishes their chances of retaining office. This limitation also operates in the case of senators of opposing parties or divergent philosophies.

There is no question but that factional and personal hostilities between senators of the same state have been a very common feature in the human environment of the Senate. These feuds seem less surprising when they are a product of partisan and ideological differences; but shared political traits are no guarantee of harmony. The history of the Senate in recent years has been replete with examples of senators from the same state who by any objective political criteria should have been allies, but who loathed one another. The relationship between Oregon's two liberal senators in 1950s—Wayne L. Morse and Richard L. Neuberger—dated to the time when Morse was dean of the School of Law of the University of Oregon and Neuberger was a law student there. Their relationship of tutelage stopped at the door of the Senate, as Neuberger struggled to get out from under Morse's paternal wing and the egotistical Morse fought to keep him there. Two years after Neuberger had come to the Senate as Morse's junior colleague, their relationship had degenerated into an ugly and continuous brawl dividing the Oregon congressional delegation into hostile camps. The correspondence between the two senators that was precipitated by a minor bill of Neuberger's to transfer a small piece of federal property to the city of Roseburg, Oregon is one of the most spiteful and vindictive exchanges between any two senators. Morse could not even bring himself to use Neuberger's first name in the salutations, but addressed him as "Dear Neuberger."[28]

Elsewhere, the fact that Georgia's two powerful conservative Democratic senators of the 1950s—Walter George and Richard Russell—participated in a personal vendetta (which dated back to 1926) and were involved in an abiding quarrel over who was to lead the Senate's Southern bloc never posed any realistic threat to Democratic hegemony in their home state. Nor did the more recent manifestation of bad blood between J. William Fulbright and John McClellan of Arkansas jeopardize the hold of Democrats on that state. It has historically been the case that conflicting ambitions for national office can also serve to drive a wedge between senators from the same state and party. For example, the active ambitions of Pennsylvania's senior senator, Republican Richard S. Schweiker, ran afoul of those of his junior colleague of the same party, H. John Heinz III. Schweiker in 1976 had reversed ideological fields in order to ingratiate himself with conservative Republicans and gain a place on the Ronald Reagan ticket during the GOP convention. Since the failure of the Reagan-Schweiker ticket to receive the presidential nomination, Schweiker has abjured his old liberal leanings and built a solid conservative voting record in the Senate. Heinz, shortly after his own election to the Senate in 1976, began to build a following in support of his desire for a place on a national Republican ticket. In the 1978 Republican primary election for governor in the Keystone state, a war of proxies was waged between a Schweiker-backed candidate and one supported by Heinz. The rivalry between the two Republi-

---

[28] A. Robert Smith, *The Tiger in the Senate: the Biography of Wayne Morse* (Garden City, NY: Doubleday & Co., 1962), pp. 355 ff.

can senators has become one of the most intense in the contemporary Senate.[29]

The elements of disharmony between senators of the same state, party, and ideology are often so all-pervasive that they cannot even agree on their source. I spoke to two liberal Democrats from an Eastern state whose terms overlapped in the Senate and whose antagonism has been widely known. The junior Senator's version of this was very simple. Speaking of his senior colleague, he recounted,

> X—— was in the [Governor's] wing of the Democratic party. They were never too keen on me for many reasons, not the least of which was that I sent a few of them to jail including X——'s law partner when I was U.S. Attorney.

The senior member of the pair attributed the dispute to an entirely different set of circumstances.

> I had a very comfortable, easygoing relationship with my senior counterpart . . . who was a Republican. We worked very well together and there was absolutely no competition. When he was replaced by a younger, more aggressive Democrat, X——, I wanted to develop the same easygoing relationship with [his] office and made every attempt to do it, but he was an aggressive, competitive, hard-driving fellow, and competition developed between us and our staffs. We had scheduled weekly working lunch meetings, and theoretically this should have worked out very well—and on those occasions when X—— and I were present, all went smoothly—but if one didn't attend the meeting our respective staffs seemed to be at each other's throats in very short order, and the meeting broke down to the point where they were no longer useful and they were abandoned.

Another force contributing to hostility between senators of the same state and party is the problem of conflicting claims over who will be chief spokesman for state and party in the Senate. A liberal Midwestern Democrat elected in the 1960s was viewed by his senior

---

[29] Wendell Rawls, Jr., "Four Races for Governor Go Beyond State Borders," *New York Times*, April 23, 1978.

colleague, also a liberal Democrat, with some anxiety: "Outwardly, he seemed pleased that I was in the Senate, but inwardly I guess it made him feel less like he was the cock of the walk."

A Republican who served in the Senate with both Democrats and Republicans from his border state asserted flatly that he preferred to share the state's representation with a Democrat. "When I sat with a fellow Republican we'd find ourselves tripping over each other back in [our state] when we went to raise money or drum up support. The Democrats stuck to their own turf and never got in my way."

Another Republican felt that interpersonal relationships were generally more serene with state colleagues of the opposite party, as his had been with the Democrat with whom he had served.

It's easier to have a pleasant relationship with a person from the other party in the same state. You know what to expect. You know what you can do and you can't do, so you're not looking for a slight all the time. He's not so apt to put you down. You operate in parallel worlds. In many cases that I observed, rivalry between members of the same party were very bitter; between members of the opposite party they are not.

He cited one important element contributing to the harmony of senators from the same state from opposing political parties.

In the old days there used to be terrible fights over patronage. There would be two people who had better things to do fighting over postmasterships. There's very little of that now, but it does come up with federal judges and U.S. attorneys. They are the chief things I would have had a scrap with anybody on. But I was blessed by having X—— as my opposite number . . . He took a position which was very sensible. After Nixon was elected, he said to me, "You got the President, you get the judges and the attorneys. It's up to you. When we get the presidency, I'll take the responsibility." That kind of arrangement makes sense.

While historically some of the most bruising battles between senators from the same state and party took place over patronage jobs, they now occur over the apportionment of credit for government contracts and projects awarded to their state. On the eve of an announcement about a major project being located in their state, the two senators begin to eye each other warily, wondering who will get the lion's share of the credit. This poses great problems when the president and both senators are of the same party, but it is by no means absent when the party allegiances are different. One Democrat whose Republican colleague was seen as a potential supporting vote on the Panama Canal Treaty complained that the Carter White House had favored the Republican with advance notice of a project.

A more elusive cause of friction between senators who share all of the objective political attributes is a desire for political equilibrium in the Senate delegation, a property that many senators impute to the voters. It was said at the time that Sen. George McGovern experienced some uneasiness when the voters of South Dakota sent liberal Democrat James Abourezk to the Senate in 1972. McGovern had been beaten badly by Richard Nixon in the 1972 presidential election; he would have to turn to the defense of his Senate seat in 1974. He was said to have feared that the South Dakota voters would decide that one liberal Democrat in the Senate from a conservative farm state was enough and that since it was he who was next up for reelection Abourezk's election two years before had jeopardized his own chances for returning to the Senate.

To summarize, relationships between senators who represent the same state, party, and political philosophy, who would seem to be the most natural of all Senate allies, are vulnerable to six practical perils which can produce conflict:

1. *Conflicts over spokesmanship.* Senators from the same state become rivals over who will be the primary spokesman for the state, the party, or the wing of the party that both represent.

2. *Competition for support.* The two senators pursue the same set of contributors, campaign workers, and interest groups, asserting conflicting claims on the resources and loyalties of these groups.

3. *The peril of political balance.* The electorate is uneasy with two senators of identical political traits and is inclined to balance off a liberal against a conservative or a Democrat against a Republican.

4. *Factionalism in the home-state party* can be a product of historical forces (i.e., an upstate-downstate division or an urban-rural split) or the result of forces unleashed by the incumbent senators and

their followers; or it may arise independently of the actions of the two senators, who may nonetheless be drawn into the dispute and find that their collegiality suffers as a result.

5. *Competition between Senate staffs* can occur despite the best efforts of the two senators to work together in harmony. The essentially vicarious nature of professional gratification among staff assistants in the Senate often leads them to advance the cause of their bosses so aggressively that relations with other senators and their staffs are impaired. Staff aides of senators from the same state who are likely to be attracted to the same kinds of issues often find themselves involved in intrigues over who will gain custody over a politically valuable issue of importance to the state. So zealously are these maneuvers carried out that the two principals must play the role of peacemakers between their staffs if their own good relations are to survive.

6. *Disputes over patronage and project credit* arise out of the need by senators to prove that they can deliver for their state and reward the politically faithful. Even with few patronage jobs available, it is important for a senator to have his own people in the federal courthouse. Having a president and a colleague from the same state of his own party can be a mixed blessing here for a senator; a number of senators felt that on the whole there were distinct advantages to being the sole state representative of the presidential party in the Senate, from the perspective of their political interests in the state.

The peculiar circumstances which cause the relationships of senators from the same state to take a direction which partisanship and ideology cannot accurately predict are paralleled by conditions inside the Senate which produce the same result. Leaving alliances with their subjective conditions aside, it is clear that even Senate blocs and coalitions do not hew rigorously to party lines.

At the risk of oversimplification and ignoring variations from one Congress to the next, the Senate Democratic majority has been composed of three groups of approximately equal strength; about 30 percent conservatives, mainly from the deep South . . . about 30 percent moderates, mainly from the western, border, and mountain states . . . about 40 percent liberals, mainly from the Midwest and East . . . .

> Senate Republicans . . . have divided more sharply into two
> wings: conservatives . . . and liberals . . . . [30]

Having votes from the other side of the aisle is often a major contributing factor to legislative success in the Senate, where strict
party-line voting is far less common than it is in the House. If the
political balance between Democrats and Republicans is close to
50-50 this support from across the aisle is a virtual necessity, but even
where one party is clearly predominant, bipartisan support for a
measure increases its political palatability.

At the earliest stages of legislative gestation when co-sponsor-
ships are being solicited, it is typical for "dear colleague" letters to be
sent to virtually all members. Highly controversial measures can
often be palliated by the presence of both Republican and Democratic names as principal sponsors. For example, all of the major initiatives to end or limit American involvement in Southeast Asia were
cast in such a way as to invite bipartisan support; the Case-Church,
Cooper-Church, and McGovern-Hatfield resolutions all reflect this
bipartisan imperative.

Cooperation across ideological lines can be even more impressive,
as when in March 1979 a resolution containing the names of Senators
McGovern and Hayakawa as principal sponsors called for the dis-
patch of an American delegation to observe the elections in Rhodesia.
When senators representing widely differing ideological positions
join in sponsoring legislation there is at least a tendency for their colleagues to sit up and take notice.

Certainly at the leadership level—and among the Senate rank and
file as well—there is a recognition that ideological lines not be drawn
with such finality and rigidity that the Senate becomes politically
polarized. The ability of the Senate to avoid being divided into per-
manently warring camps in which all positions are foreordained by a
Senator's ideology is partially a result of the manner in which issues
are defined and of political cleavage-lines not being neat and congruent, but it is also due to the fact that relations between party leaders have tended in recent years to be cordial. In some instances, close
cooperation between party leaders has resulted in alliances based

---

[30] Robert L. Peabody, *Leadership in Congress* (Boston: Little, Brown & Co.,
1976), pp. 488–489.

upon personal regard and trust as well as on political necessity or expediency. Political observers have noticed this and commented upon it. Drew Pearson, the political columnist, was present at a ceremony in 1949 welcoming to Washington the "Gratitude Train"—a gesture of thanks by the French people for American help in their postwar recovery. In attendance at the ceremony in a Washington freightyard were Vice-President Alben Barkley and Senator Tom Connally of Texas (Chairman of the Senate Foreign Relations Committee), both Democrats, and the Foreign Relations Committee's ranking Republican member and former chairman, Arthur Vandenberg of Michigan. Observing the good-natured bantering going on among the three, Pearson noted,

> There is something impressive about the way our elder statesmen cooperate in things of this kind. Barkley, Vandenberg, and Connally represent opposite sides of a lot of things. However, they are personally good friends and do a great job of representing their country on such occasions.[31]

Examples such as this suggest that whatever institutional or strategic considerations prevail, personal fondness can convert intermittent cooperation into a more durable alliance. An example of an alliance between two men of substantially different political views who were leaders of their respective parties in the Senate is that between Democrat Mike Mansfield of Montana, Senate Majority Leader in the 1960s and early 1970s, and his Republican counterpart, Sen. Everett M. Dirksen of Illinois. Their personalities were complementary: Mansfield was reserved and deferential, and Dirksen was flamboyant and flexible.

> Mansfield deferred so totally to Dirksen that even Senate correspondents began to confuse Dirksen's functional role in the Senate as that of the majority leader, not the minority leader. Dirksen was not unappreciative of Mansfield's generosity to him, and he was prepared to requite Manfield's friendship to the full.[32]

---

[31] Drew Pearson, *Diaries, 1949–1959*, Tyler Abell (ed.) (New York: Holt, Rinehart, and Winston, 1974), p. 230.

[32] Neil MacNeil, *Dirksen: Portrait of a Public Man* (New York and Cleveland: World Publishing Co., 1970), p. 230.

The Senate floor was the scene of at least two incidents in which liberal Democratic senators rose to attack Mansfield for his passive leadership style, only to be challenged and put down by Dirksen. The most important tangible product of this alliance was the Civil Rights Bill of 1964, which would have been emasculated or defeated were it not for the careful and delicate negotiations between these two men of different parties and principles.

Another alliance—which for all of its strangeness proved to be one of considerable importance not only in the Senate but well beyond—was that between Senate Majority Leader Lyndon B. Johnson and Minnesota Democrat Hubert H. Humphrey. The ground rules of the Humphrey-Johnson alliance were established in 1952 after the defeat of Democratic floor leader Ernest McFarland. Humphrey led the fight to replace him with Sen. James Murray of Montana, and opposed the candidacy of Johnson. After a contentious meeting in which Johnson ridiculed Humphrey and his liberal colleagues for claiming support for Murray that they did not actually have, Johnson summoned the Minnesotan to his office, told him unambiguously that he did not have the votes to elect Murray, and designated him an emissary to the liberals. "Now go back and tell your liberal friends," Johnson instructed Humphrey, "that you're the one to talk to me, and that if they'll talk through you as their leader we can get some things done." As Humphrey later recalled the meeting,

> I had become his conduit and their spokesman not by their election, but by his appointment. I would be the bridge from Johnson to my liberal colleagues. I was pleased with the accomplishments of the meeting, particularly the prospect that my being spokesman might bring effective participation by liberals in the power structure of the Senate.[33]

The pragmatism of Humphrey's liberalism and the desire of Johnson to maneuver himself into a position which would make him more acceptable to liberals (in order to foster his presidential ambitions) were powerful elements in the forging of this alliance. There was, however, a significant element of personal affection which grew

---

[33] Hubert H. Humphrey, *The Education of a Public Man* (Garden City, NY: Doubleday & Co., 1976), pp. 164–165.

up between these two strikingly different men which helped the alliance endure beyond the point where simple complementarity of political interest or personal ambition no longer required it. That Hubert Humphrey—not Wayne Morse or Paul Douglas of Illinois, estimable senators by any standard—was Johnson's instrument of choice underscores an important factor in the dynamics of senate alliances: they attain their greatest durability and influence when composed of pragmatists, and are at their shakiest when constituted of those who are doctrinaire. The alliance, if it does not sanction defection, at least tolerates it; it presupposes situations in which alliance partners will be compelled to stray, and assesses no long-lasting penalties for the occasional defector. It is more common among "team players" than among thoroughgoing individualists, and for that reason contemporary Senate alliances tend to be much more loosely structured than some of the historical ones. Such individualism also militates against the preeminently human affections which serve as alliances' underpinnings.

Alliances in the contemporary Senate must be judged in the light of the individualism which now suffuses the Senate generally. For example, the Wednesday Club of liberal Republican senators, numbering no more than fifteen at any given time, has never formulated—as one member phrased it—"a unified power position." "We would get behind a candidate for a leadership position as we did once in the case of Ed Brooke and when Jack Javits was giving some thought to running, but the thing that would have driven me out would have been an effort to make it into a bloc. "

Two characteristics of the Wednesday Club create a presumption that the group owes more by way of operation to the Progressive block than to the Four. First, there is the matter of prior consultation and joint planning of the group's legislative strategy. Staff members of Wednesday Club senators agreed that they do not often formulate a common strategy and pledge to be bound by it. When the group convenes there is a "round-robin" discussion in which each member discusses those issues in which he is currently involved. It actually serves more as a clearinghouse for information than it does as a forum for developing a unified position. A unified position may emerge, but it is not the product of consensus-building within the group.

A second factor which serves to weaken the alliance properties of the Wednesday Club is the frequent failure of members to give advance notice to an ally of a defection. During the 95th Congress when the Senate was debating the question of long-term loans to New York City, Edward Brooke had reportedly conveyed the impression to New York's Jacob Javits that he would support the loans. However, during the course of the debate Brooke decided to vote against the loans, but did not warn Javits. When the vote came and Brooke was recorded in opposition, Javits was said to have been quite angered by Brooke's action.

The Wednesday Club is currently a minority within a minority in the Senate, and its most impressive bond may be this isolated and beleaguered status. There is reason to question the degree of personal fondness that prevails among its members. Certainly the ill-feeling that prevailed between Oregon's two liberal Republicans, Robert Packwood and Mark Hatfield, and the frequent descriptions of some members—Percy and Brooke in the 95th Congress—as overly ambitious and vain suggest that affection does not play much of a role in the cohesion of the Wednesday Club.

There have been contemporary alliances between senators from the same state, same party, and same philosophical persuasion which have defied the perils of this type of association, such as those between Jackson and Magnuson of Washington, Baker and Brock of Tennessee, and Mathias and Beall of Maryland; and there are alliances which span vast ideological voids, such as that between Maine's Edmund Muskie and Oklahoma's Henry Bellmon, both of the Senate Budget Committee. The current Senate is not innocent of alliances, but those which do prevail must coexist with its highly individualistic nature and be seen in that context. The modern Senate alliance is more likely to embrace a pair of senators seeing eye-to-eye on a broad range of issues than it is to encompass large groups; larger collections of senators voting together with regularity along particular ideological dimensions or pursuant to their interest in an issue or regional outlook are usually not inclined to suffer the restraints on their individualism that the personal obligations of the alliance impose. But while the Senate may no longer be run by a cabal from the poker tables of a Washington watering-hole, it could not be run at all without a measure of the regularity and predictability that the alliance provides, even if its structure is merely a network of bilateral relationships.

The socio-legislative group is an object of commitment and loyalty on the part of some members of Congress, but the role of these informal associations is vastly less in the Senate than in the House. Indeed, with the exception of the Wednesday Group of liberal Republican senators, nothing in the upper chamber approximates the durability and influence that these groups occupy in the House. It is simply much easier to become lost there, where the force and power of individual members is immersed in a sea of 435 personalities; there a congressman is prompted to amplify his influence through membership in informal associations like the socio-legislative group. On the other hand, Senate committees, for all of their formality and established position in the structure of the Senate, are often unable to restrain the individuality of the single Senator, so it is unlikely that a senator would willingly submerge his ego in a voluntary and collective association like the Chowder and Marching Society or the Acorns. The Senate is still enough of a club to obviate the necessity for sub-clubs. This is not to say that senators concerned with an issue, the problems of a region, or an ideological question will not confer or caucus informally and do so on a more or less regular basis, but they seem to feel it unnecessary—indeed, almost unseemly—to formalize these coalitions or institutionalize them. Even in the case of senators who have worked together consistently over many years and have found themselves as allies more often than not, there is little inclination to codify a partnership.

The coalescence of senators around any unifying theme, interest, or affiliation—be it party, region, ideology, committee, or issue—is typically a fragile association. Even the vaunted cohesion of the Southern bloc of a quarter century ago was less a reflection of broad agreement on a wide range of public issues as it was the product of agreement on a single issue, that of race. But even that area of agreement covered cracks wider than many believed.

All of these natural foci for enduring association in the Senate—party, committee, region, state, ideology, or issue—may foster as by-products the development of emotional attachments among senators. Unlike institutional kinship, which presupposes nothing more than the preeminently collegial graces of empathy, integrity, diligence, and restraint and which requires not even the link of partisanship to find its expression, the variety of Senate friendship manifested in the *alliance* is the result of a closer and more regular association. Most Senate friendships remain fixed at the level of the institutional kinship; even in a chamber as compact as the Senate the predominantly instrumental terms of the *institutional kinship* serve, for many senators, as the only expression of friendship. These limitations affect the alliances as well, but in it the occasions and opportunities for more intimate and cooperative contact create conditions for a higher order of personal involvement. The alliance can serve as the foyer for real social friendship or pure friendship, or else, as in the case of institutional kinship, common membership or interest may remain just that and no more.

To be in agreement with other senators on a major issue is not an unmixed blessing. Senators who saw themselves as pioneers in the effort to reverse America's policies in Vietnam did not necessarily see tardy converts to the anti-war persuasion with the eyes of a preacher with a newly baptized communicant, especially when the new parishioner attempted to commandeer the pulpit. Senator Eugene McCarthy regarded the conversion of Senator Robert E. Kennedy to the anti-war position not as the saving of a soul but as the arrival of an opportunistic hitchhiker on an idea whose time had come. Agreement on a political value or principle may be insufficient to bring together a group of senators who care more about being the acknowledged leaders as with winning over other colleagues, colleagues who might be inclined to challenge that leadership and advance their own chieftancy. There is a form of larceny peculiar to legislative bodies: the theft of issues. To be the first member in the chamber to become prominently identified with a popular issue is of such towering political value that legislators have been known to preempt a colleague known to be interested in an issue by introducing a bill first and robbing him of his potential leadership.

It is important to recognize the subjective element in alliances. Advancing toward the same goal, even a very specific one over a period of time, does not in itself signal an alliance in the absence of a feeling on the part of a senator that he is part of something larger and that his actions must take cognizance of those pursuing the same goal. A former senator who was part of the group of Senate "doves" during the Vietnam War contrasted the attitudes and actions of those who sought an early termination of the American involvement; his testimony reflects the tensions which exist between the desire for individual recognition and credit and the overall goals of a group.

I was the author of the first amendment to end the war in September 1969. Then we had the Hatfield-McGovern resolution. Hatfield and McGovern were a problem. They were actually less a problem than their staffs, but the Hatfield-McGovern resolution became a very big thing in the spring of '70.

McGovern and Hatfield wanted to be out front. [Alan] Cranston and Harold Hughes and I were constantly dealing with the issue of trying to keep the thing from becoming too partisan and too personalized and focused on McGovern and Hatfield.

By contrast, Cranston and Hughes never tried to elbow themselves out front. They worked very effectively, and called McGovern and Hatfield and said, "Look, it isn't really fair the way this thing is going. So-and-so on your staff did this or that. Why don't we meet in the cloakroom and straighten it out, and tell your staff not to do it anymore."

I think that whatever cohesion there was in the group was more a question of style and approach, as much as the philosophies. Gene McCarthy, for example, I found very difficult to deal with. It may have just been the period; it was right after he'd run for the presidency, and he just abandoned ship for two years. The man had done a fantastically important and significant thing in running and probably symbolized the peace movement more than anyone else. I had great respect for him, but he was hurt. He was withdrawing. He'd flit on and off the floor, give very few speeches, and never really participated in our anti-war organization. Sure, we were all moving in the same direction, but most of the anti-war people just wouldn't submerge their individual needs in the interests of agreeing on a single approach. Some of those guys just wanted a patent on the resolution.

I remember going to Gene in September of '69 to ask him to co-sponsor the amendment to end the war and he wouldn't do it. When I finally introduced it, I couldn't get a single co-sponsor—not McGovern, not Hatfield, not anybody, and believe me, I tried. God knows, if it hadn't been for Cranston and Hughes, who were willing to hide their light under a bushel, we'd have gotten nothing.

A willingness to submerge the senatorial ego in any form of enduring association seems to have fallen prey to the new individualism of the upper chamber. A New England senator spoke with disgust about efforts to bring together senators from those six economically depressed states to work out a common policy on energy.

You could not get the New England people together for the good of New England. Our meetings were a farce. We'd go in and everybody pretended that we were getting together on the issues, and then one member would get up and go out to the telephone, and another would excuse himself to go to the men's room and give whatever we'd done to the press so that it would hit the early editions, and by the time the delegation made its report to the press, there was nothing left for credit to the delegation.

Allies see themselves as part of a community of interest, but whatever objective political characteristics they may share—attributes which serve as the initial basis for attraction—there must be a subjective dimension to the relationship which is more than a simple reflection of common voting patterns or identity of external traits. The Senate can sometimes be a surprising place, where a member's help and support flow not to those who seem to share his formal labels and attributes but to those whose political traits are much less congruent. The personal bond of these dissimilar senators is, in a human sense, firmer than that with those whom they resemble only on paper. A Democratic Senator captured the subtlety of this interplay between the nature of issues and the nature of individuals thus:

I think that one comes in here with a certain baggage, philosophically and politically, and personal style and values and attitudes about public policy, and obviously it's not surprising that there's a tendency to seek out those who share, in a common way, the same aspirations, or motivations, or purposes. But I think the key thing here is the extent to which friendships are based on even more deeply personal things.

I can see, for example, a situation where someone could be opposed to you 180 degrees, but who you found attractive as a person independent of his philosophy and, based on the strength of that relationship, be willing to help him if it weren't too big a wrench philosophically. It might even develop into a pattern on certain kinds of issues.

And conversely, you have people who you are with philosophically, that you're with politically, who you don't like at all. As I think of it, I might not do a personal favor for someone who I'm like philosophically but without that personal note as quickly as I would for someone who I don't resemble quite so much in political terms but who I have some affection for.

The alliance then is more than a simple political relationship. As with the less-substantive institutional kinship, it is a compound of both political and personal qualities. The dominant ingredients, most typically, are similarities in philosophical values and positions on major issues. Without the leaven of mutual regard and a sense of cooperative pursuit of a common goal, however, the mixture remains inert. Less expectedly, there are relationships in which overall political agreement is less perfect but where a cooperative and helpful spirit yields an alliance both personally satisfying and politically advantageous.

CHAPTER FOUR

THE SOCIAL LIFE
OF THE U.S. SENATOR

A veteran Republican senator was reflecting upon the public images of his colleagues and their private sides which outsiders rarely have the occasion to see.

> The general view of Bill Proxmire is that he's very much a loner. He has the reputation of being a skinflint, but hell, we were able to develop a very nice friendship. We exercise together. We are the only two people who use the little gym in the new Senate Office Building. That's where I do my little weightlifting workouts to help myself tone up, and he works out there, too. We see each other informally in that fashion, two or three times a week. I guess for that reason we were able to discuss more intimately the idiosyncrasies of our colleagues and what not. As a result there are things I talk about to Prox that I wouldn't with most other people.

There are settings both inside and outside the Senate itself where contact between senators other than that of a strictly business nature occurs. To be sure, senators can be seen in small groups on the chamber floor engaging in light banter, and the same applies to meetings of committees and subcommittees, but the pace and intensity of official business in the contemporary Senate really allow for little interaction beyond the job at hand. Nonetheless, within the confines of the Capitol and Senate office building there are places to which senators may repair and pursue, if that is their inclination, contacts of a more social nature. What mainly occurs in these places is, naturally enough, a great deal of political gossip. It would be as difficult to imagine a moratorium on legislative matters in this setting as it would an embargo on assembly-line problems at a canteen in an automobile factory or professional academic discussions in a faculty cafeteria. When colleagues in any work setting come together in an environment conducive to talk about things other than those of a strictly business nature, the stage can be set for them to "open up" to each other and begin transcending relationships of the purely professional or political kind. What sometimes eventuate are social friendships. Those which arise *within* the Senate, the intramural social friendships, are the subject of the chapter.

The senator is provided with a number of locales within the Capitol complex itself in which serious matters need not be discussed, some of which are rather effectively shielded from those who would press on him such discussions. These retreats are the senators' only sanctuaries where official discussions, although not precluded, are generally limited. These are places beyond the reach of lobbyists, reporters, constituents, and even staff, where the elsewhere more limited and formal types of association may develop into more personal and human relationships. These retreats may also act to mitigate the adversary relationships that are so much a part of Senate life. Two colleagues who have done battle on the floor may find that having a drink together in the office suite of the Secretary of the Senate may take the edge off the sharpness of their disagreement. This may not produce any enduring friendship of a more personal nature, but it may allow them to see a less formidable and more human side of a colleague in a context where threat is not so salient.

A liberal Democrat from the Midwest explained the value of this kind of interaction when he spoke of his own relationship with one of the most senior members of the Senate, the chairman of a major committee who is both a Southerner and a conservative.

> We were sitting around—this happened years ago—and waiting for a vote. It's nine o'clock. There's nothing, you know. Something's been going all day. Everybody knows how they're going to vote, but we're still debating. I walked into Stan Kimmitt's office [Stanley Kimmitt, Secretary of the Senate] and Jim Eastland was there. We sat around and had a scotch and just visited together. We just socialized, and so we got acquainted on a personal basis—and we wouldn't agree on anything.

In any institution, if you're going to make any headway, you lean over backwards to get acquainted with people, you know, on a personal basis so that at least if they're chairmen of a committee you aren't going to get clobbered on a personal basis. He may be against you on the issue, but you've got a bill and you can go and say, "Look, at least give me a hearing on the bill." But if a guy doesn't know you or doesn't like you and he has the power, he can just say the heck with it, he's got too much to do and he's got other people.

These men had seen each other on the floor and in committees countless times over the years, but a chance encounter between the two over cocktails provided the occasion, in a less highly charged environment, for an important accommodation.

There are a number of these social—as opposed to preeminently political—settings to which the Senator may have recourse. Some of these settings are partisan. The institutionalization of the two-party system in the Senate is apparent to anyone visiting it for the first time. Most of the partisan space is off-limits to all but senators. First, there are the cloakrooms adjacent to the chamber. The Republicans in recent years have permitted staff to enter the cloakrooms. The Democrats are only now beginning to relax their prohibition against the entry of staff, at least to the point of allowing them to use the telephone booths just inside the door; staff, however, do not yet have free run in this cloakroom, and it can still be adjudged to be exclusively senatorial. But this is really a business space, not one given over to relaxation.

Both the Secretary to the Majority and the Secretary to the Minority have offices to which senators repair for light conversation and drinks. One former senator identified three other spaces—one partisan, one semi-partisan, one neutral, all exclusively for senators—where social interaction is as great or greater than the purely political and official contact.

I can think of three relaxing spots in the Capitol that I used. One was the private senators' dining room. There are two rooms—the first being the Republicans' that you walk through and the back room the Democrats'. Nobody but a senator can enter these rooms. Always friendly. Always sociable. If I didn't have constituents up to my elbows, as was usually the case, I would eat my lunch there to get the camaraderie and privacy that went with all Senate discussions. The second place would be the gym—a very comfortable gym with exercise equipment and swimming pools and rubdowns and showers, and several times a week I would visit the gym, get a workout, get refreshed before going out on the evening's activities, shave and put on a clean shirt.

The third place was [Felton] "Skeeter" Johnson's office. [Johnson was Secretary of the Senate.] Nobody would be in there but the secretary and other senators and they'd all be Democrats and liquor would be served. The majority of the Senate debates are boring and senators are not swayed by Senate oratory. In ninety-nine cases out of a hundred we know how we're going to vote, so the speeches are for public consumption and not to influence other senators. They are a total waste of time. Most of the Senate proceedings are a bore and a waste of time—totally—and I could not bring myself and felt no obligation to sit there hours on end listening to droning arguments . . . [which] I can read far more quickly in the *Congressional Record*, which in most cases I don't. So I would leave the Senate floor and go in and chat with one of my friends and have a drink in Johnson's office.

Senator [Everett] Dirksen's office was the usual gathering place for the Republicans, and drinks were available there. We Democrats met in Skeeter's office, where there were also drinks available served by stewards and television sets, and those of us who like to drink, as I did, and those who were interested in sporting events, as I was, would spend hours in Johnson's office watching the World Series or some particular horse race or ball game or prize fight and drink and swap . political stories and have a thoroughly rewarding, interesting, friendly time.

Over the years, the men who have occupied the position of Secretary of the Senate have seen it as one of their duties to provide senators with a place of conviviality and relaxation within their suites of offices. Francis [Frank] Valeo, a successor to Skeeter Johnson as secretary, would always have drinks available there, and in the late afternoon senators would just wander in there and sit down and have a drink and talk, and sometimes you get as many as twelve or more senators in there (but usually there'd be about four or five) and you'd just stay for a few minutes and have a drink—or maybe two if it was a long, hard day—and then go on your way, and that was just plain visiting or shooting the breeze, you know, a very relaxed atmosphere. I never saw any flare-ups of any kind in there.

The Senate gymnasium, located in a corner of the Dirksen Building, is another senators-only refuge where both socializing and political talk may take place—though most senators swear resolutely that the gym is a place where little of any political consequence takes place. There is a more or less regular "gym crowd"—a group composed of about one-half of the Senate—which uses the facilities at least once during the week. What goes on there?

Well, I suppose various people go there for various things. I go there to exercise. In the process I see a few of the guys—some go there to shower and shave, some to get a massage, and some others to exercise.

The facilities available in the Senate, while not extravagant, are certainly adequate for a well-rounded regimen of exercise, and there is little evidence to suggest that it constitutes a subterranean command post or that its purpose is anything but Senatorial fitness.

It has two pools in there, neither one of them very large, but one of them is a warm-water pool and the other's cool water and there's a sauna in there. There's a wet-steam room and a dry room for heat, and there are weights and bicycles and a rowing machine and exercise room. There's one other that isn't big enough for handball, although sometimes you go in there with a racket and hit a tennis ball against the wall—that's about all the space there is. Some of the senators now—they didn't until just the last three or four years—some of them now go over there and put on their togs and shoes and then go out and run around the park and then come back and take a shower.

I would say that about half the senators use the place. I did a lot. I tried to do it every day. It was about the only exercise I'd get, which was little enough—swim a few lengths of the pool and get a rubdown—there are Swedish masseurs there to give you a rubdown.

The use of the gym seems to be rather straightforward and, although senators encounter each other there in surroundings which are for senators' use only, it is not a place where deals are cut or bargains arranged. As one Senator put it,

There isn't so much time for a lot of talk in the baths, because usually you go there to dress for dinner and leave the Senate at the end of the day and to get yourself revived, and you only have so much time for a shower and shave and change of clothes and perhaps a rubdown, but aside from a lot of joshing that goes on there, there's not much of political consequence that goes on.

There is a discernible reluctance on the part of some senators to trumpet their use of the gym. At a time when senatorial prerequisites are under attack, when every effort to raise salaries is met by objections from the economy-minded, and when most senators seek to cultivate an image of unrelieved diligence, recourse to a facility far grander than any which most constituents can use becomes a sensitive matter. Few senators would make so bold as to leave instructions that in the event of a constituent call it should be said that the senator is getting a massage or playing handball.

One of the more puckish senators hit upon an ingenious solution for getting his exercise and relaxation while not tipping off callers to his whereabouts. One day, while sitting in the steam room of the Senate gym, fretting that his new receptionist would disclose his whereabouts to callers, surrounded by naked and perspiring colleagues with their protruding paunches, he had a stroke of genius. Inspired, he went to the phone and instructed his receptionist that he was attending a meeting of the "Committee on Navel Affairs." From that day on he was able to take his relaxation untinged by guilt, knowing his callers would be satisfied that the senator was attending to the serious business of legislation. That senators sometimes find it necessary to resort to subterfuge to conceal their interludes of relaxation suggests the extent of the erosion of senatorial leisure time. In other places in the Senate, however, senators may socialize more freely without the risk of being seen as sybarites.

The senators' dining room provides such a setting for social encounters away from the curious eyes of public, press, and staff. There is a semi-public dining room where senators may lunch with outsiders, but it is the senators-only dining room that is truly sequestered from the outside. A Midwestern Democrat described the arrangement:

> You walk in and there's a long table and there it's Republicans and you go to the next room and it's all Democrats, and they don't eat at each other's table unless it was during recess and there were only one or two of you there. You usually talk politics about this issue and that issue and one thing and another.

An Eastern Republican elaborated on the etiquette of bipartisan dining, but denied that business was discussed.

> The first table is an oval table. That's the Republican one. Beyond it is the Democratic table. There's no wall in between. Same telephone in case you get calls. The Democrats walk by to get to their table and sometimes they sit down and talk— you know, if they want to talk or if they see somebody special they want to say something to, they sit down, maybe have a cup of coffee and then go on back—but usually they go to the table of their party affiliation. Usually, those tables are not full. I've never seen them full—oh, half full or something. If you're there by yourself, or if you don't have any lunch engagement or commitment, you usually end up there and it's a fellowship thing. You rarely talk business there.

A New England Republican, now retired, felt that the conversation at these tables was a mixture of both business and pleasure.

> Sometimes business was discussed—party business you might say—in those two different rooms; more often just social stuff. If there's a good storyteller he can usually attract an audience. Wherry of Nebraska was a good storyteller and would hold forth down there. Jenner of Indiana was a good storyteller— sometimes pretty low—but always amusing.

There is much less office-to-office "visiting" between senators than might be imagined. Certainly, the office suites in the Senate office buildings are not widely used for the entertainment of colleagues. The admission of the late John McClellan that he had not been inside a colleague's office in all his many years in the Senate is as much a reflection on the limited use of office space for meeting with colleagues as it is on McClellan's own remoteness. Those senior members who are entitled to a hideaway office in the Capitol do make some use of these rooms for quiet relaxation with fellow senators. Access to these rooms is far more strictly controlled than is the case with the offices. There is no staff on duty in the hideaways and they offer perhaps the most suitable locales in the Capitol complex for quiet sessions of conversation, lunch, and drinks.

One interesting aspect of the relationship between the physical arrangement of the Senate and the extent of familiarity and socializing is whether senators in adjacent suites of offices tend to be better acquainted than those whose offices are widely separated. All the senators interviewed were emphatic in denying that such a relationship was very significant. The offices are assigned on the basis of seniority, with the most desirable ones going to those of longest standing. If anything, senators who share adjacent office space often find themselves encroaching on one another. An instance of this was when the offices of Sen. Edward M. Kennedy and the then Sen. Walter F. Mondale were adjacent to each other; Kennedy, with his vast amount of mail, wanted to expand into some unclaimed office space between the two suites. Mondale, who at the time was preparing for his bid for the Democratic presidential nomination, also coveted the space. The ensuing battle for space did not jeopardize relations between the two men, but neither did it cause them to feel any better disposed toward each other. In only a few instances has there been any relationship between office location and senatorial friendship. Edmund Muskie of Maine and Henry Bellmon of Oklahoma, whose relationship is said to be a warm one, have adjacent suites on the first floor of the Russell Building, and Georgia Democrats Sam Nunn and Herman Talmadge, also known to be fond of each other, have face-to-face office suites, but no overall patterns can be drawn from these instances.

Somewhat more significant in terms of the relationship between work space and personal interaction is the Senate phenomenon of "seat mates." Unlike a member of the House of Representatives, who can take almost any seat he wishes, the Senator receives an assigned seat—on the chamber's right side (facing the presiding officer) if he is a Republican, and on the left if he is a Democrat.

> At the beginning of every new session when there will be vacancies, they simply go down the list of senators according to their seniority, presenting them with a plot [of the Senate chamber], saying that these are the vacant seats and you want to choose one. So he may choose one—and sometimes that breaks down, because after a choice is made then they want to go back and change it because somebody else has moved. Sometimes it takes a while to sort everything out, but the answer in brief is that you get your choice by seniority from among what is available in seats.

I asked one senator if there was a tendency to choose seats in order to be next to someone you liked.

> Choose your seat because of your seat mate? Oh, no! Now, if you didn't like a certain fellow maybe you wouldn't accept the seat if it was offered to you, but the technique of the Senate is to move towards the middle and the front.

I suggested to him that in one case I knew of two senators who were friendly happened to be seat mates—Frank Church (D.–Idaho) and Claiborne Pell (D.–R.I.). "But they didn't pick it out for that reason," he responded.

> You take Church. He was very far out in front, and he was too far in front and towards the door. So you try to get towards the middle, so he moved up maybe an aisle but came towards the middle.

For some senators, local traditions and historical sentiments play an important role in the choice of seats, when seniority permits them that discretion. Norris Cotton (R.–N.H.) went to great pains to claim the desk of Daniel Webster.

> When I came to the Senate, Styles Bridges, New Hampshire's senior senator, had Daniel Webster's old desk. . . . When Sena-

tor Bridges died in 1961 and I became senior senator, I lost no time in claiming the Webster desk. . . . The desk had to be moved, because my seniority was not then sufficient for me to inherit Senator Bridges' position on the floor, but a few years later my added seniority entitled me to the aisle seat on the second row, just back of the minority leadership, so the Daniel Webster desk returned to its place.[1]

For much the same reason, Senator Margaret Chase Smith sat in the right-hand corner of the chamber. Her desk had once been occupied by Senator Hannibal Hamlin, Abraham Lincoln's first vice-president and one of Maine's most illustrious sons.

There is no uniform—or even preponderant—pattern to the choice of seats by senators, but when they have such discretion by reason of their seniority, pragmatism rather than sentiment seems more likely to govern their choices. A liberal Democrat from the East applied this practical test to his own seat selection.

I'm totally unaware of any connection between where you sat and who you respected. We changed seats with some regularity. . . . And some seats were more comfortable than others. If you're on the back row in the far left-hand corner in the Senate chamber where the junior members start, you're surrounded by clusters of aides, and there's a lot of traffic going back and forth around that corner and you can't hear as well. When you speak you're at the far end of the chamber and so it's not as desirable a seat as a seat that's nearer the middle of the chamber and off the back row and you don't have the constant irritation of aides conversing directly over your shoulder. So one tends as he moves up in seniority—I certainly did—to move your seat forward and to the right.

Despite the disavowal on the part of most senators that seat-mate compatibility, personal or political, plays a role in the selection of seats within the latitude accorded by seniority, seating charts of the Senate chamber often invite the speculation that birds of a feather flock together. There was a presumptive case for this in the 94th Con-

---

[1] Norris Cotton, *In the Senate* (New York: Dodd, Mead & Co., 1978), pp. 44–45.

gress where four of the most conservative senators on the Republican side sat adjacent to each other on the two back rows. Grouped together were James A. McClure (R.–Idaho), Barry M. Goldwater (R.–Ariz.), James L. Buckley (R.–N.Y.), and Clifford P. Hansen (R.–Wyo.). I put it to one of the members of this cluster, former senator Buckley, whether any inferences could be drawn from this arrangement. Buckley explained,

> Different people have different definitions [of what is the most preferred seat]. For me the main consideration was convenience of access. I was way in the back. I could have gotten closer in, but I wanted to be near an aisle that led in from the elevators, because then if you had anything in the hub you had a chance to grab people as they went by.

> When I was there the southwest corner did tend to be more conservative, but you can't read any patterns into it.

As is the case with so many things in the modern Senate, personal advantage and convenience rather than personal affection or even philosophical solidarity tend to provide better explanations for seat choice. If a senator is given the opportunity to move out from the back row closer to the front, away from the overhang of the galleries where he cannot be seen, there is little reason to believe that he will remain a back-bencher simply to retain his proximity to a seat mate he has come to like or admire. While there is evidence to suggest that a senator would avoid sitting next to a colleague he despises, there is only the scantiest suggestion that positive personal factors impel the choice of a particular seat.

Inferences about the degree of personal intimacy that prevails even between those who have sat side-by-side for years in the chamber are perilous. A diary notation by Arizona Democrat Henry Fountain Ashurst makes this point very forcefully.

> *February 26, 1933.* Senator Walsh of Montana . . . married yesterday at Havana, Cuba to Senora de Truffin. Although Walsh and I have been deskmates in the Senate for years, he gave me no inkling of his intention to marry.[2]

---

[2] George F. Sparks (ed.), *A Many-Colored Toga: The Diary of Henry Fountain Ashurst* (Tucson: University of Arizona Press, 1962), p. 330.

There is within the confines of the Senate itself an informal social group quite different from the gymnasium crowd, the habitués of the Secretary's office, or socio-legislative groups such as the Wednesday Club, although its membership does overlap with them to some degree. Its purpose is not explicitly political—indeed, its unwritten rules preclude the conduct of business—but it represents an element of public life in America that cannot be dismissed lightly; that is the convergence of religion and politics. Although it has always been considered politically desirable for elected officials to have a nominal religious affiliation, this has often been more of an ornament than a deeply held set of convictions. In the Senate, however, for the past two decades there has been a continuous and active religious presence in the form of the Senate Prayer Breakfast. An outgrowth of the National Prayer Breakfast movement inaugurated in the 1950s with the blessings of President Eisenhower, the Senate Prayer Breakfast is a major part of the social life of the upper chamber. A similar group, established around the same time, exists on the House side.

The group in the Senate has always been bipartisan, but even the most cursory glance at the senators who have been regular attenders over the years indicates that the gathering has had a decidedly conservative political cast, with certain notable exceptions. At its inception, the guiding spirits behind the group were men such as Frank Carlson (R.–Kans.), Frank Lausche (D.–Ohio), Homer Ferguson (R.–Mich.), A. Willis Robertson (D.–Va.), Alexander Wiley (R.–Wis.) and John Stennis (D.–Miss.). Stennis continues as a mainstay of the group and the person who does the recruiting. In more recent years, senators prominently associated with the Prayer Breakfast have been Jennings Randolph (D.–W. Va.), Mark Hatfield (R.–Ore.), Harold Hughes (D.–Iowa), Sam Nunn (D.–Ga.), Dewey Bartlett (R.–Okla.), Lawton Chiles (D.–Fla.), Pete Domenici (R.–N.M.), Wallace F. Bennett (R.–Utah), Clifford Hansen (R.–Wyo.), and Charles Percy (R.–Ill.). The estimates of the attendance at these breakfasts supplied by senators who have been members varies, but certainly no fewer than fifteen and probably no more than twenty-five can be said to be more or less regular attenders.

The generally conservative shading of the group—exceptions are Hatfield, Hughes, and Percy—is not the assemblage's defining characteristic, which is, rather, its regional and denominational character; it draws most of its adherents from the Protestant heartland of America—the South and Midwest. Although senators from the Eastern states do attend, the bulwarks of the group are drawn principally from the areas south of the Potomac and west of the Mississippi, where the fires of religion burn with a more intense flame. Although the religious fundamentalism of this area has sometimes tinged politics with populism, more typically its evangelical qualities and insistence on biblical literalism has worked to produce a profoundly conservative brand of politics on such social issues as abortion, women's rights, and matters relating to alcohol and drugs. But even on questions seemingly remote from morality, the dominant religious and cultural characteristics of the area express themselves forcefully here.

The style and idiom of the Prayer Breakfast has always been unambiguously Protestant. Theoretically and officially it is nondenominational, but the very format is not one that has ever found much favor among Roman Catholics and Jews. The very dominance of such evangelical Christians as Hughes and Hatfield in the group and the infusion of a small number of "born again" Christians have tended to make it even less consonant with Jewish and Roman Catholic ritual. There have been a few Roman Catholic members of the Prayer Breakfast, such as Lausche and Murphy, and even an occasional appearance by Connecticut's Democratic senator, Abraham Ribicoff, who is Jewish, but these are clearly exceptions. The non-denominational claims of the group must be regarded with some suspicion.

How does the Senate Prayer Breakfast operate? One of the regulars explained,

> The breakfast was held in the Vandenberg room of the Capitol on the first floor right across from the Senate restaurant every Wednesday morning at 7:30 AM. The breakfast is first. They serve you right away with orange juice, bacon and eggs— whatever you ordered, individual orders. You have your breakfast. In the old days Senator [A. Willis] Robertson would have something interesting and humorous to say. Jennings Randolph might comment on some news he heard on the radio the night before or on this or that situation. You don't get into legislation.

> Then, when you'd finished breakfast, whoever's turn it was to lead would be sitting at the head of the table, would call upon a member for a prayer. He would have asked somebody to be

prepared for the prayer, which would take about a minute. When they finished the prayer the leader would go on with his ten- or fifteen-minute prepared thoughts for the day on whatever subject he wanted to. It didn't have to be on religion but could be on anything, but usually it was on religious things or philosophy or moral situations in the country—it's safe and general.

When he'd finished, then he would go around the table for comments. Individuals could say, "I pass"—which they very rarely did, but usually they would comment on the subject of his talk or they'd bring up something else and start right off on it and then they'd go around the table that way.

Then when you'd been around the table it would be nine o'clock. If you had any time left, you'd either have a prayer to conclude it, or discuss something if somebody else had another thought he wanted to comment on—but rarely on legislation, and never directly on something that was coming up for a vote, not that I recall anyway. Now it may have, I don't say never, but it was usually broader than that. I never recall any situation where any member could be embarrassed about this position on legislation or anything like that.

The sense of the value of these sessions varies somewhat among those who have attended on a fairly regular basis. For a Republican from the East "all you want from it is a warm greeting and a willingness to listen to your thing." Another Republican summed up its value for him thus:

It enabled me to see a side—apart from the obvious spiritual ones—of an awful lot of people you worked with that didn't normally emerge. I was impressed by the deep spirituality of any number of people—fundamental, deep religious beliefs— and this is something that one rarely sees in people that one works with. And it was reassuring to see that that was there, and it's nice to get back to fundamentals periodically.

To say as most senators did that pending legislation is virtually never discussed and that overt politicking is banned does not mean that membership in the Prayer Breakfast does not have political implications. It was perhaps more the case twenty years ago than it is today, but certain senators have attended the breakfast for reasons other than companionship and spiritual refreshment. John Stennis, the leader of the group in recent years, showed a sensitivity to this when he responded to a colleague's query about why the group's activities were not better publicized by saying, "It might attract the wrong people for the wrong reasons." One interpretation of this statement was provided by a Republican who frequented the breakfasts: "I suspect he probably meant that if we had television cameras at every session some people might turn out whose interests were not necessarily spiritual." Another Republican suggested the possibility of an ulterior motive in the attendance of some of his colleagues when he said, "I didn't like the idea that you might be able to get a bill out of committee because of your association with the prayer group." This comment carries with it the strong implication that although legislative matters per se were out of bounds at the breakfast, mere affiliation with the group might produce political dividends. And there is more than a hint in the comments of some senators that there are members who used the group to ingratiate themselves with some of the powerful chairmen who were the backbones of the Prayer Breakfast. A senator who by design participated conspicuously in the group's activities might well receive considerations on legislation from an influential chairman who was one of the mainstays of the breakfast which might otherwise have been denied. The apolitical pretext did not preclude a political result.

There is one value that the prayer group provides for some senators that is not widely discussed: its therapeutic function. The breakfasts are certainly not encounter groups, but there is a lay ministry that coexists with them, providing counseling and support for troubled senators and others in public life. Over the years of its existence, several prominent non-senators have been associated with the Prayer Breakfast, among them David Lawrence of *U.S. News and World Report* and Douglas Coe, an old school friend of Senator Mark Hatfield now associated with Fellowship House, which sponsors the National Prayer Breakfast and serves as a sort of unofficial chaplain for the Senate group. Coe worked closely with Harold Hughes when the latter was in the Senate, and the two now guide most of the prayer group activity within the government. They serve as a kind of "central committee" for what Charles Colson has called "a veritable underground of Christ's men all through the government."[3]

Hughes declined to be interviewed for this book.[4] But it is clear that the Prayer Breakfast itself represents only the most superficial element of the work of this "Christian underground."

When Charles Colson was facing indictment for crimes relating to the Watergate scandal, Hughes and Coe acted as spiritual therapists to bring about Colson's acceptance of Jesus Christ as his personal savior. Information regarding their activities with senators facing personal problems is more difficult to establish, but in at least one case a prominent Democratic senator with a drinking problem was aided by the group. There is also evidence that a senator whose wife was suffering from terminal cancer was directed to a faith healer by the group and experienced a temporary remission of symptoms. A senator with a physical health problem has also been assisted by Hughes, as have others with family problems. One of Hughes's most spectacular successes was with a young congressman who aspired to the Senate but had a reputation as a two-fisted drinker and brawler. Hughes, it is said, counseled him that his excesses would ruin his chances for a Senate seat. Through Hughes's influence this man's drinking problem was cured, and he achieved his political objectives. In the case of two other senators, Hughes's ministrations failed; one literally drank himself to death. It is important to note that in a profession such as politics resorting to conventional psychotherapy entails a measure of risk. As Senator Thomas Eagleton learned in 1972, when his concealment and subsequent disclosure of a nervous breakdown led to his being dropped from the Democratic ticket, public views of psychiatric treatment for public officials tend to be less

---

[3] Charles W. Colson, *Born Again* (Old Tappan, NJ: Chosen Books, 1976), p. 135.

[4] In a letter to me of May 23, 1977, Hughes wrote, "If I were to grant the interview and communicate with you about the relationships with men that I'm aware of and that I have personally on a spiritual basis, namely that of Jesus Christ, I would render somewhat ineffective the ministry I still continue in the Congress of the United States. I have not talked publicly about such a ministry, nor do I feel it possible for me to do so. Whatever I'm called to do in the Federal system in the way of a ministry for Christ must, in my opinion, continue to remain confidential in order to be effective."

sympathetic than its attitude towards those who seek the ministrations of clergy or overcome their problems through religious experience or conversion. The practical value to a politician of a form of therapy to which no stigma attaches is quite substantial.

There are those within the Senate who find the prayer group irrelevant to their needs or even offensive. One senator objected to it on religious grounds: A Roman Catholic, he saw the meetings as being in conflict with his dutiful attendance at morning mass. Another claimed that the sessions were simply too long; they postponed his arrival at the office until 10:30 Wednesday mornings. A liberal Democrat from the Midwest said, "When I first came in they tried to recruit me, but I'm like the Unitarians; I believe in one God at most." A Western Democrat was more blunt: "I've always had an aversion to public professions of piety. I went there once and decided that it just wasn't for me."

Few senators are as outspokenly critical of these breakfasts as one liberal whose impressions of it date back to the 1960s, and who by his own admission joined for opportunistic reasons.

> As soon as you get into the Senate you hear about the prayer group, and I thought selfishly that it was wise to join it, but I did it pretty much as a hypocrite, and it was awfully sort of Southern Baptist. It was run by John Stennis who . . . was a good friend of mine, although we had practically nothing in common. So I used to go over there, and there I'd run into another senator that I really despised. He was the biggest psalm-singing, hypocritical son-of-a-bitch that I ever knew—Bob Kerr of Oklahoma.

> He was a blot on the prayer group, whereas John Stennis was completely sincere. John, however, believed in the Baptist Jesus, and I didn't stay in it very long. Harold Hughes was very big in it. He was a Holy Roller if ever there was one. A very nice guy too, but he was a dedicated Christian. He'd hold out a helping hand to anybody he thought was mildly in distress, but I was never close to him. It's interesting because, I suppose, that liberal credentials aren't sufficient in and of themselves to create friends.

I asked him what value the Prayer Breakfast had for him in the year that he attended. "It promoted personal relations," he responded: "I would never have become a good friend of John Stennis's without having joined it, and I never would have come to despise Bob Kerr quite so much."

Despite the changes in the Prayer Breakfast itself over the years, it continues to attract mostly senators from the South and Midwest, remains overwhelmingly Protestant in its composition, and is considerably more conservative politically than the Senate as a whole. However, its members are more apt than formerly to attend out of sincere religious motives and less out of desire to ingratiate themselves with powerful colleagues, although the latter impulse has not entirely disappeared. The most significant political impact of the group, as in the past, occurs in situations in which one group member is disposed to favor another on a legislative or political matter. From the point of view of the personal needs of the senator, the Prayer Breakfast is a recruiting ground for smaller and more intense prayer groups and point of contact for senators experiencing personal problems with a politically acceptable form of therapy. Most relationships between regulars at the breakfast are more personal than those of the institutional-kinship type. There is some revelation of the inner self, although what is revealed is more a glimpse into the ethical and philosophical nature of a colleague than anything of a startlingly personal nature. Despite the preponderance of non-Easterners and conservatives, the Prayer Breakfast has no political program and does in no way constitute an alliance—although special considerations may accrue to members. Aside from a small group of senators who have banded together in a more intimate and direct religious association, the associations tend to be social. Without a specific denominational common denominator, the ritual is vaguely Protestant; it is in reality a kind of "civic Christianity," but more in the mode of Billy Graham than of William Sloane Coffin.

It has been estimated that there now are at least twenty-five "born again" Christians in Congress, but according to one former congressman, John B. Conlan, who has been encouraging evangelicals to seek political office, most of these members do not openly flaunt their religious beliefs, although a group formed in June, 1979, by Senators Orrin Hatch (R.–Utah) and Gordon Humphrey (R.–N.H.) declared that they would oppose liberal legislation which they held to conflict with Christian doctrine as they interpreted it. Neither as voters nor as office-holders have evangelical Christians yet made the political mark to which their numbers in this country—an estimated fifty million—might entitle them. That one of them now occupies the White House does not mean that they have reached their potential in American politics or that they are exempt from the same sorts of crosscutting pressures which affect other groups.[5]

Social friendship in the Senate, whether over a glass of scotch in the office of the Secretary or over orange juice at a prayer breakfast, has the potential for developing into a more profound type of relationship. Once the barrier of the strictly business association (institutional kinship) is transcended, for one reason or another, the stage is set for a new order of relationships. Once the words "respect" or "trust" are augmented by terms which touch more the stuff of emotions, a higher form of personal association becomes possible. The social friendship, then, can serve as a transition. It can, of course, remain no more than a matter of drinking buddies, companions in worship, or tennis partners. It can be light and airy dinner parties from time to time, but it may also contain the seeds of fundamental human affection.

The social and cultural, no less than political, life of the modern senator has been deeply influenced by the evolution of national politics in the direction of a system in which diverse and vocal interest groups circumvent the mediation of moribund political parties to submit their claims and due bills on individual legislators. The shield of the parties, which once imposed a semblance of order on the cacophony of special pleading by interest groups in the electorate, is tattered and scarred. The passage of a system in which a senator could defend legislative inaction on the pet bill of a lobbyist by placing the blame on an autocratic committee chairman or dictatorial party leader has resulted in a new order in which each senator is personally answerable. This, in part, is the price that politicians pay for the reforms of the past quarter-century. One should never underestimate the protection afforded a senator who could defend himself by pleading that events were out of his control. But the back benches no

[5] Charles W. Hucker, "God and Politics: Mixing More Than Ever," *Congressional Quarterly Weekly Report*, vol. 36, no. 38 (Sept. 23, 1978), pp. 2565–2566.

longer provide much of a refuge in the face of the upsurge in inter-est-group pluralism.

The new system of senators going "one-on-one" with single-issue interests without the cushioning of party or leadership or even the comfortable refuge of junior status has, naturally enough, produced a new type of senator working alongside those of the older type who have been able to adjust to the new rules and rigors. What has emerged from this maelstrom is a highly adapted legislative organ-ism which can subsist on a diet of almost pure politics. Like the draft horse bred for pulling power or the sheepdog bred for the ability to control livestock, the modern Senator if he is to survive must become the complete, specialized political animal. It is a rare legislator today who is truly a man of many parts, and indeed why should he be so? Of what earthly value is an ear finely tuned to music, a poetic soul, or even a love of family and friends to an importunate representative of an interest group whose only concern is legislative "outputs"?

It is a mark of the decline of simple erudition on Capitol Hill that the most commonly used standard by which to judge the intellect of a legislator is that of the "quick study." To be known as a "quick study" is no mean praise; what it implies is the ability to seize the nub of an argument with only the most cursory inspection or brief-ing. The establishment of this standard represents a triumph of the prehensile mind over the catholic one. When a legislator demon-strates even the most marginal abilities in a field outside politics, wonderment is expressed. Praise is lavished on a young congressman who publishes a book of second-rate doggerel. Because we expect so little—aside from political skills—from politicians, even undistin-guished dabbling in another field can be occasion for elated com-ments by those who feel that elected officials should be men of many parts.

It is difficult to overstate the extent to which at least some people in the Senate are oblivious to cultural trends which even the most ill-informed citizen has grasped. Several years ago, a journalist inter-viewing a young liberal senator queried him on his reading habits, particularly on his taste in novels. The senator responded that the best novel that he had read recently was *The Best and the Brightest.* For a senator to mistake David Halberstam's methodical analysis of the United States' involvement in Southeast Asia for a novel suggests the somewhat alarming degree to which politicians can be cut off. While campaigning for reelection, one of the Senate's wealthiest members was caught in a downpour in a shopping center and dispatched one of his aides for a pair of rubbers to protect his shoes. The assistant returned shortly with the rubbers and presented them to the senator. "Where did you manage to get them?" the senator asked. "I got them from Thom McAn," replied the aide. "Please extend my best wishes to Thom," said the senator, "and thank him for the use of his rubbers." An equally spectacular example of a senator's detachment from what most citizens consider reality involved a visit to Capitol Hill by the movie star, Robert Redford, who had come to Washington to lobby on behalf of one of his environmental concerns. He was shown into the office of a senior member of what was then the Interior Committee. The receptionist, seeing Redford, left her desk with great excitement to tell her boss that Redford was asking to see him. She came upon the senator poring over a stack of papers and virtually shrieked, "Senator, Robert Redford is outside and would like to speak with you!" The senator looked up from his papers with a look of puzzlement on his face, began repeating the name, and finally said to the astonished receptionist, "What group does this Mr. Redford represent?" Akin to this is the senator who spent an entire day campaigning in his state's largest city alongside a renowned baseball player from that city's National League team. The two were mobbed by youngsters seeking autographs. At the end of the day the senator turned to a staff aide and said, "Who was that attractive black man who was standing next to me all day?" From the point of view of constituents and interest groups it is probably of no consequence that a senator mistakes a major work of non-fiction for a novel or fails to identify one of the best-known of all Hollywood personalities or a major sports figure, but there is a sadness about these incidents that suggests just how narrowly gauged many senators have become and how out-of-touch they can be with those forces ordinary citizens encounter.

There are functions in contemporary Washington which are ostensibly social, but which upon closer examination are seen to be a continuation of politics by other means. Is it really possible to describe as social an evening spent at a reception for visiting businessmen from one's home state? Is a fund-raiser, even if held in the inviting ambiance of Pisces or the F Street Club, truly recreational time? The after-hours life of today's s:nator is contaminated by business matters to a degree that would ha/e been intolerable to a senator fifty years ago. There were of course obligations imposed on the older generation of senators: the rigors of the winter social season; the mandatory calling and leaving of card; at the homes of influential colleagues; the burdens on the senatorial : pouse of entertaining the social and political deans of the capital; ¿nd the obligatory social levées en masse which nearly everyone of political consequence would attend. Yet for all of this highly structured social activity, there was a much greater inclination earlier in this century and before for federal officials to participate in events which were much more purely social. There were even activities which could justly be called intellectual, such as evenings spent in rapt discussion, replete with sparkling repartee, of philosophies of government or jurisprudence and poetry readings. Just prior to World War I a young lawyer, Felix Frankfurter, rented a house with five other men on 19th Street, N.W. and dedicated the premises as a free-wheeling intellectual salon which they named "The House of Truth." Frankfurter recalled,

> I don't know who dubbed it the House of Truth but the name stuck: namely, something about the fact that it was a place where truth was sought, and everybody knew it couldn't be found, but even trying to seek the truth conscientiously is a rare occupation in this world. The dominant quality of the house was that you were unafraid to talk about anything. That makes for an interesting society. When there are repressions, or inhibitions, or fears, or timidities, or prudences; you can't have a good society. It started out in the most innocent fashion, but it became a fashionable thing. We didn't make it fashionable, but people would say, "Gee, we had a wonderful time last night at the House of Truth," and so, since most people are copycats, other people would regard it as a wonderful thing to be asked to the House of Truth. And, indeed, a good time was had. . . .
>
> There were no sacred cows. You weren't afraid to express differences of opinion, which is the very life of good conversation. Men felt that what they said wasn't going to appear in a column, let alone appear in a distorted and untruthful fashion. . . . Our inquiries were not directed toward getting copy, but

we assumed that we were all friendly, truth-seeking and truth-speaking people. The friction of minds through the friction of tongues would make everybody have a good time, and in the second place it would make us see things a bit more comprehensively than each man saw it alone in his own mind. The free spirit of man, in short, asserted itself and gave enjoyment in its exercise.[6]

In an earlier age even a man so inflexibly dedicated to serious, indeed portentous, matters of state could be remembered for graces of a social and intellectual nature. In his recollection of his Senate colleague Charles Sumner, Carl Schurz would recall,

There are those around me who have breathed the air of his house in Washington,—that atmosphere of refinement, taste, scholarship, art, friendship, and warm-hearted hospitality; who have seen those rooms covered and filled with his pictures, his engravings, his statues, his bronzes, his books and rare manuscripts—the collections of a lifetime—the image of the richness of his mind, the comfort and consolation of his solitude. They have beheld his childlike smile of satisfaction when he unlocked the most precious of his treasures and told their stories.

They remember the conversations at his hospitable board, genially inspired and directed by him, on art, and books, and inventions, and great times, and great men,—when suddenly sometimes, by accident, a new mine of curious knowledge disclosed itself in him, which his friends had never known he possessed; or when a sunburst of the affectionate gentleness of his soul warmed all hearts around him. They remember his craving for friendship, as it spoke through the far outstretched hand when you arrived, and the glad exclamation: "I am so happy you came,"—and the beseeching, almost despondent

---

[6] Felix Frankfurter, *Felix Frankfurter Reminisces*, recorded in talks with Dr. Harlan B. Phillips (New York: Reynal & Co., 1960), pp. 107, 112.

tone when you departed: "Do not leave me yet; do stay a while longer, I want so much to speak with you!"[7]

What is remarkable about this bygone era is that even though colleagues entertained each other it was entirely possible for them to avoid talking business or to at least limit the extent to which serious political subjects intruded on pure sociability. To a degree almost incomprehensible today, many of the regularized social gatherings throughout Washington actually had rules which foreclosed any discussion of serious political questions.

The celebrated poker group organized and presided over by Franklin D. Roosevelt—which met either at the Olney, Maryland home of Interior Secretary Harold Ickes or the Georgetown home of Treasury Secretary Henry Morgenthau and also included Associate Supreme Court Justice William O. Douglas, Roosevelt's military aide "Pa" Watson, his press secretary Steven Early, and his physician Admiral Ross T. McIntyre—operated under such restrictions. The social ground rules of these "command performances," as Roosevelt styled them, were that substantive matters of policy were never to be discussed. Douglas recalled that

> These poker games had an atmosphere of relaxation and gaiety. Anyone who brought up business was never invited back. A serious word was taboo because these were the President's nights out free of worries and concerns.[8]

Traditionally, then, the social life of the public figure could be walled off—albeit by *diktat*—from the encroachments of official business. But even when this separation was not presidentially decreed, Washington social life maintained a purity and self-sufficiency which it no longer possesses. It comported perfectly with the classical standard of "sociability" set forth by George Simmel.

> Since sociability in its pure form has no ulterior end, no content, and no result outside itself, it is oriented completely

---

[7] Commonwealth of Massachusetts, *A Memorial of Charles Sumner* (Boston: Wright and Potter, 1874), pp. 261–262.

[8] William O. Douglas, *Go East, Young Man* (New York: Random Huose, 1974), p. 331.

about personalities. Since nothing but the satisfaction of the impulse to sociability—although with a resonance left over—is to be gained, the process remains, in its conditions as in its result, strictly limited to its personal bearers; the personal traits of amiability, breeding, cordiality, and attractiveness of all kinds determine the character of purely sociable association.[9]

There is little doubt that, except in a case such as FDR's poker nights, politics was discussed in gatherings of the era. It would tax one's credulity to assert that political discussions would be off-limits in a gathering of politicians, but it is necessary to distinguish between conversations in which the subject matter is political and those having a definite political objective or purpose. What the rules implied was simply that there be no lobbying, no deals made, and no favors sought in a period set aside for sociability. Pleasure was an end in itself, and social settings had not only a social pretext but a social purpose as well.

These social protocols of an earlier period stand in stark contrast to the social life of today's politician. For those in Congress, especially, there are now social rituals which are in fact political rituals with social coloration. These remarks made twenty-five years ago apply today:

> The almost exclusive position of politics as the chief employment of Washington has an influence on the life of the legislator. It means that he is forced to live almost entirely in an atmosphere of politics. It is true, of course, that many enjoy this type of life with its incessant stress of influence, rivalry, ambition and frustration—it sharpens political wits and has a brilliance of its own. It does however strengthen and even overdevelop the political orientation of men who have already entered voluntarily upon such a career. By political orientation is meant that exclusive preoccupation with political events to the point where every human activity becomes evaluated not in terms of its intrinsic value but in terms of its political signif-

[9] Georg Simmel, "The Sociology of Sociability," *American Journal of Sociology,* vol. 55, no. 2 (Sept. 1949), p. 255.

icance. . . . This type of social life offers no respite from the tensions and anxieties of the legislator's own political career—it provides a stimulant rather than a soothing calm.[10]

As an institution the Senate provides many settings and opportunities for social interaction. That there is little purely social contact outside its walls is not due to the Senate itself being deficient in points of informal contact but results rather from a combination of choice and circumstance in the lives of individual senators. There are very few social isolates in the U.S. Senate, although there are a number of members whom other senators would prefer to avoid whenever possible. Although not so chummy as the House, the Senate is by no means a stiff and icy place. It is not unusual to see one senator with his arm draped over the shoulder of a colleague, or a knot of senators convulsed by gales of laughter. Outsiders may well wonder about the content of these conversations. Is a Senator regaling his colleagues with the latest joke he has heard or retelling the witticisms of his six-year-old? Or is he boasting affably of how he ran circles around a colleague in a mark-up session or ridiculing an unpopular member who made a fool of himself in a hearing? There is probably some of the former in these contacts, but most Senate staff members insist that it is the latter that predominates. It is largely tactical humor—anecdotes relating to what a member has done or plans to do, what he has seen and heard, what coups he has pulled off, and what surprises he may have in store.

The wistful recollection of former senator Mondale about the Senate as a place where pomposity is periodically punctured by wit is

---

10 Edward A. Shils, "Resentments and Hostilities of Legislators: Sources, Objects, and Consequences," in John C. Wahlke and Heinz Eulau (eds.) *Legislative Behavior* (Glencoe, Il: Free Press, 1959), p. 349. Since Shils made this observation—more than twenty-five years ago—the pressures, if anything, have intensified. More political events with social coloration—such as coffees, fundraising dinners, barbecues, pool parties, and receptions—have multiplied. Where it was once sufficient to attend an annual Jefferson-Jackson Day dinner or a Lincoln Day dinner to fatten the coffers of the party, decentralized fundraising and the financing of individual campaigns apart from what the party can or will provide for a candidate have placed an enormous claim on the time of politicians who wish to honor these obligations.

well taken. A large number of the exchanges which never appear in the *Record* poke fun at colleagues who need to be taken down a peg or two. These are usually not the types of comments which find their way into anthologies of Senate humor.

A liberal Republican recalled being put down by one of the Senate's most irrepressible jokesters, and how he gave as good as he got:

> I had an amendment in to add $600 million to a sewage bill. The previous bill bad been vetoed by Nixon because this money for sewers was in it. I arrived on the floor well-prepared, and went on for about fifteen minutes talking about how important it was to have this money for sewers. Well, I was waxing lyrical about household effluents and sanitary tunnels and all of that, and after I finished old Norris Cotton came up to me—that old curmudgeon from New Hampshire. He said, "X——, you know how highly I esteem you and I just have the greatest respect and affection for you, but I never realized until now what you were an expert on, but now I know." And I said, "What's that, Norris?" And he said, "Shit." And I looked at him and I said, "Norris, can you think of anything more important to be an expert on in the United States Senate than that?"

Senators are not markedly different from people in any profession or occupation whose conversations tend to be dominated by discussions of the absurdities of the organization or the foibles of co-workers. In the various retreats and watering-holes in the Senate where informal contact takes place—whether it is jovial and relaxed shop-talk at the offices of Secretary Stanley Kimmitt and Sergeant-at-Arms F. Nordy Hoffmann, or the exposure of one's character in the Prayer Breakfast or of one's body in the gym nothing more occurs than the revelation of another side of a business associate. These informal settings, however, have the potential—albeit rarely exploited—to be the avenues of approach for more personal types of relationships. Most relationships, however, remain fixed at the point where after the drinks have been consumed and the lunch dishes cleared away, the senators go their own ways. This does not mean, however, that these *intramural social friendships* are unimportant. They do serve to build cohesion in the Senate—a cohesion which transcends the professional good feelings of the institutional kinship and the overwhelmingly political bonds of the *alliance;* in the hierarchy of emotional relationships in the Senate, they are clearly of a higher order than these. Like them they offer possibilities for something more intimate.

CHAPTER FIVE

A NIGHT ON THE TOWN

In the late summer of 1978, the restaurant critic of a Washington newspaper received a call from an investigative reporter on a Midwestern paper. Word was that one of the senators from the reporter's state was leading a sumptuous life in Washington, dining out at expensive and luxurious restaurants. The allegations carried with them a strong hint that these eating spots were wicked, racy places; the reporter had secured a list of them and wanted to know from the critic just how decadent they were. At the top of the list was the Evans Farm Inn in McLean, Virginia. The reporter was disappointed: the Evans Farm Inn is a family restaurant with an adjacent craft shop whose stock runs to things like scented bayberry candles, and is about as decadent as Howard Johnson's. The remainder of the list contained places equally innocuous.

The modern public image of members of Congress gathering after-hours to revel and cavort at chic clubs and restaurants on their bloated salaries has gained currency largely because of the activities of an exceptional few. In fact, there is remarkably little ostentation in senators' social lives, and almost no collective revelry. The fact is that nowadays when they do gather en masse, it is usually for some sober political objective; the small amount of entertaining by senators of other senators offers little evidence of any clandestine network of political influence in the manner of the Arlington Hotel at the end of the nineteenth century. The nature of these social gatherings suggests that, though light and airy, they rarely stray very far from shop-talk and almost never touch on matters of a deeply personal nature.

This chapter seeks to answer a number of questions relating to the activities of senators outside the Senate. What, for example, is the nature of social contacts among the senators after the workday? Do colleague relationships loom large in the after-hours social lives of senators? Is there a tendency, in the face of an uncomprehending out-side world, for senators to cleave together, drawing on each other for the type of social sustenance which can only be provided by those compelled to play by the same rules and operate under the same rig-ors? Or does the competitiveness, rivalry, and individualism, of which much has already been said, blight social relationships to the point where they do not extend beyond the extent of what is institutionally prescribed or politically advantageous? Are social encounters with colleagues outside the Senate welcomed or shunned? Are there social rituals and conventions peculiar to the Senate? Most important—but also most elusive—does participation in recreational or leisure time activities exert any influence on the political behavior of senators? Inasmuch as social involvement and common leisure-time activities are often related to fonder and more intimate forms of pure friendship, this chapter will set the stage for a discussion of these relationships of deeper human commitment.

There is of course no single pattern of leisure-time activity among U.S. senators, but all the varieties in some way reflect the nature of the capital's social life, the demands of a political career, and the peculiar qualities of the Senate and its pace of life. Some accept the politicization of their social lives, while others reject it almost entirely. Some joyfully and enthusiastically use their social contacts with colleagues to foster their political objectives, while others consider such an approach an intrusion on what is essentially a personal relationship. Some seek out colleagues socially, and speak wistfully of not being able to have more contact. Others when they leave the Senate Office Building are quite content not to encounter their colleagues in the outside world; circumstances or choice impel these senators to undertake only the barest minimum of social interaction with their fellows.

It is the rare senator whose social life revolves chiefly around his Senate associates. One former senator, John Sherman Cooper (R.–Ky.) had annual parties to which all members of the Senate would be invited and which roughly half would attend; Cooper, an immensely wealthy man who, with his wife, had an expansive view of what a Senator's social life should be, pursued a course which owed more to the past than the present. What little socializing occurs outside the

Senate is usually between small groups of two or three senatorial couples. Such socially active senators today as John Warner (R.–Va.) and William Cohen (R.–Me.) do not restrict themselves to the membership of the Senate in their after-hours activities.

· A Western Democrat said that his invitation list for dinner parties usually did contain the names of senators. He was particularly friendly with fellow Western Democrats Lee Metcalf (D.–Mont.) and Gale McGee (D.–Wyo.)

> We have a place down on the river, and we'd invite the McGees down and stay over a weekend or the Metcalfs or whoever else, and we'd do the same thing when we're out West, you know, go up and stay in their cabin—things of that sort. The social contact is very rewarding.

What transpires when these intensely political people are off alone in a setting remote both in distance and spirit from the Senate? Is serious business on the agenda?

> Well, we talk about a host of other things, but some of the things that come up are Senate matters because they're in our consciousnesses and some are funny and some are wry. I don't know that we ever got one another in a corner trying to sell a point of view, but we did talk Senate business, yes.

Some senators find that colleagues make poor social companions because of their inability to take leave of their work.

> Lyndon Johnson came to our house with his wife once. He was a very bad guest; he spent most of his time during dinner going to the telephone, trying to get someone to serve on a committee. The next day I saw Harry Byrd. He said, "Lyndon Johnson was at your place for dinner last night, right?" "That's right," I said. "I'll tell you something else," Byrd said. "He spent the whole night on the phone. I know that because it was me that he was trying to get to serve on that committee."

Although Johnson's notorious encroachments on sociability with heavy-handed politicking can be seen as something of an exception, the episode does point up the fact that many senators are sensitive about extending social invitations to their colleagues for fear of infringing on their political obligations.

You don't have a lot of time for a lot of informal visits. You're so busy yourself, but you're also reluctant even to bother close friends. You know yourself if you have a terrible busy schedule—you've got somebody coming in at 3:00, and at 3:15, and at 3:30—it's a real encroachment on your friendship and on their time just to stop by and have a cup of coffee.

The Senate is probably one of the few human institutions in which a casual visit with a colleague for a cup of coffee is interpreted as an "encroachment on your friendship." To impose companionship on a colleague strapped for time is deemed an unfriendly act. And it is time which, more than any other factor, accounts for the negligble amount of social activity between senators outside the walls of the Senate. As one Republican, representing a state not far from the capital, put it:

I really didn't have the time to [socialize with colleagues]. You were invited from time to time to dinners or Sunday affairs or something like that by colleagues. Usually we came [home] on weekends to attend political functions; weekends [there] were usually busy for a public official. . . . Saturdays, always something. Sundays, always something, and unless it was something very special, we'd come home for weekends and try to attend some state affairs. During the week you might accept an invitation, especially if he was a colleague who served on the same committee with you and he was having something at his home like dinner and invite you and your wife. You'd go, but unless it was a close thing, you were too busy accepting invitations from state trade associations or constituent groups meeting in Washington.

One senator tried to impose a system of priorities on his time in order to spend more of it with his family, but by his own admission failed.

After the Senate adjourned on most nights in Washington there was something going on in the way of a reception or dinner or an embassy or private party that you were invited to as a senator. I preferred to skip—and did, in fact, skip—nearly all major receptions and cocktail parties and embassy affairs. I was bored by them. I was developing a drinking problem and I didn't want that exposure every night. And every night without exception I would have demands to appear somewhere in my state, and on every night I would want to be in my home with my family or with a small group of personal friends, which might include other senators.

My preference as to how I spent my time would have been: alone with my wife; with a small group where good conversation was possible with people whose company I enjoyed and whose opinions I respected; third in rank would be on the political trail in [my home state]—which became first in the way my time was disposed; and fourth would be the merry-go-round of Washington affairs, which I rather carefully avoided.

A veteran Republican from the East has been considerably more successful in fending off social demands.

We have developed a very private social life. We do not entertain. We do not go out. When we first came to Washington we established fairly quickly our distance from social demands, and once it became generally known that we didn't socialize the requests dropped off.

Once a year when the [John Sherman] Coopers have an elaborate buffet, we go to that just for old times' sake. Normally, though, when we are through with the day's work we are very happy to settle down. I put my feet up on the sofa and my wife reads to me, and we have a cocktail and dinner, and about ten o'clock we do the dishes and go to bed. We rarely visit with my colleagues and we have written off embassy parties totally; they're just dreadful.

A few senators speak wistfully about how they would like to get to know their colleagues better in an informal setting outside the Senate, and lament the lack of time for contact. Others seem relieved that so little of it takes place.

I'm a bit of a loner, I guess. But I think we see so much of each other all day that we tend to try to lead our own lives when we leave the office. . . . I think you just get tired of talking politics.

I feel that there's a tendency for us to scatter and be with our families—those with families here.

There has tended to be in recent years a small contingent of Senate "bachelors"—not bachelors in the literal sense but rather in the sense of having left their families in their home state. This has been especially true of those senators representing states which are a fast air-shuttle or Metroliner ride away. Sen. Harrison Williams of New Jersey was for many years a commuter between Washington and his home in Westfield. John Pastore of Rhode Island left his family in Providence; his Washington apartment was little more than a pied-à-terre. Paul Sarbanes of Maryland and Joseph Biden of Delaware do not even maintain a token residence in the capital, but live rather in Baltimore and Wilmington, respectively. The Washington social lives of these senators tend to be rather limited. Some senators have had special problems which foreclosed active social lives; the wife of George Murphy of California was an invalid, and he undertook little in the social realm in Washington. The experience of one such senator underscores the limitations on the social activities of this group.

When I was elected to the Senate my family was very young, so I kept them at home because I didn't want to break up their education. They were in elementary school and high school, and I did the traveling. If anybody was going to do the traveling Daddy was. So I would work late nights and clear off my desk, and then when I'd come home on Friday night the weekend belonged to my family. I never brought a briefcase home.

With the exception of one person, I have never been to the home of another senator. I went to Ribicoff's place one time. Now let me explain that because it might be misunderstood. See, I didn't have anything against the others, but it happened to be that one day he asked me to go to his apartment at the Watergate, and I went because it was merely a little bit of a cocktail party. That was it. I just never had the time.

These bachelors-by-circumstance and individuals whose special circumstances limit their entertaining and socializing stand at one end of the senatorial social scale. At the opposite end is a group of senators—presently quite small—whose social lives are quite energetic. These are the true Senate bachelors—eligible and otherwise—for whom a night on the town is anything but a grim political obligation.

The state of Washington once boasted two bachelor senators—Henry Jackson and Warren Magnuson—and although both have reached mature age and senatorial eminence, the two cut a joint social swath in Washington in their younger days. Another pair of senatorial social lions were Ernest Hollings (D.–S.C.) and Joseph Tydings (D.–Md.), who in their bachelor days were known to pursue an active after-hours life. They were preceded in their social forays by a pair of upper-chamber Don Juans—John F. Kennedy, then the junior Senator from Massachusetts, and George Smathers, a Florida Democrat. In more recent years the social partnership of Edward M. Kennedy and John Tunney (D.–Cal.) was a bright ornament on the otherwise bleak Senate after-hours life.

Kennedy and Tunney once even suffered a legislative indignity because of their energetic recreations—an occurrence which underscores the perils involved in being a social lion in the Senate. The two senators were planning a skiing vacation in the Alps; they approached Majority Leader Mike Mansfield to inquire whether an important bill would come to a roll-call vote before an upcoming recess. They wanted to leave Washington early to get an early start on their vacation. Mansfield assured them that the bill would be held over until after the recess and that the only measures to reach the floor before then would be routine matters which could be handled by unanimous consent. Satisfied that they could leave town without missing the vote, the two flew off to Europe. But in a cruel twist of fate, the bill was called up for a vote in their absence. An aide to one of the senators placed a hurried call to them in the hope that they might get back to the capital on time. As the vote was being recorded, however, the two men were still in a plane over the Atlantic, so they suffered the embarrassment of a missed roll-call vote on a major bill.

This incident figured prominently in the campaign advertisements used by Tunney's opponent in the next senatorial election in California. The television spots showed a young man resembling Tunney skiing down a mountain while a voice asked where Tunney had been when the crucial vote was taken. Tunney lost the election largely because of this playboy image which he was unable to shed. Kennedy, being sui generis, suffered no retribution, but it was a lesson that others might have heeded. A casualty of a similar episode on the House side was Rep. Ted Risenhoover of Oklahoma, whose purchase of a heart-shaped bed found its way into a gossip column in the *Washington Star*. The column also reported that Risenhoover was sporting a fancy new hairstyle fashioned for him by a House barber. The playboy image again took its electoral toll when Risenhoover went down to defeat in a 1978 primary.

The scandal surrounding Congressman Wayne Hays and his relationship with a House employee, Elizabeth Ray, whose only apparent duties were sexual had a chilling effect when the story broke in 1976. Both sides of the Hill were rife with rumors that a number of important politicians were hastily seeking the advice of counsel lest their relationships with Miss Ray be revealed. The scandal did not result in an absolute decline in liaisons between male legislators and their female employees, but it did tend to make them more circumspect. The more prudent of them have tended to follow the advice set forth by Lyndon Johnson's one-time aide, Bobby Baker:

> Most of the playboy politicians of my acquaintance avoided these entangling alliances generally inherent in office-wife relationships. "Don't dip your quill in the office ink" has long been a popular vulgarism on Capitol Hill, though the considerations are more practical than moral. . . . Disgruntled employees who know not only the secrets of the files, but the politician's intimate habits and thoughts as well, have long rated with Communists in their ability to inspire fear among politicians. Because of this potential blackmail power, you'll more likely find congressman X—— sleeping with someone on the payroll of congressman Y—— than with his own employee.[1]

The Hays scandal and the later one involving Congressman Wilbur Mills—coming as they did at a time of rising public indigna-

---

[1] Bobby Baker, with Larry L. King, *Wheeling and Dealing* (New York: W. W. Norton & Co., 1978), p. 80.

tion over congressional perquisites, salaries, and outside income and augmented by Jimmy Carter's successful campaign against the Washington establishment—has served to restrain the more riotous of the congressional Lotharios. As a result of this acute assertion of civic morality, there has been a long-term trend away from any activities which might be regarded as unseemly. The public is perceived by politicians as demanding that they attend diligently to the business of governing. Already writhing under the watchful and stern eyes of the news media and public interest groups, the modern politician finds his normal caution augmented by the fear that his associations or personal relationships will be adjudged as corrupt. Pressed by an insufficiency of time to do nothing more than what is politically necessary, cut off by campaign finance reform from individual patrons who formerly sustained their careers, and expected by the public not to appear to be too obviously enjoying the good life in Washington, many people in Congress find the joy of elective office receding. Although their incumbency is less vulnerable to challengers (at least on the House side) and, as indicated by public opinion polls, they are individually esteemed by their constituents (despite the general disrepute in which Congress itself is held), retirement is the path being taken by more and more members. The most typical reason cited for this course is that politics is simply not much fun anymore.

The rise of issue politics and the attendant pressure for legislative remedies, the increasing identification of legislators with interest groups, and the compulsion on the part of each legislator to gain access to the media independent of party spokesmen has caused lawmakers to invest in every action a degree of political significance that bids many of them to reject or apologize for activities which have no obvious political connection. A number of senators now are squeamish about admitting that they do anything whatsoever for the sheer pleasure of it. Given their larger constituency and the diversity of interest groups to which they are answerable, there is often an apologetic tone in their admissions that they have interests transcending the purely political. The old admixture of politics and sociability in the life of the capital was constrained by no impermeable barriers between politics and recreation; currently, however, there must be a serious, political rationale for what was formerly justifiable in its own terms. The kind of politics that now permeates these leisure-time activities produces a form of human contact which is often not very emotionally satisfying and has a sense of grimness and obligation.

Sports and games often serve as an uncanny mirror reflecting the spirit of a nation or an age. The touch-football games of the Kennedy clan with their competitive but solidarity-building elements captured the essence of that period in American life. And the recreational activities of individual politicians are often in keeping with the image they wish to convey to the public.

For some politicians, sports and recreational activities tend to have a formalistic and ornamental quality that approximates their religious observances. It is considered desirable for a politician to have a favorite sport, in the same way that a denominational affiliation is seen as necessary. It is one of those obligatory references in the campaign resumé that reassures voters that the office-seeker is a complete person. And to have won a varsity letter at college is an unchallengeable credential that the politician is "one of the boys." Even the few real intellectuals who enter politics find that sports, like religion and military service, is a reassuring notation on the curriculum vitae. Even those whose brilliance alone would commend them find that, like Eugene McCarthy, they must be pictured with a hockey stick or a baseball bat as a symbol of their normality.

Whatever value sports may have as a politically useful totem of the active life, it is increasingly the case that sports activities for senators are being subjected to a utilitarian test. This test applies the standard of fitness, rather than fun, to these forms of recreation. The days have passed when serious politicians like Sam Rayburn would express distrust of "narry-assed men." The narry-assed (i.e., slim) man is today the very model of vitality in public life. Fearing to resemble one of Daumier's French deputies in his painting *Le ventre legislatif*, congressmen pursue a variety of active sports to compensate for the sedentary nature of their jobs and convey to the electorate an image of youthful vigor. Even in earlier days, however, a trim physique was a highly prized political asset. Huey Long, whose girth was expansive, turned his exercises into a public display. He enrolled in a private health club in New Orleans, but, like so much else that Long did, the calisthenics were little more than showmanship. In gym clothes emblazoned with his name, Long would work out at the spa before a crowd of onlookers come in off the street to watch the spectacle. He also boasted of sawing wood as an exercise, but after having cut half a dozen logs would break off the exertions and begin chatting with the bodyguard manning the other end of the crosscut saw. His antics on the golf course also revealed his impatience with bona fide exercise, along with his appreciation of its symbolic value. Long hired two young men to shag balls that he had sliced into the rough and then place the balls for him in a favorable playing position. For all the world it appeared that Long had mastered the skill. Those who had previously played with him when he could not break 115 expressed wonderment at his scorecard, being unaware of his two secret weapons.[2]

Unlike many politicians of his day, Long scorned card playing. It was cards—more particularly, poker—that was the favored recreational activity among those in public life from the time of Harding to that of Truman. It is a game which has all but passed from the scene as a leisure-time activity among today's politicians. In Congress, especially, poker amounted to a kind of institutional passion. Indeed, if it was true at that time that horse-racing was the sport of kings, poker was the sport of congressmen. Yet in the group of senators I interviewed, not a single one listed poker as a leisure-time activity. To understand the symbolic meaning of the passing of poker as a politician's pastime it is important to recognize what it is that makes poker unique.

Poker is a game of competition and companionship. There is a cohesion among the members of a poker group that persists despite the fierceness of the combat. Unlike bridge, it is a game not inconsistent with conversation. While kibitzing in bridge is a distraction, in poker it is a supplement to the game. Bridge is a game of couples; poker is an activity of the group. Bridge is a sober and disciplined game; poker is much more informal. Poker, more perhaps than any other form of recreation, is not related to a particular social class. While sailing is considered a resolutely upper-class pastime and bowling decidedly working-class, poker is not decisively class-bound. A poker

[2] T. Harry Williams, *Huey Long* (New York: Bantam Books, 1969), pp. 459–460.

game can bring together people of diverse backgrounds and provide a common bond of pleasurable activity.

Poker as a form of relaxation for politicians has had the virtue of channeling their competitiveness into a leisure-time activity where it is wholly appropriate. Where stakes are mere dollars and cents rather than policies, programs, and prestige, competitive urges can be discharged in a harmless and enjoyable way. The conversation in these gatherings usually turns on the game itself and the unalloyed delight of sheer companionability.

The Roosevelt poker game, with its restrictive rules against the discussion of serious matters, was only one of the regular gatherings of its kind that flourished in Washington. Two evenings a week President Warren Harding convened his poker group, which included some of the most influential men in Washington. The poker game served as the common denominator for such blue-bloods as Edward Beale McLean, Nicholas Longworth, and Sen. Joseph Frelinghuysen and Harding's old small-town cronies from Ohio such as Jess Smith and Dick Crissinger. The largest component of the group was composed of Harding's old friends from the Senate.[3] The puritanical Herbert Hoover expressed disgust at this conversion of the White House into a smoke-filled, bourbon-fueled clubhouse, and did not continue the tradition when he occupied the executive mansion some years later. When Roosevelt took over the game once again reigned supreme. Harold Ickes, one of the "regulars," recalled a Wednesday evening in 1938 typical of the gatherings.

> After dinner we gathered around the poker table in the living room, with a galvanized tub full of beer, White Rock, and ginger ale nearby, and also within easy reach a table containing various liqueurs in addition to Scotch, Irish, bourbon, and rye whisky. We played until after twelve o'clock, and, as usual, I was one of the big losers. We played $1 limit. It was a jolly party.[4]

---

[3] Francis Russell, *The Shadow of Blooming Grove* (New York: McGraw-Hill, 1968), pp. 446–448.

[4] Harold Ickes, *The Secret Diary of Harold Ickes*, 3 vols. (New York: Simon and Schuster, 1954) vol. 2, p. 532.

Truman, far from being the dutiful homebody his depiction of himself conveyed, was a man who thrived on the company of his legislative colleagues. While it is true that he was never a fixture of the soiree circuit, his other social activities—notably poker—were aspects of him of that others invariably recall. Clinton Anderson, who knew Truman from their days in Congress and served as his Secretary of Agriculture, recalled a number of poker games in Virginia in which he sat across the table from the redoubtable senator from Missouri.[5] Truman's devotion to the game of poker, while he was in the Senate, amounted almost to a form of madness. He had a regular cab-driver who would pick him up every morning at his Connecticut Avenue apartment. One day Truman and a Senate colleague plunged into the back of the taxi, sat on the floor, and began to use the seat as a table for a poker game. They produced a bottle of bourbon and two glasses and proceeded to play poker and drink, invisible to passersby, while the cab cruised slowly through the wastes of Hains Point.

Poker was a Senate habit which persisted well into the 1950s. It sometimes made strange bedfellows indeed. There was, for example, at the old Wardman Park Hotel (later the Sheraton-Park) a poker group consisting of House Majority Leader John McCormack of Massachusetts, Senate Majority Leader Scott Lucas of Illinois, Sen. Clinton Anderson of New Mexico, Congressman Edward Eugene Cox of Georgia, Congressman William Colmer of Mississippi, and Sen. Joseph R. McCarthy of Wisconsin. What this odd combination of Fair Dealers, Southern conservatives, and the rampaging scourge of the left found to talk about of a noncontroversial and conversational nature is not known; McCarthy was another time paired in an odd relationship involving a series of high-stakes gin rummy games with Sen. Robert Kerr of Oklahoma, whose espousal of New Deal orthodoxy was only exceeded by his advocacy of the interests of the oil companies.

With the decline of poker as the sport of politicians and its replacement by more energetic activities, recreation has begun to take

---

[5] Clinton P. Anderson, *Outsider in the Senate* (New York: World Publishing Co., 1970), pp. 73–74.

on a more pragmatic image. Where poker or gin rummy could arguably improve the acuteness of a politician's mind and hone his tactical instincts, they were rarely justified in those terms. Outdoor sports, on the other hand, can be rationalized—and indeed often are —in terms of the need for a politician to be physically fit. An appearance of youthful vigor, as defined by cutting a trim figure in tennis whites, is a political asset; the bloodshot eyes and pallor of the poker table could never be advanced as useful to one's career. (Indeed, the terms "poker-playing" and "crony" have become intertwined in common political usage; they have become insinuated into the political vocabulary as synonymous with sinister and corrupt deals.) The replacement of poker as the pastime of politicians by the more salubrious outdoor sports has tended to confer on these sports a utilitarian value very much at variance with poker's status as fun for fun's sake. Politicians seeking sociability have deserted the green baize table for the grass court.

There exists in the Senate today a more or less constant group of tennis regulars, senators whose main extracurricular contacts with colleagues are over the tennis net. Before the start of the business day, usually around 7 AM, senators Lloyd Bentsen (D.–Tex.), Jacob Javits (R.–N.Y.), Lowell Weicker (R.–Conn.), Minority Leader Howard Baker (R.–Tenn.), Bennett Johnston (D.–La.), and Ernest Hollings (D.–S.C.) can be found playing tennis together. The tennis courts at St. Alban's School in Cleveland Park are favored by Senate tennis enthusiasts, although at Sen. Edward Kennedy's home, "Hickory Hill," in McLean, Virginia there is a magnificent tennis court which is often the site of senatorial tennis matches.

It is a measure of both the pragmatic standard applied to sports and games and the increasingly individualistic nature of the Senate that jogging and running have become the outdoor activities of those physically able to engage in them. There was a time when only those senators regarded as somewhat eccentric would run or jog. But the example set by William Proxmire and J. Strom Thurmond has changed running from a curiosity pursued by loners to the new Senatorial passion in sports. There can be no greater psychological—not to mention physical—contrast than that between poker and running: Poker was the game of the Senate era of chummy and boisterous camaraderie; running is the "game" of the individualistic Senate. The competition remains, but its purpose is redirected, for running is competition against oneself with a result of physical well-being. Card playing is simply not seen in those terms; it is a preeminently social activity, while running is often a solitary one.

The best-known theoretician of running, the veritable high priest of the sport, James Fixx, has noted how obsessively individualistic are so many of its practitioners and how expressive of the "Me Generation" this activity has become.

> Running has nothing, absolutely nothing, to do with caring about other people, or with compassion or with self-sacrifice. On the contrary, devotees of the sport are likely to be incorrigible loners, sufficient unto themselves in their sweaty enjoyments. . . .

> Don't imagine, incidentally, that the loneliness of the long-distance runner is nothing but a literary fancy. It's true; runners do tend to be solitary souls. Furthermore, far from being troubled by their solitude, they revel in it.[6]

Golf, at one time, was an important Senate sport, but now is the activity only of older senators. Of recent senators, Edmund Muskie, Eugene McCarthy, and Milton Young (R.–N.D.) were active golfers. However, there are now few senatorial foursomes to be found. For one thing, golf is an extremely time-consuming game. It also typically involves travel to a suburban course which hard-pressed senators are loath to undertake.

The old days when the Burning Tree Club in suburban Maryland was the scene of innumerable senatorial golf matches are now fading into memory. Those who remember it recall that, as with poker, important matters of business were generally barred from the course or the club house. Former senator Leverett Saltonstall (R.–Mass.) used to team up there with Sen. Prescott Bush (R.–Conn.) and Sen. H. Alexander Smith (R.–N.J.). Saltonstall recollected one technical breach of protocol:

---

[6] James F. Fixx, "What Running Can't Do For You," *Newsweek*, December 18, 1978.

It was common for senators to get together to play golf out at that Burning Tree Club, but politics were never supposed to be talked. They were occasionally, but very little. I never sat around out there. There were some that generally sat around and had drinks and so on. I never did. I went out and played golf generally and changed my clothes and came home, but George Mahon of Texas [Chairman of the House Appropriations Committee] was there one day after the Senate Armed Services Committee had submitted a defense package to Appropriations. I submitted it on a Friday and George Mahon was presiding, and Saturday I had played golf and I was going home and George was just coming in. I met him outside the door of the Burning Tree Club. I said, "George, what did you think of that package I submitted yesterday?" I said that I thought it made a good deal of sense or something like that. He said something friendly about it. Well, anyhow, we went back on Monday. He submitted his ideas. Now I won't say that most of them—but a very substantial amount of them were ideas from my package and that was the thing that was done and it was done in a five-minute conversation outside the club house.

In the sports activity of the modern individualistic senator there is no need for conventions or etiquette banning the discussion of political matters. The lonely runner, after all, is not apt to be badgered for a vote or asked to discuss legislative matters. The lobbyist who might corner a senator at the poker table or the clubhouse of a golf course is unlikely to don sneakers and jogging suit to catch one of the younger senators "on the run." One lobbyist did attempt to intercept Senator Proxmire in this fashion, and was sternly rebuked.

Unlike New York, where various occupational and social groups have established proprietary rights on certain eating places, Washington dining is much less structured. Theatre people in New York can be found at Sardi's, the jet set at "21", the dance and music crowd at the Russian Tea Room, and the Upper East Side young married couples at Elaine's or the Sign of the Dove. Congressional dining in Washington is less of a collective phenomenon and more subject to individual tastes; few senators congregate in any one place for luncheon or dinner.

However, as recently as twenty years ago, there were certain natural haunts for members of Congress. Harvey's—when it was on Connecticut Avenue—the old Occidental, Duke Ziebert's, and Paul Young's were the preferred downtown spots. The few choices available at the time on Capitol Hill were the Monocle, just a block away from the Senate office buildings, and the Rotunda. The decline of a sense of community in the Senate along with a dramatic expansion of the number of restaurants in Washington has resulted in there no longer being a single culinary command post. The Monocle, Paul Young's, and Duke Ziebert's attract fewer senators than formerly, though they still have some Senate loyalists.

Lunches downtown are generally ruled out by most senators; they prefer to take their lunches in their offices, hideaways, or in the private and semi-public Senate dining rooms. Some senators even have lunches brought up to them in the cloakroom. Senators scatter when it comes to evening dining on those few nights when they are free of political events. Choices are dictated by personal taste and not by social or political mandate. So Abourezk of South Dakota could indulge his fondness for Lebanese food at Bacchus and Muskie enjoy Chinese fare at the Moon Palace. But the Washington restaurants which formerly blanketed their walls with pictures of senators and congressmen who patronized them are almost extinct. The clientele of downtown restaurants has changed to a remarkable degree; It is now the lawyer and the lobbyist with their expense accounts whom the restaurateurs seek to attract. A restaurant seeking to base its clientele only on members of Congress would soon find itself bankrupt.

Few senators of recent years could be rated very highly as the kind of epicurean to whom an haute cuisine restaurant would appeal. Many senators have felt that a public reputation for elegant dining could result in being seen as decadent. Accordingly, Huey Long would make speeches on the floor extolling the virtues of "pot-likker"—the by-product of the cooking of pork and greens—and dilate on the advantages of dunking one's cornpone in the brew rather than crumbling it. Privately, however, Long was something of a connoisseur of fine New Orleans cooking. Allen Ellender, who followed Long to Washington as a Louisiana senator, set up a kitchen in his hideaway office where he cooked Creole gumbo.

The stark difference between the few real Senate gourmets and their colleagues for whom meat and potatoes are the staff of life is revealed in a story told about himself by Hubert Humphrey. The Minnesotan was on a trip to Paris with the elegant Sen. William Benton of Connecticut. Benton lured Humphrey into a four-star restaurant. Knowing Humphrey's simple, small-town tastes, Benton proceeded to order for the two of them. By the time the main course had been eaten, Benton evidently dropped his guard and allowed Humphrey to order his own dessert. Humphrey summoned the waiter and ordered a chocolate sundae.[7]

The preoccupation with diet and fitness—and the political dividends that redound to the slender and trim politician—have tended to make the ground-beef patty and the cottage-cheese scoop the standard of Senate luncheon fare. The dreariness of these repasts is accentuated by the fact that they are often eaten in solitude.

An opportunity for social interaction mentioned by virtually every senator I interviewed is official travel. Fact-finding missions, inspections of domestic and overseas military installations, visits to meetings of the North Atlantic Assembly and the Interparliamentary Union, and the holding of hearings outside Washington can throw colleagues together in situations in which social contact becomes almost inevitable. These social opportunities are heightened when their spouses accompany the senators. Being in the company of other senatorial couples, especially when abroad, seems to provide a natural and neutral setting for socializing. It is much more difficult to hold yourself aloof from colleagues when you find yourself with them in a foreign capital where few people speak English. The bond in this situation of being American, if nothing else, often serves to break down the inhibitions to socialize.

Fifty-eight senators took trips abroad during 1977. Members of the Foreign Relations Committee led the Senate in foreign travel; Judiciary Committee members were second. Western Europe was the travel objective of most senators; Panama was the next most favored destination. The fact that the Panama Canal Treaty was up for ratifi-

---

[7] Hubert H. Humphrey, *The Education of a Public Man* (Garden City, NY: Doubleday & Co., 1976), p. 159.

cation in the Senate probably accounted for the popularity of that country. Japan in 1977 was a poor third, although in most years it is a favorite objective, along with Canada and England, for privately funded visits.[8]

· Except for those trips which involve a high degree of visibility—such as the Panama outing of 1978, where scores of newsmen were in the Senatorial entourage—most trips involving two or three senators attract little attention, and thus allow almost complete escape from the curiosity of the press. They provide an occasion for members who normally have little chance to become well-acquainted to see the non-official side of a colleague. Although fast friendships may not develop, useful little glimpses are often provided.

A liberal Democrat and his wife found themselves seated next to a very conservative Southerner and his wife at the Italian Riding Academy in Vienna where the famous Lippizaner horses perform. This senatorial mission to Vienna had been provided with a block of tickets so circumstances rather than choice placed the two couples together for the evening. Just before the performance began, the Southerner, who had been consulting the program notes, leaned over to the liberal and pointed out a passage in the notes indicating that the Lippizaners are black when born but as they mature become much lighter. "It would be nice if people were that way," observed the Southerner. Recalled the liberal, "I don't know what it was about the statement—maybe it was the wistful way he said it—but it really gave me some insight into the guy."

In the statements of some senators there was the hint that being thrown together in a foreign capital with colleagues can be an uncomfortable situation.

> When you live with somebody for thirty or forty days in and out of a suitcase, and on a plane traveling around, you can either get pretty friendly or pretty mad with each other. On the whole, I think, we got friendlier rather than more distant, but I've heard of it going the other way.

[8] Mark Gruenberg, "Congress Sets New Travel Spending Records," *Congressional Quarterly Weekly Report*, vol. 36, no. 39 (September 30, 1978), pp. 2647–2658.

Such experiences can solidify relationships which were very casual prior to the trip. The presence of spouses in one instance, served to facilitate the contacts.

> In '62 and '65 we were on a trip with Senator Mansfield and the Mansfield mission. The trip was made with our wives. The Pells were on the trip and the Muskies, too. I had known them both before the trip, but hadn't been particularly close to them. I think that the wives' being there made a big difference.

This form of extramural social contact does seem to have the greatest potential for fostering friendship in those cases where senators are not well-acquainted prior to the trip abroad. A trip is usually insufficient to make friends of enemies, partly because if senators have any choice in the matter they will travel with those whom they like. Several senators told me that they actually turned down trips overseas because of their allotted traveling companions. Conversely, others said that they requested to go on a trip just because someone they liked had made arrangements to go. However, if a trip is of sufficient importance or likely to reap political dividends, a senator will of course go even though he may be in the company of a colleague he dislikes. On discretionary trips he will tend to be more selective and try to plan them in conjunction with a colleague with whom he is friendly. As in the case of so many other kinds of judgements of this nature, personal preference operates within the constraints imposed by political and institutional necessity.

Personal preference, more than any other factor, determines where the modern senator chooses to live in the capital area. Washington, D.C. is one of the world's capitals-by-fiat. Like Madrid, Ottawa, Brasilia, Islamabad, and Lilongwe, Washington did not evolve from being a nation's cultural, economic, and trading center into its seat of government through a natural process of evolution; rather, it was established by decree. Not, perhaps, so arbitrarily as by the thrust of a regal finger onto a spot of wilderness on a map, as in the case of Ottawa, or by a desire to open up a hinterland, as in the case of Brasilia, but still in its own way quite artificially did the confluence of the Potomac and Anacostia Rivers become the capital of the United States. Washington was the price exacted by Jefferson as part of a larger bargain with Hamilton. A swampy and unhygienic place, it became tolerable for year-round living only after the Civil War. Even then, the end of the short congressional session in April saw congressmen fleeing to their states and districts. Those compelled to remain behind would repair to summer homes along the extensions of Massachusetts and Connecticut Avenues or to the sleepy Southern village of Falls Church, Va. to escape the malarial miasmas. They would return in the fall when the dangers and unpleasantness of life in the capital had abated. Washington was a seasonal city, both for climatic and political reasons.

In the raw early years a strict form of residential segregation prevailed—a burlesque on the constitutional separation of powers—wherein congressional members' dwellings were clustered around the Capitol on the east side of Tiber Creek and executive branch members accommodations were on the lee side of the White House. The members of Congress

> lived the winter wholly in each other's company save as they might venture across the wastes of the Tiber to the executive quarter. They worked together, daily assembled in the noisy auditoriums of the Capitol, with no offices but their desks on the floor itself. They lived together in the same lodging houses. They took their meals together around the same boarding-house tables. Privacy was no more to be found during leisure than at work, not even privacy when they retired in their lodging houses "they lay two in a room, even the senators."[9]

This enforced communalism produced not cohesion but resentment at having to share bed and board in the capital city's few places of accommodation. Compelled to live with those with whom they worked, members of the early Congresses availed themselves of the little latitude they had by segregating themselves again into messes, or "fraternities," with those of their own state or region.

> In a heterogeneous society most members sought provincial companionship, setting themselves apart from men different in their

---

[9] James Serling Young, *The Washington Community, 1800–1828* (New York: Columbia University Press, 1966), pp. 87–88.

places of origin and differently acculturated. They transformed a national institution into a series of sectional conclaves.[10]

This regionalism reinforced by cohabitation was alleviated by the simple growth and diversification of the capital and by the development of a more expansive national focus on the part of congressmen and senators, but well into the twentieth century a residence in Washington for most members was little more than a pied-à-terre.

married members of Congress rarely brought their families to Washington. The reason was simple. The pay of Congressmen was $5,000 per year, and while that was a good deal of money then, their constituencies expected a Congressman to maintain his dwelling among them. Most Congressmen had children and so, unless they were rich, it was a financial necessity to keep their families at home and their children in the local schools. They lived as quasi-bachelors in hotels like the Driscoll on Capitol Hill, the Cochran, and the Riggs House.[11]

The advent of jet aircraft, reliable long-distance telephone service, telecopiers, and the legions of electronic aids to long-distance communication, along with the development of Washington as a very livable city and the reluctance of politicians to be separated from their families, even seasonally, has led to a system whereby the pied-à-terre is now in the provinces and the effective residence is in the capital. Convenience, taste, and income seem to be the most important factors today in a senator's choice of a Washington home. Washington real estate being a prime form of investment, most senators now purchase a home in or near the District of Columbia, but in a departure from the residential ecology of the early nineteenth century, there are no real senatorial enclaves.

There are, to be sure, preferred places to live. Senators are not to be found in such urban neighborhoods as Anacostia or the less fashionable suburbs such as Silver Spring, Maryland or Springfield, Virginia. They make the choices that would be made by any person

[10] Ibid., pp. 99–100.

[11] Arthur Krock, *Consent of the Governed and Other Deceits* (Boston: Little, Brown & Co., 1971) p. 247.

earning almost $60,000 per year. They choose places to live which range in the spectrum of quality from "comfortable" to "fashionable." Whether they are closer to the latter than the former seems to be dictated by independent sources of income.

· Capitol Hill, for all of its convenience, is not the preferred location for senatorial homes, for it is a neighborhood which has a high crime rate. The Hill neighborhood, however, has recently been gaining in popularity, due to extensive renovation of the Victorian and Federal-era houses in the vicinity. Whereas only nine senators of the 95th Congress chose the Hill as a place to live, thirteen members of the 96th Congress live there. Next in proximity to the Hill is the Southwest Redevelopment Area, which boasts a number of luxury high-rise structures, garden apartments, and townhouses. This, too, is an area which has been judged "unsafe." It currently has one senatorial resident, Harrison Williams of New Jersey; in the previous Congress it had been the home of three members.

Georgetown has always been a popular spot in Washington. Formerly an independent town, this section of the District of Columbia antedates Washington itself. There are a large number of eighteenth- and nineteenth-century townhouses and some of the best shopping in the capital in this area. Among the most expensive places to live in the District, it has attracted senators of considerable wealth. Rental rates for even the most modest townhouse in Georgetown proper begin at more than $900 per month. The colonial ambiance of Georgetown has attracted such Senate "aristocrats" as Claiborne Pell of Rhode Island, Percy and Stevenson of Illinois, and Byrd of Virginia.

Those members who prefer apartment living and the convenience of a downtown location favor the area of Foggy Bottom and the Watergate complex adjacent to the State Department and the Kennedy Center. Six senators live in this area; they find themselves about ten minutes closer to work than their eleven Georgetown colleagues.

At present the largest concentration of senators (twenty-two) lives in the large area of Northwest Washington west of Rock Creek Park and north of Georgetown. This section of the District encompasses such fashionable neighborhoods as Cleveland Park, D.C. Chevy Chase, upper Foxhall Road, Wesley Heights, American University Park, and Spring Valley. The minimum price for a house in this area is now well over $100,000. Freshman senator J. James Exon of Nebraska complained in 1979 that he had been forced to pay $125,000 for a house there, the value of which as a structure was about $40,000.

The second-largest concentration of senators is found in McLean, Virginia. With the exception of Potomac, Maryland—where only one senator, John Glenn, of Ohio, lives—McLean, with its spacious lots and gracious homes, is probably Washington's most fashionable suburban address. Eighteen senators reside there. Almost equal to McLean in suburban grandeur is the Bethesda-Chevy Chase area of Maryland, where eight senators live. Next in popularity is the northern Virginia county of Arlington, which is among the handiest to Washington; five senators live there. The independent city of Alexandria, which abuts Arlington, is the home of four, most of whom do not live in the eighteenth-century Old Town area but in the newer areas along Shirley Highway and the Capital Beltway.

The rest of the senators are scattered about: Spark Matsunaga and Gaylord Nelson in the newer neighborhood of Kensington, Maryland; Robert Stafford and Paul Laxalt in Falls Church, Virginia; Orrin Hatch in Vienna, Virginia; Mike Gravel and John Melcher in Maryland's Tantallon subdivision along the Potomac, and Pete Domenici in Rockville, Maryland.

There are two long-distance senatorial commuters, Paul Sarbanes of Maryland and Joseph Biden of Delaware; they maintain no Washington residences at all, living in Baltimore and Wilmington respectively. John Warner of Virginia does maintain a token Washington residence but spends his weekends at his farm at Middleburg, Virginia, about forty miles from Capitol Hill.

The geographical distribution of senators' residence in the Washington metropolitan area does not invite comparison to the cheek-by-jowl existence of senators which existed in the nineteenth century, but neither is it a picture of great dispersion. If a line were drawn along Capitol Street (North and South) and the Anacostia Freeway, 83 of the 100 senatorial homes would lie west of that line. (This is simply because all of the fashionable neighborhoods, with the exceptions of the Capitol Hill area and the new developments on Maryland's Potomac shore, are found to the west of that axis.) The areas of the District west of Rock Creek Park, Georgetown, and McLean account by themselves for more than one-half of senatorial residences.

Can anything be read into these patterns aside from the obvious conclusion that senators locate in the better neighborhoods? Bearing in mind that the 96th Congress is composed of fifty-nine Democrats, forty Republicans, and one independent, it is intriguing to note that Republicans outnumber Democrats in the Virginia suburbs by nine (twenty to eleven), that Democrats outnumber Republicans in the District proper by eighteen (thirty-five to seventeen) and in the Maryland suburbs by eight (eleven to three).

Without knowing the calculations that went into each senator's choice of location, the state of the real-estate market at the time, or any number of less tangible factors, it is perilous to draw any political conclusions from these patterns. There is nonetheless the provocative possibility that the party allegiance of neighborhoods has prompted Democratic senators to locate in the heavily Democratic District of Columbia and suburban Montgomery County (Maryland), and Republicans to live in Republican-dominated Virginia.

There are even a few ideological residential clusters of senators, which on the surface at least is rather intriguing. The Bethesda-Chevy Chase group is uniformly liberal. The Arlington-Alexandria-Falls Church group is predominantly conservative. Despite the substantial measure of homogenization which suburbanization has created in the metropolitan Washington area, the three major political jurisdictions, (the District of Columbia, Maryland, and Virginia) still retain some century-old political distinctions and contrasting political cultures. That these factors might play a role in senators' choice of residence cannot be dismissed entirely.

In those instances in which strong liberals and strong conservatives do find themselves in close quarters outside the Senate, there is little evidence that being neighbors draws them together socially any more than adjacent office space does within the Senate office buildings. This was evident in the recollection of an aide to a liberal Democrat, who was with his boss in a Senate elevator when they encountered a conservative senator from the Midwest. "Nice paint job you got on your house," said the conservative to his colleague, by way of greeting. The Democrat thanked the Midwesterner as he left the elevator, whereupon the aide turned to him and asked how the Republican knew his house had just been painted. "Oh, he lives around the corner from me," the Democrat responded. The aide told me with amazement, "I've worked for my boss for five years, and that was the first time I knew that he lived around the corner from Senator X———."

Social friendships outside the walls of the Senate represent, in a sense, an emotional increment over the intramural ones (which have served to reassure senators that it can be appropriate to extend the relationship to another sphere). Intramural social friendship is condoned and facilitated by the many points of informal contact within the Senate; a senator can ease into it without any great effort on his part. The extramural relationship takes effort and also involves the risk of being rebuffed, either because the object of an overture is one of those senators who prefers to segregate his professional and personal worlds or because he simply does not wish to pursue a social relationship outside the Senate with the member who makes the overture. One senator explained his own frustration with colleagues with whom he had established intramural social rapport:

> As I look at it now, most of the senators I was close to didn't do any entertaining of colleagues. We did quite a bit; my wife gave quite a number of dinner parties at our Georgetown house to which she invited Senators and their wives, but it was a one-way street. We would entertain them, but they would rarely have us back. For example, I don't think Sparkman ever invited us to a party. I guess we went to the Fulbright's once or twice. Lister Hill, never.

The reluctance of some senators to initiate social relationships with colleagues after hours may be the result of their implicitly heeding the wisdom of Alben Barkley, who admonished freshmen members of the Senate in 1945, "You cannot afford to entertain one senator unless you entertain all senators, because, being prima donnas, they are very jealous of one another."[12]

Another view of the inhibitions which cause senators to check their emotional commitments at the door of the Senate and avoid stepping too deeply into the personal life of another senator is that such involvements impair their freedom of action as politicians.

---

[12] Alben W. Barkley, *That Reminds Me* (New York: Doubleday & Co., 1954) p. 254.

Doris Kearns said that when Lyndon B. Johnson was Majority Leader in the 1950s,

> Increasingly, he came to view all relationships as continually shifting political combinations based largely on shared self-interest. And to a considerable degree he was accurate for politicians form alliances and not friendships. Individuals and institutions achieve their ends through continual barter. But deals are not bonds. Indeed intense emotional involvement with anything—with issues, ideology, a woman, even a family—can be a handicap, not only consuming valuable time, but, more importantly, reducing flexibility and the capacity for detached calculation needed to take advantage of continually changing circumstances.[13]

Much the same observation has been made of the present membership.

> Senators, while always grandly courteous with one another are rarely chummy. No time to be? Perhaps. But more important, they can't afford to be, don't want to be. A Senator can't trust a single one of his colleagues on the next issue called up. Senators resist getting closer to one another than arm's length lest it mitigate their freedom to fight.[14]

This view of human intimacy as politically incapacitating may well be correct in many cases; there are probably many senators who would feel squeamish about savaging a colleague in whose home they were recently entertained. But this incompatibility between knocking heads and forming friendships can be exaggerated. Some of the most self-confident senators are able to deal with this conflict in such a way that neither political options nor personal relationships are made to suffer. It is, however, the unusual senator who will run these risks. For many—perhaps most—senators the attitude of a middle-aged executive from California is one to which they can subscribe.

---

[13] Doris Kearns, *Lyndon Johnson and the American Dream* (New York: New American Library/Signet Books, 1976), p. 83.

[14] Bernard Asbell, *The Senate Nobody Knows* (Garden City, NY: Doubleday & Co., 1978), p. 80.

During our interview he expressed a sentiment that I had heard in various forms from many men. He said he didn't have any close male friends because the only guys he met were at work. "I avoid socializing with the guys who work for me. I think it's bad business. If you want to get the job done you've got to keep an impersonal kind of objectivity." He added that he really liked many of the men he worked with but he just couldn't take the risk of getting too friendly with them.[15]

Although extramural social friendship may serve as a demarcation point which separates the largely professional relationships from the more personal ones, the fact that two Senate colleagues are tennis partners or enjoy dinner parties together does not mean they will inevitably share their innermost secrets. Again, the ability of senators to discipline these relationships can be impressive. Good as they are at keeping their distance, in only a few cases is there any evidence that senators who dine, play tennis, or vacation together attain pure friendship. Indeed, these extramural social friends may be no more than what one observer calls "activity friends";[16] in this type of relationship, individuals find they share a common interest but have no inclination to pursue the friendship further. As in the case of institutional kinship and alliances, social friendship may be sufficient unto itself and not call forth the need to deepen the relationship. It is entirely possible, indeed it is probably typical, for people who are such social friends never to discuss anything of a deeply personal nature.

This tendency for people to develop special-purpose friendships-or "differential friendships," as George Simmel characterized them —has been seen as an outgrowth of an increasingly complex and specialized society whereby

> personalities become too individualized for a complete reciprocity of understanding and in consequence they incline more to relationships which involve only one facet of the per-

---

[15] Herb Goldberg, *The Hazards of Being Male* (New York: New American Library/Signet Books, 1977), p. 129.

[16] Darrell Sifford, "Friendship: You Get out of It What You Put into It," *Philadelphia Inquirer*, March 2, 1978, p. 3C.

sonality at a time. These differential friendships . . . demand
that friends refrain from obtruding themselves into one
another's interests and feelings not included in the special
relationship. The failure to observe this limitation would seri-
ously disturb the friendship. Within the segment of the total
personality that the relationship does involve, the feelings,
although limited at the periphery, are not necessarily shallow.
They may be sincere, deep, and abiding, and centered at the
very core of the individual's personality.

The development of differential relationships with acquain-
tances, friends, and relatives, with their varied social demands,
safeguards the individual's privacy and protects him against
undue emotional involvement in the lives of others.[17]

This effect is visible in both intramural and extramural social friendships in the Senate. Dinner parties or tennis matches do not compel
senators to peer deeply into each other's souls, exchange highly personal confidences or self-revelations. Perhaps as a consequence, they do
not appear to inhibit a senator from doing political battle with a colleague who was his host at dinner the previous evening.

The argument that all personal relationships may diminish a senator's room for maneuvering and inhibit him in battles can be overstressed. (The political inhibitions which might result from a too-
close personal friendship are most likely to cause problems in the
pure friendships which are the subject for the next chapter.) The benefits which flow to the senator in a merely social friendship are
nonetheless principally those of a personal nature: companionship to
alleviate the burdens of the job, a valuable glimpse into the character
of a colleague, finding a person with whom to share a special interest, and an opportunity to become acquainted with the family of a
colleague. In the contemporary Senate, with its high level of profes-
sionalism, these personal benefits can be written off as attractive but
marginally important extras. There is certainly no impairment of formal senatorial power that arises from being socially distant or aloof;

---

[17] Margaret Mary Wood, *Paths of Loneliness* (New York: Columbia University
Press, 1953), p. 101.

no evidence was found of any such senator being denied a chairmanship or even an elective leadership post in the Senate. Indeed, the recent history of party leadership on both sides of the aisle is replete with instances of the most dour and restrained personalities imaginable achieving positions of leadership.

The political benefits to be reaped from a social friendship clearly flow from the intramural rather than extramural variety. Sociability in the institutional context can be very useful to a senator. According to a veteran Washington journalist, "You get a better spin on the ball." However, unlike the senatorial alliance, social friendship usually sets up no serious expectations on substantive matters. It is clearly a more personal relationship than that found in the alliance or the institutional kinship, which is essentially a damage-limiting pact; social friendships are more positive than that.

Legislators seem to sense a value in developing relationships with colleagues on a basis that is not strictly political. This was noted by Stephen K. Bailey and Howard D. Samuel in their case study of Mississippi congressman Frank E. Smith, who served in the House in the 1950s.

> In his first six months as a member, Smith had made it a habit to spend as much time as possible on the floor and in the cloakrooms. His chief purpose was to meet the other members and to give them an opportunity to meet him. . . . For the same purpose, as often as possible he ate his lunches in the House dining room, sitting with whomever he chanced to meet. . . . The process of getting acquainted with other members, in the long run, would promote his own effectiveness as a member of the House.[18]

As diffuse as the benefits of these kinds of intramural associations might appear, they can provide a senator a substantial amount of what Hubert Humphrey called "wiggle room"—favors and considerations which may not be substantively significant but which have considerable procedural value and can be a great help in fostering a career in the Senate.

---

[18] Stephen K. Bailey and Howard D. Samuel, *Congress at Work* (New York: Henry Holt & Co., 1952), p. 131.

There are, of course, senators who use the social opportunities afforded them to pursue politics by other means. Although it is less true now than formerly, the social cultivation of powerful members of the Senate by junior members is a very calculated technique used by some. This social courting is less prevalent today because chairmen tend to be less autocratic, junior members less deferential and power more evenly distributed and individualized. Older senators and former senators who were interviewed were very emphatic on the point that this social cultivation was once widely practiced. Both inside and outside the Senate it also involved ingratiating one's self with the ranking minority member of a committee. Some senators continue the practice, but it is significant to note that the cultivation of fellow senators is less pronounced now than that of influential people outside the legislative branch, as with the blatant social cultivation by one very prominent member of the Senate Foreign Relations Committee of Secretary of State Henry Kissinger. There is some mild romancing of members of the Democratic and Republican Policy Committees by members who want a preferred committee assignment, but such requests do not typically involve any wining and dining. The attitude of the newer and younger senators to the old practice of cultivation was expressed thus by a border-state Democrat:

> Most men don't get to the Senate unless they are reasonably competent, able, and tough. Men like that kiss very little ass.

Social friendships inside the walls of the Senate, facilitated by a physical environment that permits senators to come together and establish informal relationships, may or may not be of a politically useful nature, depending on personal choice. The opportunities in the Senate dining rooms, gymnasium, cloakrooms, offices of the secretariat, or Prayer Breakfast for senators to encounter each other and for relationships to flourish provide an atmosphere in which serious political discussion is not obligatory, indeed, may even be avoided. It is natural, of course, for such encounters to touch lightly on politics, because that is the métier of the senator. Once having encountered a colleague in such a setting, the stage may be set for a more personal type of relationship, but this is neither a natural nor inevitable consequence of such contacts.

Social relationships outside the walls of the Senate among colleagues are limited in frequency partly because of time constraints, partly because the reluctance of some to become emotionally involved in the life of a colleague, partly because senators are so saturated with each other's company that they would sooner spend leisure time with those not associated with the Senate, and in some instances because of the fear that it represents an encroachment. Such social contacts as do occur among colleagues after hours are deeply colored by politics, as when senators are drawn together after hours for events such as fund-raisers—often for the benefit of other Senate colleagues—which are social in style but not in substance.

The private lives of senators are a mirror-image of the individualism that now prevails in the Senate itself. Even in the pursuit of physical activity this individualism manifests itself; the trend away from group sports and games to more solitary forms of recreation is an expression of this individualism. Increasingly, moreover, a strongly utilitarian test is applied to sports and games—fitness rather than fun is both the standard and the justification.

There is much intelligence but little real erudition in the modern Senate. Professionalization and specialization have taken their toll on the interests of senators. One long-time observer used a nice simile: "They have minds like polished brass helmets. They deflect intellectual notions the way they reflect light—they bounce off like English peas." The modern Senate represents the apotheosis of the "quick study"—the efficient but narrowly gauged mind.

There are no longer any Senatorial gathering-spots or enclaves. The carefree life of the Senate social lion of years past has given way to more sedate entertainments. Senatorial "wickedness" is rarely proclaimed publicly, and casual affairs are conducted with modesty and discretion; the political penalties involved in ostentatious liaisons are too heavy for even the most tumescent senator to bear.

The concept of "sociability" as distinct from either deep personal attachment or a strictly business relationship has a tangible expression in senatorial social friendship. It is not merely a construct; it has real-life manifestations. It is, most typically, companionability without self-revelation, geniality without the sharing of inner confidences. It constitutes "the play-form of association and is related to the content-determined concreteness of association as art is related to reality."[19] Many of these Senate social friendships remain fixed, for the duration of the association, at that point of sociability. Those few relationships which do eventuate in pure friendship retain, of course, the external characteristics of social friendship—dinner parties, common vacations, exchanges of office-visits, and joint trips abroad—but these activities, social in form, become augmented by a more significant emotional bond. It is a bond all the more remarkable for having been forged within a profession and an institution in which such relationships have often been judged improbable, if not downright impossible.

Without question, most people pass through the Senate without establishing such a relationship with a colleague. Distinguished careers, spectacular legislative achievements, and the loftiest posts of leadership have been attained by those who knew no such relationships; obscurity, frustration, and lack of distinction have often been the lot of those who enjoyed them. Their relevance and importance are for the emotional and spiritual man, not the political or legislative man. Some senators enjoy such relationships only with those wholly divorced from politics; others are drawn to political men and women, but only to those who have never served in the Senate. Some go through life without ever being touched by them at all. The forces which inhibit such relationships in senators are not radically different from those which operate to impede them in other spheres of activity. These forces, however, are accentuated by the nature of human relationships in this unique institution.

Despite the tiresomeness of such a cliché as "the loneliness of power," it is valid; there is much loneliness in the Senate. It is not a loneliness which comes from any lack of attention or even adoration by those fascinated by senators or obligated to them in some way, nor is it a loneliness which comes from insufficient contact with colleagues. It is rather the loneliness of living a life in which relationships must be screened so mercilessly. Manipulators by instinct, senators fear to be manipulated. Gregarious by necessity, they are wary lest gregariousness lead them into perilous involvements.

---

[19] Georg Simmel, "The Sociology of Sociability," *American Journal of Sociology,* vol. 55, no. 2 (Sept. 1949), p. 255.

Needful of approval by temperament, their vindications come from masses of voters they can never know, while the affections of those with whom they are most closely engaged are usually withheld, and often of little consequence.

Yet would the American people, the representatives of organized special interests, or the press and television approve a Senate in which more loyalty was owed to colleagues than to constituencies, sentiment ruled in place of sober political calculation, members disdained specialized questions in favor of broad intellectual pursuits, and politicians were boon companions? The modern Senate is highly adaptive and functional in terms of what the American people want from it: a legislative mill, a political commodities market in which issues are traded, a symphony orchestra in which each performer is a soloist, a secular consistory from which benefices and indulgences are issued, and a theater in the round where position-taking is the standard of the player's art. Far from being obsolete, the Senate is the perfect, modern American institution, fully in keeping with the nation it serves: fragmented, lacking in a sense of community, competitive, given to vulgarity and posturing. But when motivated by the gravity of challenge or touched by some nobler impulse it can, like the people it represents, be efficient, purposeful, and compassionate. There can even be found in the Senate those who, in defiance of professional inhibitions, come to regard some few of their colleagues as friends within the terms of a definition acceptable to ordinary men and women.

CHAPTER SIX

FRIENDSHIP, PERSONAL AND PURE

When the concept of institutional kinship was introduced in Chapter 1 it was accompanied by an argument justifying considering this form of interpersonal relationship among senators as a manifestation of friendship. The reader was asked to accept this restricted and limited form of human association as an expression of friendship because of the peculiar institutional context in which it occurs. In a highly fragmented, individualistic, and competitive Senate where institutional norms no longer serve to guide or chasten, some measure of cohesion is retained through a network of individual compacts between senators (based upon actual experience) that colleagues would be restrained, diligent, empathetic, and trustworthy. Not for its conformity to some ideal but for its validity in a very special context was this form of association advanced as an example of friendship.

In considering the evidence of pure friendship in the Senate, only a similar plea to consider the context can avert the accusation that genuine intimacy is impossible among United States senators. If we are prepared to accept that fondness can exist without deep personal involvement, that political imperatives can be permitted to dilute fidelity with inconstancy, that differences in ideological and philosophical values cannot readily be transcended by even the most compatible personal qualities, and that those senators deemed to be closest rarely have much insight into one another, we can begin to approach the subject of pure friendship in the Senate and examine its few tangible expressions. The rarity of such expressions was commented upon by a congressional observer of long standing who commented, "There aren't too many epiphanies in the United States Senate."

For those in quest of David and Jonathan or Damon and Pythias in the contemporary Senate, the pursuit is likely to be disappointing. What emerge are scattered pairs or groups of senators, whose most obvious shared characteristics are partisanship and ideology (or, if not always precisely shared, at least not dramatically incompatible), drawn together in relationships which transcend extramural social friendship in their degree of intimacy. In some of these relationships there is considerable familiarity among the families of the senators, some evidence of shared confidences on personal matters, and, in one such group, more than a suggestion that political behavior is influenced by the closeness of the personal ties, or at least that political appeals are made and responded to on a basis other than strict self-interest. The principal caveats which attach to the consideration of these friendships are: first, that there are few of them; second (as outlined above), that they be considered intimate not by normal standards but by the idiosyncratic ones of the Senate; and, finally, that some types, for a variety of reasons, seem to be diminishing. While there is nothing to suggest that senators as a group are incapable of forming close personal ties with those outside the Senate, they tend to refrain, for a variety of reasons, from establishing the most intimate ties with their colleagues.

The expectation that a senator's closest friends would be those with whom he is in more or less continuous political accord is a natural one, and our interviews with members of the Senate did not refute this expectation. Virtually all of the senators asserted that it would be extremely difficult to sustain a close association with a colleague with whom clashes over issues occurred on a regular basis. There was, moreover, a consensus that working together for the achievement of the same political goals on a regular basis operates to bring senators together both in a political and personal sense. Cooperation rather than conflict on legislation results in greater frequency of contact, and out of this friendly political association can develop an intimacy that opposition simply cannot produce. However, as amply documented previously herein, it is not appropriate to infer personal closeness from political agreement, nor is it safe to deduce hostility in any consistent way from ideological dissimilarity. Most senators are able to compartmentalize their political feelings from their personal ones to a remarkable degree. Ideological agreement, then, does not automatically signal personal closeness, although every intimate friendship that I was able to identify occurred among men who were relatively close philosophically. The only senators for whom ideological compatibility came even close to constituting a strict requirement for personal friendship were those doctrinaire liberals or conservatives who acknowledged that they would find it difficult under any circumstances to feel personally close to an ideological opposite. But here the numbers were so small that it is impossible to say with any certainty that this attitude is characteristic of all those holding intense ideological views.

While ideological compatibility is associated with personal closeness, most of the relationships among those senators who share philosophical outlooks are not intimate. Even those who are primed to understand the Senate can fall prey to mistaking political compatibility for familiarity. Washington columnist Drew Pearson ran afoul of this misconception when he attempted to enlist a group of senators to intervene in the tragic personal life of Senator Thomas Hennings from Missouri.

Tom Hennings had a drinking problem. The senior senator from Missouri was fighting a losing struggle against the bottle. An early incident symptomatic of this was in 1952, when he was serving as chairman of the Senate Elections Committee; he had deserted the effort of the liberals on the committee to deny a Senate seat to the demagogic Joseph R. McCarthy, and had fled to a room on the sixteenth floor of the Plaza Hotel in New York to drink himself into a stupor. (He had devised a cover story that he was in Lincoln, Nebraska, but repeated calls to that state revealed that he had never arrived.) The liberals' effort to deny a seat to McCarthy failed. By 1955 rumors were circulating that Hennings had withheld the documents most damning to McCarthy in the previous year's censure hearings, for fear that the Wisconsin Republican would blackmail him on his drinking. By the spring of 1957, Hennings's binges were increasing in their duration, and his marriage was breaking up. At this point, columnist Drew Pearson, who liked and admired Hennings, went to a number of liberal Democratic senators who had been long-term allies of Hennings and attempted to convince them to pay a call on the Missourian to offer their help. Pearson recorded the incident in his diary:

I talked to Paul Douglas (D.–Ill.) and to Wayne Morse (D.–Ore.) about a "visitation" on Tom. Paul was dubious, said he didn't know him well enough. Wayne was emphatically for it. It seems one trouble is that Tom doesn't know many other senators. . . .

Luvie [Mrs. Pearson] and I stopped in to see the Mike Monroneys. Mike says he doesn't know Tom very well either, and doesn't know who does. Apparently, Tom has led quite an aloof life as far as his colleagues are concerned.[1]

I asked a former U.S. Senator who knew both Hennings and Pearson, as well as Morse, Douglas, and Monroney, how it was possible for the colleagues of the stricken senator to stand on ceremony and express reluctance to pay a call on him because they did not know him well enough. The ex-Senator explained that Pearson had made a mistake common to those outside the Senate; knowledgeable outsider that he was, he assumed that since Hennings tended to vote with the other three liberal Democrats there was a close personal relationship. He said, "Tom was independent. He wasn't a member of any built-in group in the Senate. He voted with the liberals, but that's where the relationship ended."

The saying of Thomas Heywood, the seventeenth-century English writer, in his *Hierarchie of the Blessed Angells*, "I hold he loves me best that calls me Tom," does not apply to the U.S. Senate. Though many of his colleagues called Hennings "Tom," it was hard to find those who knew him—much less loved him—enough to penetrate the recesses of his tortured soul, even among those who most closely shared his public principles.

If simple compatibility of political values is not always sufficient in and of itself to give rise to personal intimacy, what is it that can move the relations of ideologically similar senators in the direction of personal intimacy? Two general factors present themselves as being capable of emotionally augmenting a relationship of political agreement: significant shared experiences, such as attendance at the same school, involvement in the same state political organization, or joint

---

[1] Drew Pearson, *Diaries, 1949–1959,* Tyler Abell (ed.) (New York: Holt, Rinehart, and Winston, 1974), pp. 232, 339, and 386.

participation in some important cause—more simply, having been at the same place and the same time for the same purpose; and common spiritual or social values, such as membership in the same religious denomination or possession of certain social affiliations. In those Senate friendships of the most intimate and pure variety, these two factors can spell the difference between simple ideological compatibility and genuine personal fondness.

The spiritual and social values are acquired from the family early in life. The significant shared experiences which can serve to convert political compatibility into pure friendship develop later in the career of the individual. These latter factors may become important either prior to Senate service—as with those who have attended the same school, served together in the military, or been part of the same state political organization party faction; or occur within the Senate itself, as in the case of those drawn together by the common prolonged pursuit of a shared legislative goal, or by the structural features of the Senate during a particular historical period. But despite the apparent ability of these factors to transform relationships and cause "birds of a feather to flock together," similarity can sometimes breed contempt.

It is not surprising that some of the closest relationships among senators are those involving some fundamental religious or social similarity or a common experience of great personal meaning. Of those friendships based upon common experience, the most important historically has been the mentor-protégé friendship. Shared political experience, generally in the same state political organization, is the wellspring for this relationship. There are, however, a few unusual cases where introduction takes place outside the world of politics, notably at college or in the armed forces. These relationships, which often express themselves not so much in terms of friendship but more in terms of unusual insight or understanding, are those of the "old school tie" and the "old soldiers." Sometimes this flicker of insight or understanding is provided by the sharing of a personal tragedy; we will look at this "tragic nexus" at the conclusion of this chapter.

The more primal ties of social or religious solidarity are prepolitical or extrapolitical, but in practice tend to give rise to friendships among people whose political philosophies are harmonious. It can be argued that it is ideological agreement which is the essence of the relationship, but in the cases of three Senate groups, the Catholics, the evangelicals, and the socialites, a bond of considerable power, distinct from party or ideology, adds firmness to the association.

Both of these sets of factors—significant shared experiences and common values must be treated with caution. For while they may help to explain some friendships, their influence is merely nominal in other types of relationships between senators who hold them in common, and there are pure friendships which develop without their influence. In a few instances they may even lead to conflict. What began as a mentor-protégé relationship between the two liberal Democrats from Oregon, Wayne Morse and Richard Neuberger—and had its origins in the period when Morse was Dean of the University of Oregon School of Law and Neuberger was his student—ended in strident hostility. A devout belief in Catholic doctrine shared by Eugene McCarthy and Robert Kennedy was insufficient to avert deep personal enmity, and their eventually shared opposition to the Vietnam War—a struggle which brought many others together—served only to accentuate their personal differences.

Particularly close relationships can develop between senators who can trace their association to a common college or law school. Given the tendency of politically inclined students to seek each other out, and the fact that a number of senators attended the same school at the same time, several long-term relationships of this nature exist in the Senate. One such relationship survived a head-on clash for the same Senate seat: In the election of 1968, Republican congressman Charles McC. Mathias challenged incumbent senator Daniel Brewster. Mathias defeated Brewster, so the two never served in the Senate together, but Brewster's feelings about his old classmate at the University of Maryland Law School retained much fondness.

> Mac Mathias and I are old friends. We were classmates in law school and, through much of our last year in law school, he stayed at my house in Baltimore County. He is the godfather of my oldest son and I was an usher in his wedding. This friendship has remained steadfast through the years in spite of vigorous political differences and in spite of the fact that he defeated me. . . .

He has conducted himself always—and in that particular campaign—as a complete and thorough gentleman. . . .

Let alone is there no bitterness against Mac Mathias, there is *great* respect and affection for him! To give you a recent example, on January 20, 1977, my wife Judy and I walked in side by side with my old friend in the U.S. Senate to witness Mr. Carter's inauguration. . . .

Only today my wife received a personal note from Mac congratulating us on our new baby.[2]

Mathias's close personal ties to Brewster and his knowledge that his old classmate was an alcoholic added an agonizing twist to their 1968 campaign against each other. Brewster's drinking problem had developed to a point where it had become a matter of public record. He had attended a State of Israel rally in Pikesville, Maryland in 1967 and been so drunk that he was unable to address the gathering. This was reported in the Maryland press. Mathias, however, had chosen not to capitalize on Brewster's troubles. It can be argued that the Mathias campaign slogan, "Reason for a Change," was a veiled reference to Brewster's drinking himself into insensibility, but Brewster himself, chose to place the most favorable interpretation on Mathias's conduct of the campaign.[3] It is worthy of note that when Brewster was indicted for accepting a bribe in exchange for a favorable vote on a postage-rate bill, Mathias testified on his behalf, voluntarily. Brewster in turn supported Mathias for reelection in 1974.

The relative restraint with which Mathias conducted the 1968 campaign and his willingness to speak up on Brewster's behalf is unquestionably evidence of a remarkable man. His reputation for fair-mindedness and balanced judgment resulted, at a very early time in his Senate career, in the unusual situation of having senators voting for a freshman's bills simply because of the name they carried as sponsor.[4] Whether Mathias would have been so generous to an oppo-

[2] Blaine Taylor, "Phoenix—The Rise, Fall, and Resurrection of Senator Daniel Brewster," *Maryland State Medical Journal*, vol. 26, no. 7 (July 1977).

[3] Ibid.

[4] Mark J. Green, with Bruce Rosenthal and Lynn Darling, *Who Runs Congress?*, introduction by Ralph Nader (New York: Bantam Books, 1975), p. 209.

nent whose friendship he had not long enjoyed is a question; his long and intimate association with Brewster cannot be dismissed as a factor in his behavior.

Long and intimate knowledge of a colleague, as in the case of Brewster and Mathias, can serve to restrain enmities which might otherwise arise in political competition. It also enables the partners in this type of relationship to offer advise and counsel—advice which, if it came from another source, might be rejected. Having known a person in his younger and less guarded days gives a colleague a superior insight. To have shared a dormitory room or have dated the same women establishes an early bond and an understanding which may prove quite durable.

Two old college friends were serving the same Southern state in the House when a vacancy occurred in one of the state's Senate seats as the result of a resignation. The one who was senior in terms of service quickly emerged as the front-runner for the Senate seat. However, it was widely known in the political circles of the state that this senior member had a drinking problem. This was brought home very forcefully when the state committee met to give its endorsement and the front-runner came in "very tight" indeed. The state's premier political figure, then serving in a cabinet post in Washington, had come down for the meeting, and was so appalled at this that he took the other congressman aside and asked him if he would run in the other man's stead. The more junior congressman declined, saying that it would crush his colleague to be dropped for the nomination, and besides, the two had made a personal pact on who would get the first open Senate seat. The junior member did assure the premier politician that he would keep an eye on his colleague from his vantage point on the House side.

Two years later another senatorial resignation occurred and the loyal friend then got his Senate seat. This enabled him to observe the senior senator more closely; his drinking problem had worsened and the junior member decided to intervene.

> I talked to him about his drinking on many occasions. We were a year apart in age and had been classmates at the university. . . . After I joined him in the Senate, he would invite me to his office for a drink. I would go but not have anything to drink. When I invited him to my office I never served him

a drink, and when he visited my home I never offered any liquor. I didn't want to contribute to his problems.

Another such relationship existed between a Midwestern Democrat and an Eastern colleague of the same party.

> X—— and I had the same job as undergraduates at college and in law school; we were both secretaries in an undergraduate organization at Harvard. He'd gone to school in England and I'd gone to school there, so we had a lot of friends in common. We had some shared experiences, so it gives you a running start when you get in here that you see some people that had some common experiences, values, and attitudes. It's a very congenial and comfortable relationship.

Old college friends reunited in the Senate need not have a relationship of very great closeness or intimacy, but they may find that their long-standing acquaintance may take the edge off political differences which might otherwise have been a source of difficulty. This was the case with a conservative Republican from the West and a liberal Republican from a border-state. As the Westerner recalled the relationship:

> X—— and I were good friends, but we rarely voted together. We'd been friends since way back in college; we played on a football team together at Yale. He was so much more liberal than anyone I'd ever felt comfortable with, but I'd really come to respect him over the years.

It is clear that this relationship was more along the lines of an institutional kinship between two men of vastly differing philosophies.

The old school tie, then, has within it a length of association which might produce deep personal ties of the pure friendship variety, and indeed there is some evidence that this has happened. But it is as likely to produce relationships of considerably less intimacy, for political differences—or the many other factors which inhibit senatorial closeness—may intervene and reduce the effect of the long-standing relationship to a less profound type of relationship, or simply relegate it to a quaint and static background memory.

There were actually very few school cohorts in the 96th Congress. John Culver of Iowa and Edward M. Kennedy of Massachusetts were undergraduates at Harvard at roughly the same time; theirs has developed into an essentially extramural social friendship. The same applies to Culver's relationship with Maryland Democrat Paul Sarbanes, who attended Harvard Law School at the same time as the Iowan. Spark Matsunaga (D.–Hawaii) and Ted Stevens (R.–Alaska) were also at Harvard Law together in the early 1950s, but there is no evidence of any particular closeness between them.

In the 96th Congress there were Harvard-trained senators in abundance (fourteen in number) and Yale and Columbia were also well-represented (Yale with eight graduates and Columbia with four). There were few cases of age-cohorts, however, and even among them there is little evidence that simply having attended the same school at the same time gave rise to pure friendship. It seems that the passage of time and the fact that association may not have been continuous may cause old ardor to cool, if there was any to begin with. A senator may also wish to make as little as possible of his youthful adventures and interests, and be content to inter them with his diploma and yearbook. And the contemporary Senate may not provide the most estimable setting for rekindling a friendship. Neither time-schedules nor current interests may provide much of a basis for such a resumption. If the only thing two senators have in common is having attended Harvard, its effect on their relationships in the Senate will be minimal.

Unlike his British counterpart of years past—with whom flourishing the school colors or invoking the glories of an elite regiment might have changed a vote, because anyone who rowed with the "blues" or served with the guards couldn't possibly be a bad chap—the modern U.S. senator is much less impressed with such sentimental references. I asked one senator if there was any solidarity among former Princeton undergraduates serving in the Senate, and his response was, "absolutely none." In the few recent examples of pure friendship based on common college experience, the early tie was usually more close than that of simply being classmates.

Memories of having faced military combat together often produce close ties among ex-soldiers. As memories of the rigors of combat abate, a fond nostalgia often emerges. One of the senators in the group I interviewed had served in an armored unit during World War II with a colleague. "We were always warm friends," he recalled.

"I think that the war experience enhanced our friendship a lot." A somewhat different experience in the military resulted, with Bob Dole (R.–Kan.) and Philip Hart (D.–Mich.), not in an intimate friendship, but in a warm personal regard which mitigated ideological differences. Both men, grievously injured during World War II, spent time together undergoing treatment in the same veterans' hospital. "They had a very special relationship that political differences couldn't disrupt," explained one observer of their personal interactions in the Senate. It is possible that if the ideological barriers between these men were not so imposing, the relationship would have been even closer.

Mentor-protégé friendships can develop between senators who were unacquainted prior to their Senate service but most relations of this nature have tended to have their origins in common participation in state political organizations and were often the product of powerful state machines. Given the tendency of these machines, historically, to mandate a set of policies to its senatorial representatives and to recruit those whose views comported with those of the party leaders, there is a built-in set of partisan and ideological values which can prove hospitable to friendship. These state organizations typically established mechanisms for mobility and succession to offices. Promising or simply loyal people were placed in orderly queues for movement into vacant posts. Younger people were groomed by their elders to move up. The very regularity of succession procedures had the effect of reducing or even eliminating inter-generational challenges. Younger men, knowing that loyal time-serving would eventuate in higher office, were unlikely to challenge those ahead of them in line. The process was more orderly then than now. There was less overt scrambling, and the younger individuals, while not necessarily models of filial piety, were nonetheless inclined to bide their time. Pressure might even be exerted on the elders to step down before death or disability, to allow the channels of mobility to be opened.

Depending on the state, one might move from local office to a state assembly seat and then be tapped for a congressional seat, moving from there to the Senate. In some states, even, the progression began with municipal office. Strong state party organizations, whatever their shortcomings, often operated to moderate ambition, dampen interpersonal conflict, and provide a regularized process of political succession. It is interesting to note that the few recent examples of mentor-protégé relationships in the U.S. Senate have occurred between senators who were products of the same strong state party organization.

The best-known and most institutionalized of these, until recently, was the Minnesota Democratic Farmer Labor party. Since the fusion of the Democratic and Farmer Labor parties after World War II, some of the best known figures in the national Democratic politics progressed through DFL ranks. The endorsement of the DFL convention averted most primary election fights, and even when they occurred the party went into the general elections unified. When Hubert Humphrey left his Senate seat to become vice-president in 1965, state Attorney-General Walter Mondale was appointed by Governor Karl Rolvaag to an interim term. Then Mondale won the seat in his own right in 1966. In 1971, when Eugene McCarthy left the Senate, the unanimous choice to succeed him was Humphrey. For almost three decades, the DFL was this nation's only liberal machine. Although it did not eliminate interpersonal enmities, it muted them to a remarkable degree. In its later years, Humphrey was unquestionably the patriarch of the DFL; the man who benefited most fully from his largesse was Mondale. Their relationship was a close one, and Humphrey never attempted to restrict Mondale to the role of junior partner. Nonetheless, the relationship was indelibly stamped with the seal of mentor and protégé.

In the early years of the Mondale-Humphrey relationship this mentor-protégé connection was overt; it was a wholly natural outgrowth of Humphrey's willingness to assist Mondale's career and Mondale's acceptance of this guiding role.

Humphrey has been said to have had other protégés in Minnesota politics. Such a role has been ascribed to Eugene McCarthy, who recalled, however, "They used to consider me a protégé of Humphrey's but I think I had to be introduced to him the night I got elected." This was certainly not the case with Mondale, who stood loyally by Humphrey during the agonies of the 1968 presidential campaign, never publicly divulging his private differences with him over his dogged refusal to abandon the military course in Vietnam set by Lyndon Johnson.

The relationship became more complicated when Humphrey returned to the Senate in 1972 as Minnesota's "junior" senator. In Humphrey's absence from the Senate Mondale had come into his own. He had become autonomous, and can even be said to have assumed the unchallenged position of Minnesota's chief spokesman, especially as Eugene McCarthy's interest in the Senate began to ebb. With Humphrey's return, however, Mondale began to chafe under the burden of having as a junior colleague such a larger-than-life figure. He was falling again under the older man's penumbra. It was not the case that Humphrey asserted any tutelary role; he staunchly denied any such motive in a letter to me:

> Humphrey's shadow has not prohibited the growth and development of political leaders in Minnesota. I believe it can be fairly said that I have given as much as I have taken, that I have encouraged young men and women to enter public life, and that that I have helped them whenever possible. I have never been accused of trying to keep other people from succeeding lest it dim my life or overshadow my work.[5]

Despite this avowed effort to avoid being overbearing, Humphrey's very presence necessarily created problems for his younger, but "senior," colleague. Without the slightest intention of stealing the scene, Humphrey upstaged Mondale. An event which occurred in the first week of September 1975 is a testament to this. Mondale had flown from Washington to St. Paul to be present at the visit of the Bicentennial Freedom Train to the twin cities. Mondale appeared at the train station with his son and began to address a large and appreciative crowd. At one point, however, Mondale noticed that the crowd was distracted by a commotion at the opposite end of the train. Walking down the tracks was Hubert Humphrey, wearing an engineer's cap and holding the hand of a small child in full engineer's regalia. Mondale gave up trying to hold the crowd's attention and merely watched as they flocked around Humphrey, who had dramatically, but unintentionally, upstaged Mondale.

The shadow of Humphrey, which for so long had obscured Mondale, finally receded when Humphrey retired to private life. This permitted Mondale to attempt such daring initiatives as testing the presidential waters in 1973–74. Mondale's gratitude for what

---

[5] Letter from Hubert H. Humphrey to author, July 21, 1976.

Humphrey had done for him in the past was genuine. No one who heard his eulogy to Humphrey could fail to be moved by its sincerity and feeling. To be the protégé of so generous a patron could be useful, but Mondale eventually reached the point where he wished to be judged on his own accomplishments and not on the renown of his mentor. That Humphrey would have sought out and assisted Mondale in a less cohesive state political organization is, of course, a distinct possibility. The DFL, however, was more conducive to these types of associations than were state parties without acknowledged leaders or regularized mechanisms of succession.

Only two relationships in the contemporary Senate seem to approximate the mentor-protégé model, and both are products of strong party organizations at the state level. In the earlier part of his first term, Sam Nunn (D.–Ga.) was said by many to be a protégé of his senior colleague, Herman Talmadge, scion of a Georgia political dynasty. Nunn was a political neophyte, completely unfamiliar with Washington; a friendly Georgia congressman had some of his influential friends in the capital show the ropes to the junior senator from Georgia. Nunn was said to have been an attentive and respectful junior colleague of Talmadge's while Talmadge assisted him. It took Nunn little time to become acclimated, and since then he has risen swiftly in the estimation of his colleagues. Talmadge, on the other hand, has recently suffered from accusations that he diverted campaign contributions for his personal use. The relations between the two men continue to be close; Nunn, a man of more than ordinary ambition, might have tried to avoid being too closely identified with a colleague in trouble, but when Talmadge made the decision to enter a hospital for treatment of an alcohol-abuse problem brought on by his political troubles, Nunn was on hand to offer counsel and advice to his one-time mentor.

A durable mentor-protégé relationship has existed between Louisiana's two senators, Russell Long and J. Bennett Johnston. The name of Long in Louisiana is even more powerful than that of Talmadge in Georgia. Long, moreover, continues as the unchallenged expert on federal tax laws and autocrat of the Finance Committee. Long's star is firmly attached to the Senate firmament, and Johnston is said to be a diligent lieutenant of his. One way in which Johnston benefits from his close association with Long is that colleagues may be tempted to go through him to reach the influential chairman of the Finance Committee.

The nature of the Senate in the 1950s gave rise to an abundance of mentor-protégé relationships. The hierarchical nature of the institution itself and the tendency of younger senators to attach themselves to influential senior members or party leaders, whose patronage and protection made it easier to obtain a favored committee assignment or achieve passage of a politically important bill, made such relationships politically important for newcomers. The self-consciously manipulative nature of some of these relations makes them suspect; the sincerity of the attachments varies from those which were purely entrepreneurial to those which produced a very definite fondness over time—although they may not have started out that way. Some were clearly alliances, but others evolved into relationships of significant closeness. Many of these relationships appear on their face to be highly asymmetrical; that is, the tangible rewards seem to flow from the mentor to the protégé. In practice they were more nearly balanced with the protégé reciprocating with deference, gratitude, loyalty, companionship, and solace.

The relationship between senators Lyndon Johnson and Richard B. Russell of Georgia was one such mentor-protégé relationship.

> Richard Russell found in the Senate what for him was a home. With no one to cook for him at home, he would arrive early in the morning to eat breakfast at the Capitol and stay late enough at night to eat dinner across the street. And in these early mornings and late evenings I made sure that there was always one companion, one Senator, who worked as long and as hard as he, and that was me, Lyndon Johnson. On Sundays the House and the Senate were empty, quiet, and still, the streets outside were bare. It's a tough day for a politician, especially if, like Russell, he's all alone. I knew how he felt for I, too, counted the hours until Monday would come again, and knowing that, I made sure to invite Russell over for breakfast, lunch, or brunch or just to read the Sunday papers.[6]

---

[6] Quoted in Doris Kearns, *Lyndon Johnson and the American Dream* (New York: New American Library/Signet Books, 1976), p. 110.

Bobby Baker, Johnson's long-time aide in the Senate, acknowledged the closeness of the Johnson-Russell relationship, but saw in it a fundamentally manipulative motive on the part of the Texan.

> LBJ sensed that for all [Russell's] power he was lonely. Though it isn't well known, Dick Russell did a lot of solitary reading and drinking—the mark of a lonely man. Lyndon Johnson took pains, therefore, to make his family Dick Russell's family. Soon, Russell took most of his weekend meals with the Johnsons: afterward, LBJ would take him for long drives and pick his brains. The Johnson daughters were encouraged to call the Georgia Senator "Uncle Dick," and Lady Bird Johnson—always charming and gracious—went out of her way to make him feel at home in her home. There were some who snickered behind their hands at LBJ's obvious courtship of the powerful Georgia senior, but there's absolutely no doubt that his campaign worked.[7]

Harry McPherson, another long-time Johnson aide in the Senate, also saw that in the most profound sense Johnson's attachment to Russell had a specific political purpose; although he might have open-handedly invited the Georgian into the bosom of his family, he once commented in a moment of candor that he was preoccupied with "keeping Dick Russell from walking across the aisle and embracing [Minority Leader] Everett Dirksen."[8]

The inescapable conclusion to be reached from these accounts is that Johnson was using the old man to further his political ambitions and that his show of feeling for Russell was largely contrived. I put this interpretation to a former senator who was privy to both Johnson and Russell during his years in the Senate. I suggested that Johnson had "adopted" the old bachelor and brought him into his family circle for essentially political reasons. The former senator dismissed this interpretation by saying, "If there was any adopting, it worked the

---

[7] Bobby Baker, with Larry L. King, *Wheeling and Dealing* (New York: W. W. Norton & Co., 1978), p. 42.

[8] Harry McPherson, *A Political Education* (Boston: Little, Brown & Co., 1972), p. 130.

other way. They had a relationship that was both political and personal. The personal relationship was one of great warmth. Even when Johnson moved on to the White House and the two of them disagreed over Vietnam policy, the warmth of feeling persisted."

Even where the relationship between elders and juniors in the old Senate did not mature into a fully developed mentor-protégé relationship, it was customary as well as prudent for a new member to pay a visit on one of the influential elders and solicit, albeit ritualistically, advice on how he should proceed in his Senate career. One of the pronounced differences between the initial Senate experiences of older senators and younger is that the former went to the senior members to solicit general advice, while the latter did this rarely. During the 1950s it was the practice for a new senator, especially if he were a Democrat, to solicit the advice and counsel of Majority Leader Lyndon B. Johnson. Having made a favorable impression on Johnson, the new senator could anticipate that substantial rewards would flow his way. Often Johnson would preempt the newcomer by making the overture, but he left little doubt that his attention would have to be reciprocated. As one member of the Senate "class of 1956" recalls:

> Lyndon Johnson was extremely cordial from the time that he received the unexpected news that I'd been elected, and phoned me the morning after the election. He took a keen interest in me until I voted "wrong" on Rule XXII [which stipulates the number of votes required to terminate a filibuster]. It was my first vote. He had thought that my vote was in his pocket, though I'd never told him that. Then he didn't really speak to me for six months. That was his way. He spoke to me only when he had to in the course of business, but otherwise gave me to know that I was ostracized. Then the Civil Rights Act of 1957 came along. The crucial issue was the jury trial amendment, and depending on the passage of that amendment depended the passage of the bill. I believed in the jury trial amendment, but, more importantly, I added a proviso to it which put an end to blue-ribbon juryism and thus insured racial non-discrimination in the selection of federal juries, and that brought over the votes necessary for the passage of the bill. And when that happened and I had played a crucial role in the passage of legislation that Johnson strongly desired,

then I was strongly in his embrace again and nothing was too good for me.

First he put me on the McClellan Rackets Committee, and that was getting front-page billing. Then, when the first vacancy occurred, he put me on Foreign Relations, when I had been in the Senate less than two years and in those days you usually waited a full term or more before obtaining an appointment to the Foreign Relations Committee. So he befriended me.

Johnson wanted his favors returned in kind, but he also demanded that he be recognized as the author of a junior Senator's good fortune.

I remember that my maiden speech was on a dam project [in my state]. Johnson, for some other reasons, had decided that he would help me get that dam approved in the Senate, and so he went to some of his Southern brethren and asked them if they couldn't support the federal dam . . . and asked them to read my speech and so forth. So the Senate passed the bill, and I had some notion that it happened because of the persuasiveness of my argument and the effectiveness of my speech. En route back to the office after having won the victory, I remember Clint Anderson grabbing hold of me and turning me around in the corridor and saying, "Have you thanked Lyndon Johnson?" and I said, "No, I hadn't," and he said, "Well, I hope you're not laboring under any misapprehension that this bill has passed the Senate by virtue of your leadership and not by virtue of his intervention. I think the first thing you should do is to get back to the Capitol and look him up and thank him for his help."

Well, it was that sort of advice that I needed from time to time—that senior senators were willing to give to me. But that was a different period; the freshman senators weren't expected to really exercise all the prerogatives of their position then. That's all changed. It would have been unseemly for me to participate in a debate on major national issues within a few weeks after I had been elected to the Senate. It was expected of freshmen that they should remain silent for at least six months in deference to their seniors, and when they did make a speech it should be on a matter that related to their own states, where it would be assumed that they had some measure of competence.

But all of that has changed and I don't know whether it's for the better or the worse. There was a discipline in the Senate that helped to prevent the kind of chaos that occurs so frequently today in the presentation of legislation.

This wistful reflection on the passing of the hierarchical Senate of bygone days may reflect this senator's own seniority and impatience with the vocal upstarts in the modern Senate, but his lament over the demise of the norm of apprenticeship is also a condemnation of the argument that tutelage, age, and experience are without value. Certainly in interpersonal terms, a Senate with natural leaders and norm-setters was one with fewer uncertainties. While it is true that apologists for the Senate as it was tend to confound age and sagacity, it is equally incorrect to confound callowness and brashness with wisdom—perhaps more so. If the elders demanded fealty and deference, they were also prepared to confer protection and assistance. Thus, in some ways the old Senate was more efficient. With influential senior mentors who were able to swing a dozen votes behind the bill of a freshman it was far easier to build winning coalitions than at present, when highly individualized appeals must be made and party loyalty may count for little.

The decline in mentor-protégé relationships is a product of both the modern Senate and the decline of strong state party organizations. With the new dispersion of power, senior members, even chairmen, have less largesse to bestow. Fewer advantages accrue to the junior member who might be willing to place himself under the tutelage of an elder. Older members, moreover, are less inclined to assert the prerogatives of longevity. There is less gratuitous advice given to new members. There is a heightened sense among the few remaining grandees that each senator is a force in his own right. Often now, when called upon for advice by a newly elected senator, the elder will be sparing in his counsel. This was the case with a newly elected conservative senator who solicited the guidance of veteran conservatives.

Cliff White [F. Clifton White, a conservative campaign adviser] arranged a little dinner for me in Washington just a month after I was elected. It was attended by some of the conservative wing of the Republican party—John Williams who was just going out, [Carl] Curtis, [Paul] Fannin, a few people like that. It was a very charming, lovely dinner, but when I said, "Do you have any words of advice?" what sort of dribbled back was to the effect that anyone who was able to get that far certainly didn't need any advice.

The thing that struck me immediately about the Senate was the fact that anyone you wanted to ask a specific question of was more than happy to accommodate, but if you're asking for an agenda, no, that wasn't forthcoming.

With the rise of personal campaigning, as opposed to running as a loyal partisan, the responsibility felt for a new colleague of the same party has diminished. Tutelage and advice is rarely sought or proffered. In fact, it is more likely to be sought than proffered, because gratuitous offers of advice might well be resented. When sought, it is more likely to be solicited for details than for general guidance. Committee chairmen or members of the Steering Committee are approached for favored assignments, but granting such a favor incurs no long-lasting personal debt on the part of the supplicant; it certainly does not result in any enduring relationship of patronage and dependency. The new senator is now very much on his own. This is generally viewed as a positive change from the old veneration of the elders. But it also casts the freshman out into the senatorial turmoil without any natural or predictable hand-holds.

The possession of common ethical and religious values has long been noted as a major determinant of personal attraction.[9] While it is not a widespread practice in the Senate to select one's most intimate friends on the basis of shared spiritual and social values alone, the interaction of these values with shared political philosophies is capable of producing bonds of unusual closeness. In some instances shar-

9 "Religious Ethnocentrism and Its Recognition among Adolescent Boys," *Journal of Abnormal and Social Psychology,* vol. 47 (1952), pp. 316–320 and "Similarity of Valuings as a Factor in the Selection of Peers," *Journal of Abnormal and Social Psychology*, vol. 47 (1952), pp. 406–414.

ing spiritual and social values may even cause marginal differences on policy to be relegated to an unimportant status in order to maintain the integrity of the friendship bond. Three groups of senators in the modern Senate can be identified as intimate friends, based on their possession not only of common political philosophies but of shared religious and social values as well. These are the Catholics, the evangelicals, and the socialites.

Arthur M. Schlesinger, Jr., in his biography of John F. Kennedy, uses a quotation from Mary McCarthy's *Memories of a Catholic Girlhood* to illustrate the effect of Catholicism on Kennedy: "If you are born and brought up a Catholic, you have absorbed a great deal of world history and the history of ideas before you are twelve, and it is like learning a language early; the effect is indelible."[10] Schlesinger also comments on Kennedy's "Irishness," which came out in so many ways—in the quizzical wit, the eruptions of boisterous humor, the relish for politics, the love of language, the romantic sense of history, the admiration for physical daring, the toughness, the joy of living, the view of life as comedy and tragedy. And it gave him a particular slant on American society."[11]

There is perhaps no attribute of an American politician more difficult to evaluate in terms of political effect than religion. In part, the elusiveness of this characteristic can be explained by the nominal quality of the religious beliefs of so many public people. Religion's role in the formation of intimate friendships among politicians is equally hard to pin down. It is often difficult to isolate religion as an independent element or to assert that religion *per se* is the dominant force in the behavior of a politician, when it is so commingled with ideology, partisanship, state or regional loyalties, and social class. Omnibus designations of public figures such as "Boston Brahmin" or "Southern Bourbon" point up the problem of sorting out just what it is that constitutes the defining characteristic. Is it philosophical, regional, denominational, stylistic, or partisan affiliation that is being identified—or is it all of these? When examining the closest relation-

---

[10] *A Thousand Days: John F. Kennedy in the White House* (Boston: Houghton Mifflin Co., 1965), pp. 106–107.

[11] Ibid., pp. 78–79.

ships of U.S. senators this problem of commingled and mutually reinforcing factors makes isolating a single element very difficult.

It is widely believed among some Senate observers whom I interviewed—staff members, journalists, lobbyists, but, significantly, not senators themselves—that the Catholicism of certain members drew them into a relationship of great intimacy. These members were Eugene McCarthy (D.–Minn.), Mike Mansfield (D.–Mont.), Edmund S. Muskie (D.–Me.), Edward M. Kennedy (D.–Mass.), and the late Philip Hart (D.–Mich.). This tie was not of equal closeness among the five, but rather produced clusters of close relationships.

The origins of the Mansfield-Edward Kennedy relationship found its origins in the deep affection that Mansfield felt for President John F. Kennedy. Mansfield, a product of the "Johnson system" in the Senate, was compelled to be in Johnson's corner rather than Kennedy's during the 1960 nominating process, but his support for Johnson in his home state of Montana was listless and merely symbolic. The Kennedy forces succeeded in capturing the support of the Irish-Catholic miners in Butte—the group from whence Mansfield had come. His formal support may have been for Johnson, but his heart was with Kennedy. Once in the White House, Kennedy came to have great fondness for the Majority Leader, and defended him strenuously against those who unfavorably compared the reticent Montanan to his predecessor, Johnson. Mansfield reciprocated this feeling of warmth. On the day Kennedy was assassinated, Mansfield delivered the most heartfelt and moving eulogy to Kennedy uttered on that tragic day.

After John Kennedy's death, Mansfield transferred his affection to the late president's two younger brothers, but he was also subjected to a countervailing pull as the floor leader responsible for the Johnson legislative program. He knew the enmity that existed between Johnson and Robert Kennedy, but steered a careful course between his loyalty to Johnson and his affection for the Kennedys. But when Robert Kennedy on March 2, 1967 delivered the speech in the Senate which signaled his defection from Johnson's policy on Vietnam, Mansfield—who was still firmly in Johnson's camp on the war issue—applauded the declaration and extolled its importance. However, as is often the case with people in the quandary of having a friend express a dissonant opinion, Mansfield placed the most felicitous interpretation on the speech, characterizing the Kennedy position as having much in common with that of the Johnson administration. The speech was in fact a passionate indictment of the President's Vietnam policy, but Mansfield interpreted the differences as being unimportant. He was said to have been the only senator who placed that construction on Kennedy's remarks.[12]

Another occasion when Mansfield was put to the test of having to choose between his personal loyalty to the Kennedys and his political fidelity to Johnson occurred one evening when Washington hostess Perle Mesta, an old Johnson supporter who had been excluded from the Kennedy White House social circle, gave a party in Mansfield's honor which conflicted with the celebration of the Robert Kennedys' fifteenth wedding anniversary. Washington gossip columnists, ever vigilant in those days for any hint of conflict between the votaries of the New Frontier and the adherents of the Johnson Great Society, interpreted the rival social functions as a test of individual loyalty. The Mansfields dutifully attended the reception in their honor, graciously proposed a toast to Mrs. Mesta, and then left for the Georgetown home of the Edward Kennedys where the anniversary party was being held.[13]

The assassination of Robert Kennedy in 1968 caused Mansfield untold grief. Lady Bird Johnson described Mansfield on the morning after the assassination as looking bewildered and having "a staring look in his eyes."[14]

The personal relationship which had grown up between Mansfield and Robert Kennedy was paralleled by a close political cooperation, which once saw Mansfield interpose himself between Kennedy and Mansfield's deputy, Russell Long (who regarded Robert Kennedy with mistrust). In 1967, Kennedy was anxious to have the Senate take a roll-call vote on a welfare measure he considered important. Although absent from the Senate, Kennedy had asked Joseph Tydings (D.–Md.) to keep vigil on the amendment. Long, a superb parliamentarian, maneuvered the bill around a bewildered

[12] Victor Lasky, *Robert F. Kennedy: The Myth and the Man* (New York: Trident Press, 1968), pp. 389–390.

[13] Ibid., pp. 247–248.

[14] Lady Bird Johnson, *A White House Diary* (New York: Holt, Rinehart, and Winston, 1970), p. 680.

Tydings and denied the liberals their up-or-down vote. Only through Mansfield's intercession did the bill later come up for a vote.[15]

After the death of Robert, Mansfield transferred his affection readily to the last remaining Kennedy brother. When Edward Kennedy, for both personal and ideological reasons, decided in 1969 to mount a challenge to Russell Long for the position of Majority Whip, one of his first telephone calls announcing his decision was placed to Mansfield. Mansfield characteristically neither encouraged nor discouraged Kennedy.[16] The vote in the caucus was taken in secret, but when the result was announced and Kennedy unseated Long, Mansfield could not conceal his delight, proclaiming Kennedy "a link with the younger generation." In Long's unofficial tally of the vote in the caucus, Mansfield was listed as one of Kennedy's thirty-one votes. Some uncertainty has been expressed as to how Mansfield actually voted,[17] but a senator who was present recollects vividly that Mansfield cast his vote for the Massachusetts senator.

The events which occurred later that year on Chappaquiddick Island cast a dark shadow on the career of Edward Kennedy, and on his relationship with Mansfield as well. Mansfield's immediate reaction, in the aftermath of Chappaquiddick, was to issue a statement of support for the beleaguered Kennedy. When Kennedy returned to the Senate, he was embraced warmly by Mansfield. But as Kennedy's effectiveness as Whip plummeted, Mansfield was said to have felt let down by him. Accordingly, when Kennedy was challenged for the post he had held for a mere two years by Robert Byrd (D.–W.Va.) Mansfield was again in a quandary—whether to support the dutiful but remote West Virginian or continue to express his confidence in a man he genuinely liked but in whom he had been disappointed. Kennedy lost the battle to Byrd, and again Mansfield's vote is not known due to the secrecy of the procedures. The recollections of several of those present indicate, however, that Mansfield's vote was once again cast for Kennedy. One observer suggested that Mansfield has simply tended to back incumbents on leadership votes. But if

---

[15] Robert L. Peabody, *Leadership in Congress* (Boston: Little, Brown & Co., 1976), p. 368.

[16] Ibid., p. 372.

[17] Ibid., p. 380.

Mansfield were consistent in this, he would have backed Long in 1969. Mansfield's high opinion of Kennedy was well-known, and his personal fondness for him may in some ways have been the strongest that he felt for any of the Kennedy brothers.[18]

Another relationship of unusual closeness occurring within this group of liberal, Roman Catholic Democrats was the one between Eugene McCarthy and Philip Hart. The religious connection here is even more clear-cut than in the relationship of Mansfield and the Kennedys. McCarthy himself places the origin of their friendship at the point when their children were attending the same Catholic prep school. The bond of their Catholicism did not arise from the fact that they went on retreat together but rather from the sharing of common spiritual values and their application to public life. The two men came to the Senate in 1958 and found themselves on the same side in many battles; this commonality of political values, however, provided only the preconditions for a relationship which would in the fullness of time be as spiritual as it was political, although the two elements were often mutually reinforcing. The identity of their political values, however, has been overstressed. Hart lagged far behind McCarthy on opposition to the Vietnam War, and he was less critical of the operations of the FBI and CIA than was McCarthy, but the relationship never soured because of these differences. McCarthy's eulogy to Hart leaves little doubt that whatever political agreements there were, it was a spiritual association that defined the nature of the relationship and caused it to endure. McCarthy has written,

> Philip Hart was a man out of his proper time. He was meant for the Age of Faith, or at least for the declining years of that age, when men like Thomas More could make their final defense, beyond the civil law, in religious belief. Philip Hart spoke seriously of God, of Heaven, of the religious obligations as they bore upon private life and upon political action. "Would there be segregation in Heaven?" he asked in a Senate hearing. "What of our obligations to practice, as a society, the corporal works of mercy?" He could have said, as Thomas More said just before his death, that he had been in all things

---

[18] Ibid., p. 382.

the King's good servant, but God's good servant first. Philip Hart was the good servant of his own time, of his family, of his country, of its laws, and of its political institutions, especially of the Senate. But in all of these, because of his own compelling religious beliefs, he was God's good servant first.[19]

The McCarthy-Muskie relationship was also a close one. Both were part of the "class of '58," along with Hart. In this relationship the situational factors surrounding the Senate fight for a major civil rights bill in 1964 combined with the political values shared by both men to draw them together. On the late nights of the Southern filibuster, they and Hart spent a considerable amount of time together, dining together on the way home and, as McCarthy recalls, "ate a lot of bad food together." Muskie and McCarthy, who were seat mates, were also frequent golf partners. The closeness of their relationship was all the more remarkable given their personalities. Each had considerable intellectual ability and in his own way found it difficult to deal with those less well-endowed intellectually. Muskie would deal with them with temperamental tongue-lashings; McCarthy with the keen edge of his verbal knife. Men like these rarely like each other, yet McCarthy and Muskie stayed close until the bitter struggle over the Vietnam plank at the 1968 Democratic convention, when conflicts of principles and ambition intervened. The estrangement became more complete in 1972, when the two clashed directly in the primaries and McCarthy characterized Muskie as "the most active representative of Johnson administration Vietnam policy at Chicago." But it is clear that even as late as the eve of the 1968 Chicago convention, if McCarthy could have tolerated the Democratic nomination falling into any hands but his own, he would willingly have let it fall into Muskie's. Indeed, just before that convention McCarthy had toyed with the idea of calling Muskie and throwing his support behind the senator from Maine. When at last Hubert Humphrey received the nomination and telephoned McCarthy for suggestions for a running mate, McCarthy put forth Muskie's name.[20]

---

[19] Eugene McCarthy, "Philip Hart," *New Republic*, January 15, 1977, p. 13.

[20] Abigail McCarthy, *Private Faces, Public Places* (Garden City, NY: Doubleday & Co., 1972), pp. 420, 429.

The role that is played by religious or cultural affinities in the choice of closest friends is uniquely elusive. Senators are naturally reluctant to admit that interpersonal choice is influenced by such considerations. Occasionally, this is candidly acknowledged. Abigail McCarthy, wife of the former Minnesota senator, regarded such affinities as a most natural basis for association.

> In general, our friendships based on previous associations grew out of two groups: the network of Catholic liberals with whom we shared mutual friends and acquaintances and the less diversified group of "new" Democrats typified by the ADA of that time and the AVC [American Veterans' Committee]. These two associations often overlapped.[21]

The tendency for groups to overlap, as Mrs. McCarthy points out, makes it difficult to sort out the individual effects of such things as religion and ideology. When, for example, in January 1976 it was necessary for Majority Leader Mansfield to choose a Democratic senator to reply to President Ford's State of the Union address, did he choose Edmund Muskie because of the Maine senator having an unchallenged position in the party? Given the fact that senators of the stature of Humphrey, Bayh, Jackson, and Church—all potential or announced Presidential candidates—had an equally meritorious claim on spokesmanship, why would he choose Muskie? Mansfield probably liked Muskie more than the others, but what was this liking based upon? It could be argued that Muskie and Mansfield were both liberals, but so were the others. However, Humphrey, far and away the most prominent, could expect little in the way of personal favors from Mansfield. Although both had been Lyndon Johnson's lieutenants in the Senate, their friendship had, in Humphrey's words, "been damaged by my years as vice-president, when I worked the Hill arduously, pushing Lyndon Johnson's 'Great Society' legislation, supporting the president on Vietnam [and] impinging, I'm sure, on the majority leader's prerogatives and power."[22] Still, the reason for Mansfield's choice of Muskie could be as simple as the fact that the

---

[21] Ibid., p. 163.

[22] Hubert H. Humphrey, *The Education of a Public Man* (Garden City, NY: Doubleday & Co., 1976), p. 431.

Maine senator had assumed the chairmanship of the Senate Budget Committee and professed no Presidential ambitions for 1976—statuses enjoyed by none of the other claimants.

So Mansfield favored Muskie with the spokesmanship and handed over to him the Majority Leader's office for the televised rebuttal. That Mansfield felt warmer to Muskie than he did the others has been affirmed in the interviews; that the religion the two men shared figured in the warmth of this association likewise finds some support there.

There is a moderately strong suggestion in the interviews that religion has played a role in the choice of colleagues as friends, and that the forces of religion and ideology are reciprocal. It is a more elusive task, however, to make the case that religious affinity is a guide to specific political behavior.

The evidence to support the view that their religious beliefs served to draw this group of Senate liberals closer together as friends is more than circumstantial. Muskie, who is very stinting in his friendships with colleagues, can only be said to have been truly close with Hart, McCarthy, and, latterly, Eagleton, who is also a Catholic. The departure of McCarthy from the Senate in 1971 was said to have caused a void in Muskie's life, and "he seem[ed] genuinely to regret the loss."[23] McCarthy, equally discriminating and demanding in his choice of friends, maintained intimate ties only with Muskie and Hart. Hart's affection for Muskie and McCarthy, but especially for McCarthy, went beyond mere social friendship. On McCarthy's role as the herald of opposition to the Vietnam War, Hart confessed, "Gene McCarthy turned my children around. He gave them hope."[24]

In their biography of him, Theo Lippman, Jr., and Donald C. Hansen described the periodic meetings of Muskie with Hart and McCarthy in the late 1960s and his sense of loss when they ended.

> Muskie, Hart, and McCarthy would get together for supper and talk on summer evenings when their families were out of town. These sessions gradually faded out over the years, to

[23] Theo Lippman, Jr., and Donald C. Hansen, *Muskie* (New York: W. W. Norton & Co., 1971), p. 213.

[24] Abigail McCarthy, op. cit., p. 352.

Muskie's sorrow. In 1970, he discussed their passing. "I think it is one of the real regrets of the past few years. You get to know the senators in that way. The time available for this kind of comradeship and discussion is much more limited than I thought it would be. In that sense, the Senate really isn't a deliberative body, in the sense that we find opportunities actually to get into policy questions in an informal way, that makes it possible for us to pick each other's brains and probe each other's instincts and feelings about these issues. That is a great loss. The cloakrooms aren't that sort of place. The committee hearings aren't. Markup [bill drafting] sessions aren't. There is just very little opportunity to sit down in a bull session to talk about the state of the nation and the state of the world, to examine each other's ideas on the national goals and the objectives we ought to be following internationally."[25]

Muskie's lament for the companionship of his two favorite colleagues dwells almost entirely on the demise of what seems like little more than an informal political discussion. He speaks of "examining each other's ideas on the national goals" and of "opportunities actually to get into policy discussions in an informal way." It is a lament for the engagement of the mind; there is no hint of a communion of the heart. What a distant and restrained form of intimacy this was! Even with the inviting and great-spirited Hart, the friendship reached a certain point and then could go no further. A line was drawn for Muskie which could not be transgressed, beyond which lay the uncharted and forbidding realm of emotions and feelings.

Philip Hart was "Muskie's dearest friend in the Senate."[26] The relationship, however, lacked the quality of self-revelation and the readiness to probe deeply into the personal life of even his most cherished associate. This hesitance to express himself in the language of affection Muskie attributed to his own reserved nature.

"Well, Phil Hart and I, you know, we can communicate without ever talking. And I'm more comfortable that way. When we do talk, we might talk about the Senate or a piece of legis-

[25] Theo Lippman, Jr., and Donald C. Hansen, op. cit., pp. 105–106.

[26] Bernard Asbell, *The Senate Nobody Knows* (Garden City, NY: Doubleday & Co., 1978), p. 448.

lation. But the kind of intimate talk that—well, there the shyness still comes in. I can't dig into, for instance, his personal life or his feelings. He's dying of cancer, you know. It would be wrong to do it, anyway. But I couldn't do it. In large part, because I'm—I find it very hard to talk the language of love and affection. I feel it. And I can demonstrate it. But I can't talk about it. I just can't."[27]

The close association of the liberal Catholics had begun to fade by the early 1970s with the departure of McCarthy from the Senate. Hart's death the day after Christmas of 1976 deprived the group of its central figure. Although Mansfield was not at the core of the group, his retirement in 1977 removed one more element of cohesion.

Their last reunion was in the first week of June 1976 when a tribute was given to Hart personally at the Muskie's home. Several of the friends eulogized him, but it was Kennedy's statement to Hart that stuck in the mind of one of those who was there. "He didn't want what he said to be maudlin. Everyone there knew why they were gathering; it was to say goodbye to Phil. Teddy managed to keep the equilibrium of the group at a time when they all might have broken down in tears. He injected a little humor. He kept up the spirits of the group when they all knew they were probably seeing Phil for the last time."

Despite death and retirement from the Senate, the old bonds are not quite extinct. Late in 1978, when Muskie was on his way to China, he arranged a detour to Tokyo, where Mansfield is now serving as U.S. ambassador. "Just to spend a few hours with Mike," said an aide. "In a place like the Senate where friendships are so rare, you don't forget very easily the few that you have made."

As the friendship group of liberal Catholics passed from the Senate scene, another association based on shared religious beliefs was developing. It symbolized the emergence of a new force in American politics, evangelical Christianity. While evangelical, the group was not exclusively Protestant; indeed, two of the four members were Roman Catholics. The partisan and ideological composition of this group was somewhat more heterogeneous than that of the liberal

[27] Ibid., p. 301.

Catholics. The members of the group, in the 95th Congress, were Sam Nunn (D.–Ga.), Lawton Chiles (D.–Fla.), Pete Domenici (R.–N.M.), and Dewey Bartlett (R.–Okla.). Bartlett retired at the close of the 95th Congress and died early in 1979. Although all four senators were regular attendees of the Prayer Breakfast, their religious association was far more intense than the more diluted and generalized ritual of the breakfast.

The prayer lunch of Chiles, Nunn, Bartlett, and Domenici, like the Prayer Breakfast, took place on Wednesday. Several hours after the breakfast, in room S-138 of the Capitol, broke up, the four senators, along with former senator Harold Hughes and Douglas Coe of Fellowship House, reconvened in one of their offices and for an hour and a half prayed together. Unlike the tepid homilies and philosophical discussions which characterize the breakfast, this ninety minute devotion was recognizable Christian prayer. It was, moreover, a far more obvious and dominant force in the lives of the participants than the breakfast is for its regular attendees. Religion suffused the lives of these senators; at least one also began his staff meetings with a period of prayer.

As in the case of the other pure friendships in the Senate, a substantial measure of ideological agreement served as the general background of the association. Both Chiles and Nunn could be counted as moderately conservative Democrats; Bartlett and Domenici were consistently conservative Republicans. Using the Conservative Coalition support scores as an index of a Senator's conservatism, in 1977 Chiles and Nunn with identical scores of 80% approximated the scores of Bartlett (79%) and Domenici (89%) in the same year.[28] While other ratings show greater variations in the roll-call performance of the four men, they were fairly close on at least one ideological test.

But as in the case of the Senate liberals, ideological compatibility alone did not account for their closeness, although it seemed a necessary ingredient in bringing them together. Evidence of this was provided by a staff member of one of the evangelical four.

> There was a section of the 1978 energy bill which related to stripper wells, of which there are a few in Florida, but many in Oklahoma. Bartlett was interested in getting co-sponsors for

---

[28] *Congressional Quarterly Weekly Report*, vol. 36, no. 1 (January 7, 1978), p. 8.

the bill, and sent out a "dear colleague" letter to pick up co-sponsors. It was not a part of the bill in which Chiles was passionately interested. Nonetheless, Chiles went on as a co-sponsor. If the same letter had come from John Tower (D.–Tex.), who's another oil-state conservative, I doubt whether Chiles would have gone on as a co-sponsor.

Co-sponsorship is not a very exacting test of the extent to which personal friendship among senators extends to the legislative realm. But there is evidence that the relationship of the four evangelicals occasionally prompted them to act above and beyond the call of duty and perform favors which would be greater than those owed to other colleagues—even those with whom alliance relationships were shared.

On the same piece of energy legislation, Chiles was the recipient of very important personal considerations from Domenici which entailed the New Mexico senator going considerably out of his way to assist the Floridian. This occurred when the two houses of Congress had enacted materially different versions of the Carter Administration's energy bill, and the legislation was then sent to a House-Senate conference to reconcile the differences. The Senate had added a Chiles amendment to the bill relating to natural gas use in Florida. The House bill contained no such measure, and Chiles had hoped to have the amendment added in conference. Normally, the job of looking after the interests of the state would have fallen to a fellow Floridian on the conference committee—in this case, Democratic Congressman Paul Rogers. Rogers, who represented the Eleventh Congressional District, had recently announced his retirement; he has been described as being "inactive" in the business of this conference. The Chiles amendment was thus in serious jeopardy, as the House conferees were determined to drop the measure from the bill. It appeared as if the amendment to protect Florida's natural gas users was doomed.

At this point Pete Domenici intervened. Domenici was a Senate conferee. Chile's staff had been reluctant to press Domenici to rescue the amendment and were willing to accept a compromise that would have reduced its effect. Domenici, however, approached the Chiles staff, sat down with them, and instructed them with great exactitude about how to proceed, going out of his way to see that the Chiles amendment was retained. "He didn't have to spend the time doing that," a staff member recalled. "He took the initiative to rescue an amendment which would have been dead without his intervention."

On defense matters, Sam Nunn is regarded as one of the brightest and best-prepared members of the Senate Armed Services Committee. His opinions are held in the highest esteem by his colleagues. He would normally be sought out by colleagues for voting cues and advice on national defense legislation. In the case of the other evangelicals, however, Nunn served as more than just a cue-giver. "They really defer to Nunn on defense matters," an observer noted. "You can certainly make the case that it's his expertise, but the other three really walk through the mine-field behind him. They're uncommonly attentive to what he has to say on military matters."

A pattern of mutual aid and extraordinary consideration on legislative matters characterized the relationships of the evangelicals in the Senate. It was paralleled in the personal realm by intimate social relationships which embraced the families of the four senators, and which were intensified when one of their number, Dewey Bartlett, fell gravely ill with cancer. As in the case of the liberal Catholics, whose attention came to focus on the stricken Philip Hart, the bond of friendship among the evangelicals thrived in this adversity. Bartlett's three colleagues provided great emotional support when he was undergoing painful chemotherapy treatments, and their prayer sessions served to boost Bartlett's morale during periods of hospitalization.

The most demanding test of the political ramifications of a close friendship is whether it would cause a senator to change his behavior and entertain an argument that he had been prepared to reject. In such situations, friendship serves as a tool for "persuasion or at least suggestion." It can command attention and even, in rare instances, cause minds to be changed.

It is often difficult to document such changes, since senatorial conceit—as well as caution—does not often allow for interpretations suggesting that anything but the merits of an issue dictated a position or a vote. An interesting example of how close personal friendship does facilitate access and allow for persuasion, suggestion, or even mind-changing involved two members of the evangelical group. Domenici was a member of the Committee on Environment and Public Works, which was responsible for reporting out the Clean Air Act of 1976 to the Senate by a 13 to 1 vote. The bill, supported by Domenici, risked emasculation at the hands of an amendment from the floor proposed by Frank Moss (D.–Utah). Chiles, however, was publicly opposed to the committee bill and favored the Moss amendment; there had been a considerable amount of pressure on him from Florida lobbyists on a provision of the bill which would have excluded polluting factories from certain zones. When the bill came up for a vote on August 5, 1976, Chiles went to the floor prepared to support the Moss amendment and oppose the committee bill. What happened then was described by an observer:

> Domenici got a hold of Chiles and began making the case for the committee bill. Unbelievably, he turned Chiles around, and he did it on the merits of the bill. He got him to reverse himself on a long-standing and publicly held position. It took guts for Chiles to turn around, but it was the force of Domenici's argument that did it. I can't think of more than one or two other members who could have accomplished that. He got him to listen to an argument that he'd been primed to oppose, and ended up getting his vote.

It is significant that Domenici was reported to have turned Chiles around on the merits of the committee's bill. But it is equally important to recognize that Chiles might have been less willing to consider exhaustive representations on behalf of the committee's position from just any senator. A close friendship might not in itself be enough to induce a senator to reject the pressures of lobbyists from his own state, but it might well enable a colleague to present arguments to him which, coming from another source, would be rejected. On issues of little direct political consequence to a senator, a vote might be granted solely as a favor to a valued friend; but where the countervailing pressures of state interests are forcefully expressed, more is involved: close friendship will sometimes act here to produce superior access, leave a colleague open to suggestion, and create the conditions for him to be persuaded of the need for a change of heart or mind.

America's aristocracy has contributed few of its number to the Senate in recent years, but the few that have served at the same time have tended to gravitate toward each other socially and personally. Three of the senators I interviewed were members of socially prominent families. All had attended elite preparatory schools; two attended Harvard and one had been an undergraduate at Princeton. All three indicated that their closest personal friends in the Senate were individuals from the same social milieu. But here again the intimacy of the association was not independent of agreement on fundamentals of political ideology. Liberal socialites chose other liberal socialites as intimates; the moderate Republican socialite chose as friends blue-bloods of the same political stripe. In one instance, the chosen colleague, Paul Douglas, was not himself a socialite, but his wife was socially prominent; ideology played a major role in this attraction as well. As an Eastern liberal whose name was in the *Social Register* (not ex officio) described the relationship:

> Paul Douglas (D.–Ill.) and I were very close. His wife was Emily Taft, of the liberal wing of the Cincinnati Tafts. She was his second wife and was a howling liberal.

Social ties combined with ideology to influence the choice of closest friends by a Republican socialite. The closeness of relationship with one of his aristocratic colleagues is evident from the description provided by the late Leverett Saltonstall.

> [H. Alexander] Smith [R.–N.J.] and I discussed personal things. Well, Smith was the kind of fellow who wanted, sort of, support—that isn't a fair word—he wanted "confidence," if you will, and quite often he'd come up to my office, but more often I'd go down to his office. He was an older man. We had many of the same friends and I think this caused him to confide in me.

Saltonstall also designated senators Prescott Bush (R.–Conn.) and Raymond Baldwin (R.–Conn.) as his other closest Senate friends; both were men of wealth and standing in high society. He singled out a Democratic senator, Joseph Sill Clark of Pennsylvania—a Philadelphia blue-blood—as a social friend. The two senators often dined at each other's homes in Washington when they were in the Senate.

A liberal Democratic socialite found that his introduction to the Senate was facilitated by his family ties to Saltonstall.

> When I first came here Leverett Saltonstall, whose sister-in-law is married to my uncle, helped me from the more social and political viewpoint to know my way around the Senate.

There is little evidence to suggest that membership in this country's social elite causes these senators to act in defense of the interests of their class. Indeed, the very prominence of such aristocratic liberals as Joseph Clark and Claiborne Pell (D.–R.I.) hints at the opposite effect. Class interests may figure, however, in their choice of issues as areas of specialization. For example, the traditional interests of the American aristocracy in the arts may account for Pell's choice of the Subcommittee on Education, Arts, and the Humanities. The small number of certifiable blue-bloods in the modern Senate and the fact that they are divided by partisanship and philosophy tends to limit their collective influence. There is no evidence of their acting in unison in recent history.

The values that they hold in common seem to express themselves more in the social and personal realm than in the political sphere. Their family connections provide introductions to their social counterparts in Washington, and provide a ready-made social circle. The cachet which attaches to membership in the upper crust is somewhat diluted by the fact that all members of the U.S. Senate are listed in the Washington *Social Register* and in the *Green Book*. (Among the many advantages of incumbency in the U.S. Senate is that instant elite status is conferred on anyone with a certificate of election to the upper chamber.) Nonetheless, within this ex officio elite of one hundred legislators those whose claim on social prominence is less protean often tend to gravitate to one another; their closest friendships are usually forged with those with the proper social credentials—or at least the proper pretensions.

It is an unusual relationship which would cause a senator to expose to another such personal problems as drinking, marital discord, financial difficulties, or even serious physical ailments. Such a relationship would have to be a very close one among ordinary people; among politicians the disposition to confide in anyone, especially a colleague, on such sensitive subjects, which entail peril to one's career, is rare. Unlike confidential discussions with lawyers, clergymen, or physicians, such conversations are not privileged. The risk involved is monumental; it reposes in the confidant the ability to unmake a career or ruin a reputation. A U.S. senator who acts in close professional association with a limited number of colleagues runs a particularly great risk in expressing such confidences unless his confidence in the colleague's discretion is ironclad. The tendency among politicians in general, and senators in particular, is to remove matters of this kind as far from political associates as possible. Thus the pure friendships of senators, if they have any at all, tend to be with those who are neither senators nor indeed even politicians.

One well-known Democrat mentioned the name of a prominent Washington attorney as the single person in whom he would confide. Another mentioned his law partner from his pre-Senate days. A third mentioned a businessman from his state with little interest in politics. The most intimate friend of another was his roommate from college. Most senatorial pure friendships in the group interviewed were friendships of long-standing that antedated Senate service. Given the presumption of ulterior motivation and instrumentalism and the rigorous screening on the part of senators regarding those who speak to them in the language of friendship, it is not surprising that so many of them reserve pure friendship for those who knew them in their former lives as private citizens. The simple length of duration of such personal associations accounts for a good deal of the closeness, but another important factor is that these relationships preceded their eminence as senators and hence are less contaminated by suspicions of being opportunistic or insincere. The closeness of many of the relationships of senators with those apart from politics suggests that fewer perils are involved in such associations. Pure friendships of senators, accordingly, are not marked so much by their absolute deficiency but rather by the rarity with which they involve other Senate colleagues.

Claude G. Bowers, the first biographer of Sen. Albert J. Beveridge, who served from 1899 to 1911, dwelt at unusual length on the personal friendships of his subject. His account of the progressive from Indiana indicates the existence of six deeply personal friendships, and aside from a passing mention of Sen. Charles G. Dawes—whose friendship with Beveridge antedated their Senate service—not one of his intimates was another senator. Beveridge's closest friend was David Graham Phillips, a novelist and reformist journalist; their relationship dated back to their days as roommates at DePauw University. Equally ancient were his ties to financier George W. Perkins. In his early days in the Senate he initiated lifelong personal ties with New York publisher Frank A. Munsey and the editor of the *Review of Reviews*, Dr. Albert Shaw. Social relationships also existed between Beveridge and *Saturday Evening Post* editor George Horace Lorimer and *Harper's* editor Joseph Sears.

Beveridge had the gift of friendship and Bower's description of his relationship with Phillips leaves little doubt that it was an intensely personal one.

> Whenever either found time from exacting labors to relax, their minds traveled to each other. Time and again Beveridge in a flood of feeling would urge his friend to join him wherever he might be. "Come up here Graham, I am always hungry to see you"—and he was. Nothing in the correspondence of the two throws a tenderer light on the novelist and his loneliness than the letter he wrote on the birth of Beveridge's first child. "You get everything, don't you? . . . I envy you, Bev, I do—that baby." Thus the friendship was like a poem until the end when Beveridge took charge of Phillips' funeral. It had its effect on Beveridge's life."[29]

What characterized these extra-Senate pure friendships for Beveridge—especially that with Phillips—was a willingness to confide, a disposition to reveal plans and hopes, a desire to spend leisure time in each other's company, a fundamental agreement on values, and a readiness to intervene in times of crisis in the life of a friend. These are operational manifestations of pure friendship, and although Beveridge's relations were established along these lines with a half-dozen other men, not a single one was a Senate colleague.

Pierre Salinger's account of John F. Kennedy's intimates sets forth several categories of friends, none of which included anyone from his days in the Senate. Sen. George Smathers of Florida, who served with Kennedy in the 1950s, partied a good deal with the future president but was not a confidant. His truly personal friends, apart from family members, were either school and Navy buddies or those associated with Massachusetts politics, according to Salinger.[30]

The verdict for the relationships of many people in political life delivered by Stimson Bullitt applies convincingly to many in the Sen-

[29] Claude G. Bowers, *Beveridge and the Progressive Era* (Cambridge: Riverside Press of Houghton Mifflin Co., 1932), pp. 158–172.

[30] Pierre Salinger, *With Kennedy* (Garden City, NY: Doubleday & Co., 1966), p. 97.

ate: "A politician has few friends, and among them he is sure of few but those he knew when he was still unknown."[31]

Even when the extra-institutional pure friendships of U.S. senators are considered along with those which occur within the chamber itself, it is difficult to say that evidence of widespread intimate ties is very impressive. The inhibitions against intimate friendships between American men are powerful; the transient nature of many professions, politics among them, results in a periodic uprooting which makes it difficult to establish the basic familiarity with others that is a precondition for friendship. The workplace—which would be the most natural setting for intimate friendship, because of the sustained personal contact on a daily basis—is as likely to produce competition as teamwork and cooperation. Business relationships, if they do develop, often tend to remain just that: positive associations on a five-day, forty-hour-a-week basis which only occasionally extend into the social sphere and rarely become intimate. The same forces which restrain social friendships restrain more intimate ones as well: the fear that close personal ties with business associates will confound decisions that ought to be made strictly on the basis of the welfare of the organization: the loss of the freedom to maneuver; the closing off of options which might be available in the absence of close personal ties; and the raising of expectations of support and the general introduction of emotional factors into situations which more properly ought to exclude them.

These are not simply operational problems but normative ones as well: How much friendship is good for an organization? Can people who are friendly work to foster organizational values which are compatible with the maintenance of their friendship? There is a relationship between agreement on values and personal attraction. Precisely how this relationship operates has been a subject of enduring debate among social psychologists. The cause and effect are unclear: Does personal liking proceed from agreement on corporate or political values, or vice versa?

---

[31] Stimson Bullitt, *To Be a Politician*, rev. ed. (New Haven: Yale University Press, 1977), p. 12.

The widespread aversion on the part of senators to meddling in the personal affairs of colleagues and to opening up one's life to their scrutiny may well be functional in terms of the way in which the Senate operates. As Bernard Asbell put it, "Their personality flaw is institutionalized in the Senate, and indeed becomes an operative strength."[32] When senators are viewed as thoroughgoing political beings whose only needs are the satisfaction of their constituencies and the advancement of their careers, this sweeping statement is perfectly valid. Yet there is another Senate that lurks behind the institutional, political Senate which—although not so salient, obvious, or very often even visible—is a part of the institution nonetheless. To recognize that the Senate is made up of people is to acknowledge that there exists a human Senate. Senators are extraordinary people, to be sure, and their humanity is often concealed behind elaborate shields of party labels, ideological attributes, and political positions; but their response to those events which wound or assault any human being are different only in degree, not in kind, from the reactions of ordinary people. They may be inured to political attacks, but they are no better suited than any of us to rise above sickness or the death of a loved one. Indeed, due to the nature of their careers, they may even be called upon to bear a heavier burden than the private citizen. So remorseless are the claims on their lives, so public are their activities, so exemplary must be their behavior, that their vulnerability in human terms is often very great.

It happens, then, that the great and revealing personal sharings of self which do occur from time to time between senators take place when their veneer of reserve and composure is stripped away by those emotions which affect any human being. These moments take place more typically in the house of mourning than in the house of rejoicing.

A few years ago an incident occurred in which these veneers were stripped away and a profound mutual understanding was achieved between two senators of radically different political views. It occurred in the context of personal tragedy, and produced between them a bond which had hitherto been absent. The two senators—one a veteran liberal and the other a freshman conservative—had found

---

[32] Bernard Asbell, op. cit.

themselves on an elevator in the Capitol. The liberal considered the conservative an inflexible and doctrinaire spokesman for positions he regarded as repugnant; they had not clashed directly, but each regarded the other with cold disdain. A few weeks before the meeting in the elevator, the wife of the conservative had been killed in a tragic accident. The wife of the liberal was suffering from inoperable cancer. Finding themselves alone in the elevator, they exchanged no greeting at first. Then, the liberal turned to the conservative and said, "I was terribly sorry to hear about your wife's death." The conservative thanked him and said, "You know, I was going over our checkbook the other night and trying to balance it, and all at once it came over me the times I criticized her for the way she kept the accounts. If there were any power in the world that would help me to call back those angry words over silly little things like that, I would do it." With tears welling up in his eyes, he grasped the liberal by the arm and said, "I know what you've been going through, too. Words of comfort from you have a special meaning." The two adversaries wept silently together.

Accounts of their subsequent relationship tell of its transformation. Both continue to tread their separate political paths, but the old ascribed hostility is gone. Their opposition is gentler. Their disposition to accommodate is greater. They are not intimates, but no longer are they enemies.

CHAPTER SEVEN

LONERSHIP, LEADERSHIP, AND FRIENDSHIP

One day in the late 1880s, young Congressman Henry Cabot Lodge of Massachusetts encountered on the House floor the diminutive Congressman Samuel "Sunset" Cox of New York, who began to reel off some jokes from his repertoire. He sent the flinty Boston patrician into gales of laughter with tale after tale. Then, with a trace of bitterness, he told Lodge, "If I were six feet tall instead of five-feet-six and had never made a joke I should be in that chair [gesturing towards the Speaker's place] and not on the floor. The people like those who make them laugh, but they will never give the highest places to anyone whom they do not think serious."[1] Lodge, a little man himself, may have taken Cox's utterance at face value. Whether by nature, or by design, he was to show a gravity of purpose and soberness of demeanor. He shunned close relations with his colleagues, and finished his career as Floor Leader of the Republican Party in the Senate.

While it is by no means the case that political leadership in the United States Senate is the province of hermits and lone wolves exclusively, there are certain circumstances which favor the leadership of the man apart if that remoteness is seen as contributing to the furtherance of the objectives of the group whose stewardship he seeks.

After Robert Byrd had been in the post of Majority Leader of the U.S. Senate for two years, *Washington Post* congressional correspondent Robert Kaiser interviewed a number of people who had had occasion to observe the taciturn West Virginian at first hand. Commenting upon the remarkable degree of success Byrd had achieved,

---

[1] Henry Cabot Lodge, *Early Memories* (New York: Charles Scribner's Sons, 1913), p. 331.

a Senate staff member rendered a rather sweeping judgment on the human qualities required of a floor leader: "You have to be someone who has no interests other than the Senate—the kind of person you wouldn't want to have dinner with."[2]

Byrd, a man who has on occasion been seen having a solitary stand-up lunch in the Democratic cloakroom, is one of the Senate's most conspicuous loners. He is also the Majority Leader and a man esteemed as being one of the most meticulous legislative craftsmen and parliamentary virtuosos in the Senate today. There is more to Byrd's "lonership" than a noticeable absence of a sense of humor or the eschewal of conviviality. He is a man who by most accounts has no personal friends in the membership of the institution whose fate he so largely determines. This apparent paradox—that a man who stands apart from any personal intimacy with colleagues is able to attain one of the few posts in the Senate subject to what is in fact a personal referendum—is the subject of this chapter. Also addressed is the related paradox that such a man may be perceived as a friend.

What is a loner in the context of the Senate? In the course of an interview with a senator designated by many of his colleagues as a loner, there emerged a picture of what lonership means in practice.

> My relationship with my colleagues does not generally extend to the social realm. We see each other all day and I try to lead a life of my own when I leave the Senate. I think I just get tired of talking about politics.

> There's a wonderful feeling of bonhomie and camaraderie within the Senate itself and many of my colleagues share in it, but as a general rule I like to be doing something different. . . . When I go out in the evening with [my wife], it's rarely with another Senatorial couple.

> I have very little time for leisure activities. I don't like playing tennis early in the morning, so I've not joined any of those groups that play in the morning. I take a briefcase full of work home in the evening, so I don't get a chance then. I've taken up

---

[2] Robert G. Kaiser, "Majority Leader Byrd Has Made Converts in Two Years," *Washington Post*, October 28, 1978.

running for exercise. . . . I attended the Prayer Breakfast a couple of times, but that's not quite my dish. I don't know why. . . .
I attended [college] with X—— but I didn't know him particularly. . . . I think that service in the Senate inhibits real friendship more than it fosters it. I can't really say that I feel very
close to any of my colleagues in a personal sense.

The U.S. Senate has had more than its share of loners aloof from
emotional involvement with colleagues. These were not people who
were necessarily politically solitary but were individuals whose
closeness of attachment with fellow members never transcended the
level of an alliance. They were able to establish the good cordial relationships found in institutional kinships and even to operate as part
of the more or less continuous grouping of politically and personally
compatible senators that meets the test of an alliance friendship, but
their social contacts outside the Senate with colleagues were limited,
sporadic, and innocent of any of the truly intimate relationships one
might find in a pure friendship.

These were personal "loners" as opposed to political "loners", the
latter being those who avoid becoming part of any particular bloc in
the Senate. Thomas Hennings of Missouri, whose problems were
beyond the reach of the liberals with whom he so often voted, was a
personal loner. Frank Lausche, an Ohio Democrat in the 1950s and
1960s and pillar of the Senate Prayer Breakfast, was more of a political loner, as was Estes Kefauver of Tennessee. The political loner is
often the "anomalous" senator, perhaps a Northern Democrat who
does not behave like other Northern Democrats, or a Southern Democrat markedly more liberal than his fellow Southerners of the same
party. Sometimes he is a senator who is simply independent-minded.
Wayne Morse of Oregon was often unpredictable in his actions but
was in no sense a social loner; for all of his maverick tendencies, he
had considerable social contact with his colleagues. And some senators are loners both politically and personally.

The personal loner has often been a person of considerable influence in the Senate. The senator who became one of the most powerful chairmen ever to preside over the Senate Foreign Relations
Committee, William E. Borah, was a confirmed, consistent personal
and political loner. Journalist Henry L. Stoddard's comments on him
when compared with those of Borah's biographer, Claudius O. John-

son, underscore not only the fact that institutional kinship and loner-ship are not incompatible but also the great imprecision with which the term "friend" is often used. Stoddard's view of Borah was that

> if you were to study the Senate rollcall you would find that Borah votes more independently of party, of friends, and of opponents more than any other senator. Nevertheless, he has more friends among his colleagues than have most senators, and his attitude on legislation sways more votes. Why? Because of confidence in his integrity and ability, and because he makes no personal issues. He accords others the privilege he exercises of having his own opinion. There is nothing vitri-olic about Borah; he never assails those who disagree with him; he fights their views but not them.[3]

Contrast this with Johnson's emphatic comments on Borah's per-sonal attachments.

> The Betas [Borah's fraternity brothers at the University of Kansas where he was an undergraduate] may have been somewhat disappointed in him, but Borah left no enemies on the campus. Neither did he leave any warm friends. He has never had an intimate friend, one to whom he would pour out all his hopes and fears, one to whom he would reveal his soul. If a man does not find such a friend in college, he is not likely to find one anywhere else.[4]

Stoddard's description of Borah is a virtual checklist of the attrib-utes of a senator capable of institutional-kinship relationships. So, in a sense, is Johnson's, especially insofar as Borah was able to avoid making enemies. But Johnson reiterates his judgment on Borah's absence of personal friends by observing, "He never let gratitude cor-rupt his soul and turn him from his appointed path," and—even

[3] Henry L. Stoddard, *As I Knew Them* (New York: Harper & Bros., 1927), p. 526.

[4] Claudius O. Johnson, *Borah of Idaho* (New York: Longmans, Green & Co., 1936), p. 18.

more pointedly—"He never had an inseparable companion nor a friend with whom he shared his innermost thoughts."[5]

When the Borahs moved to Washington, it was Mamie Borah who fulfilled the social obligations of the senatorial family in order to release her husband for matters of business. Even in his recreations, Borah was the consummate social loner: solitary early morning jaunts in Rock Creek Park astride his thoroughbred, Jester. Borah's nickname, "The Lone Rider of Idaho," seemed to fit both his political life and his personal life, especially the latter. Left to his own devices, he would have preferred to have spent his time locked away in a room with histories and biographies. While kindly and not without a sense of humor, he lacked "the capacity of making an individual feel at once that he is in the presence of a friend."[6]

Borah was more emphatically a personal loner than a political one. The terms of the alliance of the "Sons of the Wild Jackasses" of which he was a member were not unduly restrictive, so Borah could maintain his position within the Progressive constellation while going his own way on a number of issues. As was pointed out in Chapter 3, this group of Western Progressives was more an alignment than an alliance in the manner of the Four. Lonership—both personal and political—was not necessarily irreconcilable with Borah's membership in this loosely structured group. His relationships with his fellow Progressives were warm but not close; his nightly calls to Burton Wheeler during the Court fight were less an expression of intimacy than they were a cordial gesture from a colleague who had been a more or less consistent co-belligerent for more than a decade.

Henry Cabot Lodge's claim on the leadership of the Senate Republicans in 1919 was not strengthened by any close attachments with his colleagues; he had few. His closest friend in public life had been Theodore Roosevelt, a man of his own social milieu; their friendship had survived Roosevelt's decision to wage an independent presidential race in 1912. Lodge's feelings of loss at Roosevelt's death were profound. But with the possible exception of the lordly Elihu Root (R.–N.Y.), Lodge was on close personal terms with none of

[5] Ibid., pp. 18, 33.

[6] Ibid., p. 334.

his colleagues. "Root," as Claude Bowers recollected, "sat near Henry Cabot Lodge, and by their manner the two gave the impression of holding themselves aloof from their inferiors."[7]

But while Lodge was stinting in his intimacy with colleagues, he was not incapable of gestures of consideration to them. Shelby Cullom of Illinois, Lodge's predecessor as Republican Floor Leader and a man who had clashed with him on occasion, testified to the existence of a side of Lodge that was not always apparent.

> I have seen it repeatedly stated that Senator Lodge is unpopular in the Senate—that he is cold and formal. From my long acquaintance with him, extending over some seventeen years, I have found this not to be true. In times of trouble and distress in my own life, I have found him to be warm and sympathetic.[8]

Robert A. Taft of Ohio, who dominated Republican politics in the Senate for more than a decade in the 1940s and 1950s, was not without personal friends in his private life, but he shunned close personal associations even with those with whom he worked most closely in his legislative career. Both a personal and political loner in the Senate, "Taft [was] a legislative artist who always worked best when alone."[9]

In his three terms in the Ohio legislature, this bleakly honest, intellectually arrogant son of one of the most affable of all American presidents made no close personal friends among his fellow legislators. Relaxed in the company of old school friends, he came across to the public and his colleagues in the words of one associate as a "cold hearted son of a bitch."[10] While a staunch opponent of American interventionism in foreign policy, he forged no lasting ties with the isolationist bloc; while tolerating, even goading, Joseph McCarthy in his depredations against "communists" in government, he was never part of the McCarthyite coalition.

[7] Claude Bowers, *My Life* (New York: Simon and Schuster, 1962), p. 74.

[8] Shelby M. Cullom, *Fifty Years of Public Service* (Chicago: A. C. McClurg & Co., 1911), p. 352.

[9] William S. White, *The Taft Story* (New York: Harper & Bros., 1954), p. 199.

[10] Quoted in: James T. Patterson, *Mr. Republican: A Biography of Robert A. Taft* (Boston: Houghton Mifflin Co., 1972), pp. 103, 166.

The frequency or infrequency of his dealings as the head of the hierarchy with other Republican senators had no necessary relationship to them as individuals or to the degree of fondness or lack of it that he felt variously toward them. When he met a senator frequently it was only because that senator at the moment was occupied with something in which Taft had great interest. *Issues* determined his Senate associations, personalities were all but irrelevant.[11]

Taft's alliances were not bounded by overall ideology but by the test of a colleague's fidelity to particular issues which Taft cherished. He established relationships with Progressives such as Burton Wheeler and Robert La Follette, Jr. largely because of the aversion to foreign entanglements that they shared with the Ohioan. In the general manner of alliances, the respect and friendly feelings that emerged from his association with Wheeler and La Follette grew out of experience, for "in developing friendships in the Senate [Taft] was moved neither by cronyism—for he remained cool and unconvivial—nor even by partisanship, but by cautiously discovering who among his colleagues could be trusted to fight for the causes he held dear.[12]

Unlike Borah, Taft was capable of making enemies, especially if he sensed in a colleague a hostility to those principles which he cherished. Firm in his conviction of the rightness of these principles, he could call forth great hostility. George Aiken of Vermont, a fellow Republican, considered Taft a narrow and reflexive reactionary. "Every time he stood up to speak, I wanted to fight him," recalled Aiken.[13] Taft's hindrance of fellow Republican Raymond Baldwin of Connecticut was so unremitting that Baldwin finally just gave up; he arranged a meeting with his state's Democratic Governor, Chester Bowles, and beseeched him to appoint him to a state judgeship so that he could resign in good grace from the frustrations of the Senate, even though a Democrat would certainly be appointed in his place. From Taft's point of view, Baldwin represented the Eastern internationalist wing of the Republican party, which Taft considered anathema to

[11] William S. White, op. cit., p. 202.

[12] James T. Patterson, op. cit., p. 253.

[13] Quoted in Ibid., p. 266.

his own isolationist principles.[14] That Taft bore the sobriquet, "Mr. Republican" was somewhat ironic in light of his tendency to harry those of his own party who menaced his strongly held principles.

However, Taft did go out of his way to mollify fellow-Republican Arthur Vandenburg of Michigan who, after World War II, recanted his old isolationism and lined up with the aggressive internationalism of the Truman administration. He was willing to propitiate Vandenburg because of the Michigan Senator's chairmanship of the Foreign Relations Committee, but privately considered Vandenburg something of an apostate and a man morbidly addicted to flattery.

Taft was not a consistent conservative; his was a private set of principles, not a coherent conservative dogma. Viewed in classical and abstract conservative terms, many of his positions were anomalous, indeed inconsistent. He favored public housing, which conservatives considered socialistic. Despite his own moneyed background, he subscribed to what amounted to a devil theory of the Eastern banking community. When support for a Jewish homeland was the almost exclusive property of liberal Democrats, Taft's pro-Zionist views were highly conspicuous among Senate Republicans. He placed an exceedingly high valuation on those issues for which he chose to fight, and he was a relentless adversary to those of his colleagues who threatened those cherished objectives—but even with those with whom he agreed most consistently he was a man apart.

> It did not occur to him to linger with colleagues, to swap stories, or to pause for a drink after work. Though he did his share of entertaining, he never grew very close personally to any of his colleagues. To an extent his failure to develop close friends stemmed from the difficulty most adults have in establishing truly warm friendships with new acquaintances, and to an extent it marked the kind of private man he had always been. Besides, he had Martha [Mrs. Taft] to confide in, and he still relaxed most readily with his old college friends. . . . Not desiring any new intimacies, he simply did not trouble himself to look for any in the Senate.[15]

---

[14] Sidney Hyman, *The Lives of William Benton* (Chicago: University of Chicago Press, 1969), p. 406.

[15] James T. Patterson, op. cit., p. 341.

Taft guarded the approaches to his inner self with resolute wariness. He actually lived under the same roof, in 1940, with Sen. Wallace White of Maine, who for five years would serve in the position of Republican Floor Leader as Taft's front-man. But the amiable White was no intellectual match for a man with such rigorous standards. White did Taft's bidding and earned Taft's loyalty, which was tenacious; but for Taft intimacy did not necessarily proceed from loyalty.

For Borah, who ascended to the chairmanship of the Foreign Relations Committee by the inexorable process of seniority, the absence of personal friends among his colleagues was immaterial to his rise. But even if the post had been elective, his tendency to avoid making enemies might have been sufficient to turn away a challenge. For Taft—who not only made no personal friends among his colleagues, but wounded some along the way—his unanimous election to the post of Floor Leader, becoming congressional partner to the first Republican to occupy the White House in two decades, might seem a singular prize for someone so unloved. In the U.S. Senate, however, such events are not exceptional.

This portrait of the human—or inhuman—qualities of Taft, would be, however, incomplete without reference to some of his other gifts, which were simultaneously political and personal—and which commended him to his colleagues as a leader. While he was without any deep personal attachments to them, he had a deep appreciation of their individual needs as senators. The accuracy of his advice and tough-minded appraisals which were never tainted by false optimism were strengths that redounded to the benefit of the Senate, the party, and the individual senator.

> Long before he reached any place of official leadership he had become an untitled leader in the Senate because he gave no overt sign of wishing to be one and because of the rare quality of advice he gave to his colleagues. Many came to his office and the relationship was on the whole coolly impersonal and much like that of a senior student calling upon his professor for a required conference about his work or future. . . .
>
> Other powerful senators have told me frankly, if in an understandably private way, "Bob could give you a sense of *security*. . . ."
>
> [Taft] moreover . . . was careful not to offer a merely optimistic prognosis of a fellow senator's doubts and sufferings. Every

man has perhaps had the experience of going to one friend when he wanted to be reassured and quite a different friend when he wanted a surgical survey of his difficulties. Taft was the surgeon type.[16]

Taft's "surgical" friendship with his colleagues was not warm and endearing, but

his unselfishness, his willingness to work, and his capacity for retaining information forced his colleagues to rely on him, whether they liked him personally or not. His style of leadership could scarcely have differed more from the convivial approach of McNary or Barkley or from the shrewd and personable manner of Lyndon Johnson, but it was remarkably effective. . . . .

His colleagues sensed another trait crucial to the success of his leadership: his trustworthiness. Taft, they realized, meant absolutely what he said, he never failed on his word, and if he seemed blunt, he was never personal. He played no favorites, adopted no cronies, shunned even the appearance of bowing to pressure groups. He was, they said, a man of integrity. By that they meant he was true to himself. . . . Taft, said Walter Lippmann, "was . . . at the core so genuine and just, so rational and compassionate that he commanded the confidence of men when he could never convince them."[17]

The absence of personal friends among his colleagues and even the incapacity for forming ties of intimacy with them were the ingredients of Taft's lonership, yet three former senators whose service in the Senate coincided with Taft's all mentioned him as a friend. One of these senators, a liberal Republican, volunteered that it was indeed paradoxical that the term was applicable to their relationship.

I think Senator Taft became one of my very best friends, strange as it may seem (since I saw almost nothing of him socially). It all came about in 1948–49. When I was elected in

---

[16] William S. White, op. cit., pp. 200–201.

[17] James T. Patterson, op. cit., p. 350.

1948 there was a battle on for the leadership and I think it was Taft and Lodge—I'm quite sure it was. I would not commit myself because I was studying Taft's record. Cabot Lodge was my friend. [Taft] had been my friend. We were personally quite close and I would like to have supported him, but he simply wasn't energetic enough. I think that side of him came out in the 1960 campaign when he was running with Nixon. He was a perfectly lovely man but there was this softness about him.

According to this former senator, Taft showed solicitude and understanding of a colleague's political problems and vulnerabilities, and was capable of great gestures of gratitude when a fellow member supported one of Taft's cherished measures at some political risk to himself.

I recall an amendment on the Taft-Hartley Bill. It was a tough call for me, but after I studied it I found myself leaning towards it, but was still unwilling to come right out and say so. When Taft's staff man came to me to get a commitment, I told him that I wished that I could commit myself, but I just wasn't sure about the repercussions at home. I told him that he could tell Senator Taft not to worry, that I'll do my best. Now, of course, I didn't tell him a thing. Well, I voted for it finally, and Taft came to me and grabbed my hand and thanked me over and over again. He said that he knew it put me in a difficult position but that it was the saving vote for him. He was very good that way.

So Taft, the man with no close Senate friends and little ability or inclination to forge close ties, was seen as a friend by some of his colleagues. At least in one case he was supported in a leadership fight over a colleague who was indeed a close personal friend. While not inclined toward intimacy with his fellow members, he was "friendly" enough and sensitive enough to their needs that when these modest gifts were combined with his perceived mastery of the legislative process and skills as party spokesman, this Senate loner could be proclaimed both as leader and friend.

Taft's hand-picked successor for the post of Republican Floor Leader was William Knowland of California. The Californian, who was elected unanimously to succeed Taft, was an Oakland newspaper publisher who had served in the assembly and senate of his native state. He saw combat in World War II before his appointment to the U.S. Senate in 1945. He shared Taft's personal aloofness, but lacked his parliamentary skills and found himself perpetually at odds with the Eisenhower administration, despite being in the enviable position of commanding a Republican majority for a popular Republican president. He was, however, elected to the Republican leadership post in the two succeeding Congresses.

Knowland was more conclusively a member of a Senate bloc—the so-called "China Lobby"—than Taft, and was on the whole a more consistent conservative. He was, according to one observer's recollection,

> [a] strapping man with a great fold of muscle and flesh at the back of his neck. I sometimes feared he would burst out of his skin when the level of contention became high. His mind had a single trajectory—flat—and at point-blank range. His integrity was that of a bull, admirable in its way, but unsuited for political leadership. He was entirely predictable, and permitted more skillful men to tie him (and thus his party) inflexibly in fixed positions.[18]

In terms of basic political characteristics, however,

> nothing approaching fundamental disagreement divided [Taft and Knowland]. True, Knowland had been far more pro-Europe [on foreign policy] than had Taft, but he had more than compensated for this failing by his long, dogged preoccupation with the sins and shortcomings, real or alleged, of Democratic policy in Asia. . . . As to domestic affairs, there was no divergence of substance. In the personal sense, too, Knowland embodied much that Taft had always approved—solidity, a certain stolidity, a gravity of approach that was sometimes very near to humorlessness . . . .[19]

---

[18] Harry McPherson, *A Political Education* (Boston: Little, Brown & Co., 1972), p. 74.

[19] William S. White, op. cit., pp. 256–257.

But it was more than just a lack of humor; it was a quintessential rudeness and a lack of skill in interpersonal relationships. When it appeared as if Wayne Morse was about to embark upon a filibuster over the "tidelands" controversy when Knowland was whip, a more sensitive and flexible man might have been able to avert what developed into a twenty-two hour talkathon. Knowland, however, would make no conciliatory gesture to the Oregon maverick, despite Morse's own desire for a face-saving pretext for avoiding the filibuster.

Knowland's rigidity often expressed itself in a callousness to the needs of colleagues which caused them to resent him deeply. In 1958, for example, Republican colleague John D. Hoblitzell of West Virginia, who was up for reelection, informed Knowland that he was in danger of being beaten in his contest with Democrat Jennings Randolph and asked that Knowland defer several important votes. Knowland was incensed that Hoblitzell would place his own political needs before those of the Senate, and refused to accommodate the West Virginia Republican, who retired to the cloakroom muttering imprecations against Knowland. Hoblitzell went down to defeat.[20]

Even when asked for advice or when having his opinion solicited, Knowland would be uncommunicative and abrupt. His successor, Everett Dirksen, a vastly more accommodating leader, said of Knowland, "You ask him a question, and he'd say, 'No comment.' You ask him another, and he'd give you a grunt."[21]

Knowland's ambition for the presidency led him into an ill-starred campaign for the governorship of California in 1958. He left behind no legacy of fondness. His associations with colleagues were of a formal, indeed stiff, nature. Whether it was these deficiencies in Knowland or the circumstance of working as leader under a Republican president with whom he was chronically at odds that most hampered his success is difficult to assess. The combined effect of the two problems, however, produced a stewardship that was satisfying neither in institutional terms nor in terms of the needs of individual senators.

---

[20] Neil MacNeil, *Dirksen: Portrait of a Public Man* (New York and Cleveland: World Publishing Co., 1970), p. 166.

[21] Quoted in Ibid., p. 312.

As with Borah, Taft, and Knowland, the current Majority Leader of the U.S. Senate Robert C. Byrd, is a man without close personal friends among his colleagues. In the opinion of one colleague,

> Bob Byrd is a very serious-minded man. He went through law school while he was in the Congress, and I don't think that Bob had any time for frivolity, if I may put it that way. I never heard Bob tell a joke. He's very serious-minded, very pragmatic. He's a constructionist and a good mechanic.

> These traits are very valuable, of course. Naturally you make, well, let me say—I don't want to say you make enemies—but you make people disagree with you at times. But they respect him and know that the job has got to be done. I'll tell you frankly, if it hadn't been for Bob Byrd, Mike Mansfield would have been in trouble many, many times. Bob is a pusher; Mike was not. There was something very docile about Mike Mansfield; he was the lay priest of the Senate. As a matter of fact, if he could have gotten into the clergy I think he would have turned out to be a cardinal. There was something ecclesiastical about the man.

> Now Bob's another case entirely. When Mike wouldn't dream of trying to move things along, Bob would say, "Look, this thing's been dragging along all afternoon. You're not far apart. Why don't you stop this tomfoolery and get on the ball and resolve this thing tonight." Well, now, Mike could have done that, but he never did.

Another Democratic colleague of Byrd's provided much the same kind of evaluation of the Majority Leader.

> Bob Byrd did not get to his present job based on his personal popularity. He got there by dint of prodigious work. He *is* able. He learned the institution. If I were the Majority Leader I would want him as the whip. He loves the floor. He loves the detail. He'll stay there endless hours with all of the mechanics that would bore me to death—working out schedules and making sure that people are there. But he's a guy who didn't get where he is based on personality by a long shot. I can't think of a single one of my colleagues who would count Bob as one of their personal friends.

Loner that he is, Byrd is able to strike a more harmonious balance between parliamentary interpersonal skills than other leaders with no close Senate friends. Like Taft and unlike Knowland, Byrd is not oblivious to the needs of his colleagues as people; he is not only prepared, but willing, to accommodate them. Byrd has shown himself capable of gestures of personal interest that have earned him the loyalty, if not the affection, of his colleagues. He emulated the type of considerate gesture that was one of Lyndon Johnson's strengths, based on the ability to deal with a colleague at three levels: as a member of an institution, an individual senator, and a human being.

In 1952, Westwood Byrd, the only daughter of Sen. Harry Byrd, Sr. of Virginia, died under tragic circumstances. The funeral was being conducted in Winchester, Virginia and Lyndon Johnson made the long drive from Washington to be present. To his astonishment, Johnson discovered upon arriving at the funeral that he was the only member of the Senate in attendance. That one of the most influential and respected members of the Senate was grieving without any expression of condolence from other senators was incredible for Johnson. The elderly conservative was overcome by Johnson's gesture. When a vote crucial to Johnson's national ambitions came up in the Senate several years later, the old man remembered the Texan's thoughtfulness and gave him his vote.[22]

Twenty years later, Robert C. Byrd duplicated the Johnson gesture and found, as Johnson had, that he alone among the members of the U.S. Senate had rallied to a colleague at a time of bereavement. In 1972, the wife and baby daughter of freshman senator Joseph Biden (D.–Del.) were killed in an automobile accident. Byrd traveled to Wilmington for the funeral service and stood almost unnoticed at the back of the church.

Given Byrd's undemonstrative qualities, it was a thoughtful gesture; these expressions do not come easily to him. Yet he is deft at handling the political needs of his colleagues, and can be tactful and deferential. He will address colleagues on the phone by such endearing terms as "boss" or "chief," but it is the political ego which is being recognized far more than the inner man.

---

[22] Roland Evans and Robert Novak, *Lyndon B. Johnson: The Exercise of Power* (New York: New American Library, 1966), p. 106.

A classic workaholic, Byrd rises at 6:30 every morning, then usually travels by chauffeur-driven limousine—one of his perks of leadership—from his modest home in McLean, Va., to his office, where he is in business by 7:45. He then begins a breathless round of staff discussions, committee meetings, and appointments. The majority leader always eats lunch in his office, usually a bologna sandwich prepared by his wife Erma. . . . By 8:00 P.M. Byrd is on his way home carrying a heavy briefcase. He has few close friends in Washington and never takes a vacation. Says he: "I wouldn't enjoy going away and doing nothing." His scant leisure time is spent with his wife, watching TV news and interview programs.[23]

Byrd's lonership is wholly consistent with his maintenance of institutional-kinship ties with his colleagues, but it and his role as legislative mechanic, facilitator, and procedural fine-tuner are less conducive to his membership in an alliance. Ideologically speaking, while his history is one of conservatism, Byrd has moved in a pragmatic direction. While leadership in the Senate is not necessarily incompatible with strong political views,

> a potential candidate [for Senate leadership] cannot deviate far from the mainstream of his party's ideological orientation. . . . Party leaders are "middle men" located well within the dominant wing of their party's general ideological orientation. . . . If, by an unusual combination of circumstances an ideological exception is elected, for example, the relatively liberal Senate Minority Leader Hugh Scott of Pennsylvania, he generally shifts toward his party's center in his subsequent voting behavior.[24]

An important qualification for Senate leadership, in modern times at least, is a position of relative ideological neutrality; if that is not the case at the time of selection, it soon becomes so. Taft was no hide-

---

[23] "Byrd of West Virginia: Fiddler in the Senate," *Time*, January 23, 1978, pp. 12–13, and Robert L. Peabody, *Leadership in Congress* (Boston: Little, Brown & Co., 1976), pp. 400–401.

[24] Robert L. Peabody, op. cit., p. 470.

bound conservative, and even Knowland, a person far less flexible even than Taft, had what amounted to a private agenda of cherished issues rather than an entirely consistent conservative philosophy from which deviation was difficult.

But if ideological neutrality—or at least an ideological stance susceptible of moderation—was characteristic of these leaders, what about the question of personal *affective* neutrality? While it is true that leadership in the Senate has devolved upon such relatively outgoing and friendly types as Howard Baker, Hugh Scott, Lyndon Johnson, Everett Dirksen, and Alben Barkley in modern times and, before that, John W. Kern, Charles McNary, and Wallace White, remote men sequestered from the emotions of their colleagues have also been chosen, such as Henry Cabot Lodge, Sr., Taft, Knowland, and Byrd.

The not infrequent choice of loners for top posts in the Senate may simply be a function of chance. There is also the possibility that under certain circumstances the loner's very aloofness may be perceived as an advantage in his job. He may be favored over other types of senators because he is insulated from the vulnerabilities associated with being on intimate terms with colleagues. In those periods of Senate history in which greatest emphasis is placed upon firmness and resolution in the conduct of work, senators may be inclined to favor leaders coldly determined rather than those to whom personal friendship comes readily. When the stakes are particularly high, it may seem prudent to choose a leader who will plunge ahead and get the job done with little worry about the effect of his hard-driving techniques on personal relationships. The loner's claim on leadership may also be improved during periods of great individualism in the Senate when cohesion is low and individual achievement is more highly prized than the maintenance of solidarity and a "clubby" atmosphere. The loner's quality of dispassion—which in the original sense of the term comes very near to being a synonym for impartiality—may commend him over other claimants at such times.

What appears to have made these loners acceptable or even desirable as leaders was their single-minded devotion to the institution and their perceived effectiveness. At first glance it appears that a premium has been placed upon the need for brisk, businesslike efficiency, with the loner's interpersonal limitations relegated to a position of little or no importance. In practice, however, the successful loner-leaders have demonstrated a substantial capacity for decent interpersonal relations. While having no close personal friends among members and little aptitude or inclination for sociability and intimacy, leaders such as Taft and Byrd are capable of being perceived as friends because of their ability to inspire trust, work hard, and provide accurate assessments of political and legislative outcomes, conferring by doing so a sense of security upon both the institution and the individual senator. Chosen principally for their skills as tough-minded professionals, they are able to augment these more formal strengths with an appreciation of what makes their colleagues tick. While their approach to colleagues may be reserved and clinical and their most obvious strengths—which most forcefully commends them for leadership—are parliamentary genius and stature as party spokesmen, they are able to conduct interpersonal relations with enough sensitivity to avoid complete detachment from the political and personal needs of individual members.

Loner-leaders like William Knowland seem less able to maintain this balance. Inflexibly dedicated to more general objectives, seeing individual members only in terms of their relationship to the collectivity, and preoccupied with the needs of party and institution, this type of leader runs the risk that his stewardship will in effect benefit neither the more general objects of his concern nor the requirements of the individual senator.

If the loner, with his deficient capacity for forming close personal relationships with colleagues is a highly eligible candidate for leadership, what does this say about the influence of friendship on the selection of leaders? It says that a senator's ability to form intimate ties with colleagues is unrelated to other qualities which may commend him as a leader, qualities which may be of such importance as to offset his limited capacity for deep attachments. And it appears that the criteria used by senators in their choice of leaders are different from those they use in choosing their closest friends. The comments of a Midwestern Democrat are characteristic of the group interviewed:

> I think that the important thing to keep in mind is that the qualities—the things you most admire in people on the outside—would carry over to the Hill. Now in leadership it may be a different thing. In leadership selection, I think, it's the least common denominator. I don't mean that with a negative

implication, but to be elected leader—to be elected in a political battle to that position—really means that you're acceptable to a wide spectrum of people, and it usually means that you have to be somewhat of a eunuch on the issues. It may also mean that you have to be an emotional eunuch as well. You can't have a very pronounced profile. So that some of the things that just on an abstract plane you pick to admire in a colleague may not translate to suitable evaluations for a leadership position.

A senator's capacity for personal friendship is neither a positive nor a negative attribute in evaluating him as a leader. What seems to be important, however, is how that individual's capacity—or lack of it—for close attachments is likely to influence his performance as leader. Accordingly, it was not the aptitude for personal friendship enjoyed by Howard Baker and Ted Stevens or the remoteness of Robert Byrd and Alan Cranston *per se* that influenced how they were chosen and perceived as leaders but the potential effects of these characteristics on the discharging of those tasks considered crucial for the institution, the party, and the senators as individuals. These characteristics relating to personal relations may often be perceived to have no effect at all.

Clearly, more than just the capacity for personal friendship is evaluated in terms of effect on a leader's performance. While his ability to attract or hold himself aloof from colleagues in the most deeply personal sense might be seen as influencing his conduct, he is also evaluated in terms of his capacity for the less emotionally demanding form of interpersonal association which I have called institutional kinship.

Some senators feel very strongly that openness, trust, and avoidance of conflict—the very qualities that would commend an individual as a personal friend—might put certain colleagues at a disadvantage in situations where more detached senators would be able to operate with greater certitude. A long-time Senate collaborator of Hubert Humphrey who valued the great warmth of the Minnesotan recalled the early days of the 95th Congress in 1977 when Humphrey resolved to challenge Robert Byrd for the Democratic leadership.

Hubert's shortcomings—the very things that would have caused troubles for him if he had managed to win—came out in the course of his decision whether to stay out or get in. By the time he got into it—and he didn't really belong in it—he didn't have a chance, because he can't count and never could. Hubert counted friendly smiles and pats on the back. He just thought a lot of people were for him who weren't. Byrd, on the other hand, counts votes. He won that job based on the quality of his performance—and the bottom line for me, and I daresay most of my colleagues, is performance.

The strong sense that a colleague's aversion to making enemies could detract from the toughness required for leadership tasks was expressed to me strongly by a Republican from an earlier era in the Senate who recollected his impressions of John Sherman Cooper and Leverett Saltonstall. Saltonstall had served as Republican whip from 1949 until 1957. He had attempted to win the post of floor leader in 1952 but was defeated by Styles Bridges. He continued as deputy until 1957. Cooper had challenged Dirksen for the post of floor leader of the Republicans in 1959.

I knew John Cooper the way I know the palm of my right hand. John Cooper was a very easygoing, lovely sort of guy. You could disagree with John Cooper but, my God, you could never dislike him. I mean, he was that kind of guy. Well, I'm telling you—and this is an awful thing for me to say—but even the devil could get along with John Cooper, or John Cooper could get along with the devil, whatever way you want to put it. I mean there was something about John that was just sanctified; he was that kind of guy. He never raised his voice and he was very courteous to everyone. He was like [Leverett] Saltonstall. You could never get angry with him either. You couldn't really shout at Saltonstall, and you couldn't do that to Cooper. But whether or not they could get anything done was another thing.

One Democrat drew comparisons between the considerate approach used by Mike Mansfield with his colleagues and the more tough-minded techniques used by both the Montanan's predecessor and his successor.

Mike Mansfield just wouldn't interfere with anybody under any circumstances. That's the kind of person he was, and they loved him for it. Sometimes it paid off. If Mike Mansfield got up you might have disagreed with him, but you knew he was honest and he had that respect. I know that a good number of my colleagues considered his style a relief from Johnson, but let me say this: It will be recorded in history that Lyndon Johnson was one of the best Senate leaders we've ever had. I mean Lyndon Johnson—you've got to realize this—that Lyndon Johnson was a go-getter who came out of Texas and gave us a civil rights law. He gave us the civil rights law. Now how do you think he did that? You don't think he did that by going around and kissing people? Now, Bob Byrd is a pusher. He can get under your skin. Mike just never did that.

If some senators regarded certain traits commonly associated with a capacity for personal friendship as operating, in practice, as impediments to performance in a leader, others felt that a senator unable to get close to colleagues as people might encounter difficulties of another kind. A Republican who was in the Senate at the time William Knowland was the GOP floor leader suggested that the Californian's remoteness from his colleagues was a serious drawback in his leadership.

Bill Knowland was a very stubborn, set man. He never made the effort to find out what made his colleagues tick. He just never got to know me. I was having a very bad time in my state over [a] navy yard. . . . The workers there were being paid on a scale much lower than the workers at [a] navy yard which was only fifty miles away. We got a pay equalization bill passed in both Houses and Eisenhower vetoed it. I went to Bill Knowland for help and he didn't have the slightest sensitivity to what this meant to me. He just couldn't understand why I was so agitated. He just took me for granted. Lyndon Johnson, on the other hand—who was, after all, the leader of the other party—came to me and said, "Be sure to be on the floor at such and such a time and we'll see what we can do about that veto." And when the time came Johnson had his people lined up on it and every one of them came through.

A more recent example of problems encountered by the remote type of leader was described by another Republican, who witnessed the defeat of Robert Griffin by Howard Baker for the post of Republican floor leader vacated by Hugh Scott.

> I don't think that Bob [Griffin] had much insight into his colleagues, and it got him into real trouble when Baker went after the leadership job when Hugh Scott left. He was a very stiff and standoffish person, and I think that if he'd been a little more friendly he might have gotten some more support, or at least have had some inkling as to what was coming.

There is a very strong feeling among some senators that in addition to possessing parliamentary skills and proficiency as his party's spokesman, the leader should be able to understand and address himself to the senators' individual needs (but not, significantly, to needs of a very personal nature). He should have an appreciation for the significance of issues as they relate to the states, an understanding of the constraints under which individual senators operate, and an ability to act with intelligent restraint when a party colleague is forced to part company with him on an issue. He must be able to grasp the idiosyncracies of fifty states and the one hundred men and women representing them, legislators whose concerns are not only national in scope but parochial as well. A border-state Republican extolled these virtues in Everett Dirksen:

> Dirksen himself was a great conciliator and I think he was a great leader. A lot of people considered him a blow-hard— *some* people did—but when he spoke on an issue, he knew it. I never wanted anybody to come in from outside the state to speak when I was a candidate, because I knew the issues in the state better than they did. But with Dirksen, he could come in and convince everybody that he understood the problems of the state. He'd studied them. Now mind you, he was a great performer and people loved to hear him speak, but he was able to adjust himself beautifully and talked to audiences in [different states] and convinced them that he knew what their problems were, and did so intelligently.

Robert Byrd is also said to have a like appreciation for the peculiar constraints under which senators operate, through his comprehension of the states and their voters. Byrd not only understands the peculiar needs of the senators and their states but applies this knowledge to situations in which these problems and issues force them to take positions at variance with his. This strength of Byrd's was tested in the 95th Congress over the section of President Carter's energy bill on the deregulation of natural gas; two Democrats from consumer states—Ohio's Howard Metzenbaum and South Dakota's James Abourezk—led a filibuster against the bill, a bill which Byrd and the Democratic leadership supported. It was a bitter and lengthy battle which ran into the night and produced angry exchanges. Byrd was irked at the efforts of Metzenbaum and Abourezk to block the measure. A Democrat recalled the filibuster and its aftermath:

> On the natural gas thing, some people were very personally mad at each other. I had some press people come to me and ask whether it had permanently damaged their relationships or permanently hurt Abourezk and Metzenbaum's relations with Bob Byrd, and I said, "No, not at all." It bothered Bob a lot; He got very hot under the collar, but he knew what the Midwest was going through with the gas situation and realized that they had to fight for their interests.

A former Republican senator brought up the question of certain issues "sacred" to certain groups of senators, which good leaders treat with considerable tact:

> Take cloture, for example. People are generally classed as liberal or conservative on that. There were senators who might be classed as liberal on many subjects who would never vote for cloture because they had small states and were fearful of being run over—men from small states in the West. They would say they didn't believe in it, and a good leader took them at their word no matter how desperately he might have wanted those votes.

Some senators also tended to place a very high valuation on trust as a personal criterion for leadership. In some cases this desire for forthrightness and honesty in a leader was given emphasis equal to or even greater than such institutional strengths as parliamentary mastery or proficiency as the party's spokesman. A former senator contrasted his feelings about Lyndon Johnson and Mike Mansfield as leaders:

> Take Mike Mansfield. People say he wasn't much of a leader. He was a good leader in this sense—he was believed. Lyndon was a strong leader in this sense—that he could get bills passed; but you just didn't have that trust.

The same senator felt that Leverett Saltonstall in his years as whip combined trust and a sensitivity to the political constraints under which senators work.

> There would be certain things that would come out of committee. Now I'm not talking about questions like civil rights or all this turmoil that came out of the Vietnam War, but things a little larger than state or local questions that would come out of committee. Well, you'd read the committee's report and the minority report or talk to the floor manager, but you still might wonder what was the right thing to do on that. You'd want somebody who you could believe in and who would tell you the truth—somebody who wasn't directly involved in it.

> When Leverett Saltonstall was whip I'd turn to him. One time I went to see him on a bill, and he said to me, "I'm going to vote for this bill, but you shouldn't where you come from." I believed what he told me.

Related to trust and an awareness of and solicitude for the detailed concerns of a senator and his state is another quality that some senators value—the ability to confer protection. This criterion relates not so much to state issues but more to the leader's understanding of national constituencies and interest groups and his ability to aid senators in averting disaster; to some degree this is an informational role, but it also entails counseling. There is also here, in a sense, a concern over the leader's ability to avoid institutional calamity, but it is expressed in individual as well as institutional terms. The "sense of security" that Taft was able to convey embraced simultaneously the institution, the party, and the individual.

At a time when the Senate is under pressure to produce legislative remedies by a public skeptical of its performance, a leader oriented towards effectiveness would be of great value to the institution and also beneficial to the individual senator interested in moving a particular piece of legislation to enactment. But each senator also has a private agenda of needs and goals which may not be coterminous with that of the collectivity. So while senators may esteem certain institutionally relevant strengths in a leader, they want special treatment as well. This capacity to be attuned to the needs of the individual may actually be well-met by the loner, who may be as sensitive to particular needs as he is to aggregate or institutional necessities. Toughness in moving the institution along and resolution in fostering the exigencies of party must be accompanied by an understanding of and a solicitude for the peculiar needs of the individual senator.

It has been said, apropos of the U.S. Senate, that

> for a leadership job you think about the kind of person he is, how he does his business. You want a fellow to treat you fairly. You wonder how a person will conduct himself with *particular reference to you.*[25]

Aside from valuing such general strengths as "performance," "effectiveness," and "attention to detail"—characteristics which tend to redound to the benefit of all—senators have peculiar needs as individuals which, while not necessarily inconsistent with those traits relevant to the institution or party, are sometimes different. A veteran Republican senator who recalled his own reactions to the close battle between Griffin and Baker for the part of Minority Leader said, "I actually trusted Griffin more than I did Baker, but Griffin was just the wrong symbol for the party at the time." Their evaluation of a leader or a claimant on leadership appears to be a product of both the more comprehensive and individualized criteria.

When senators take a colleague's capacity for personal friendship into account in judging his suitability for leadership, they do so not in terms of that capacity as an independent and isolated trait, but in terms of how it will influence his behavior regarding the needs of the institution and of themselves as individuals. A great capacity for personal friendship will be suspect if there is a sense that it will make the leader prey to cronyism. As one Democrat remarked, "It's perfectly

[25] Quoted in Ibid., p. 363.

OK for a man to have lots of friends, but if you feel that he's likely to give the inside track to his buddies, you want to make damn sure that you're one of them." The qualities associated with an ability to form close personal ties may also come under suspicion if there is a feeling that they may inhibit resoluteness in the leader. If a leader finds it difficult to "lean on" people for fear of alienating them, this may certainly work to his disadvantage during those times when the application of pressure is needed. A trusting and sunny disposition in and of itself will confer neither advantages nor disadvantages on a claimant for leadership—unless it is perceived as damaging the individual by making him susceptible to unwarranted optimism, especially in the assessment of votes and support for legislation.

In a like manner, the detachment from colleagues as people found in the loner type is neither an asset nor a liability per se, unless it cuts the leader off so decisively from any appreciation of the requirements and yearnings of the individual members that what emerges in effect is a callousness or obliviousness to their private needs. Here, there may occur distortions in judgement based not upon wishful thinking but on simple lack of empathy. The remote leader may also be seen as insufficiently attuned to the cherished interests of colleagues and overly prone to pressuring them to accede to actions which may benefit the party or the institution but which may violate some deeply held personal conviction or state concern.

The leader, then, may possess qualities that invite personal friendship and may indeed have many friends, but these qualities must not be seen as leading him into cronyism, unrealistic illusions, or passivity in the interest of not antagonizing colleagues. On the other hand he may be permitted remoteness if the distance he places between himself and the hearts and minds of colleagues does not produce emotional obtuseness or a lack of consideration for private needs.

What emerges from this complex of institutional and private needs and official and personal criteria for leadership is, first of all, a realization that no leader will approximate the ideal for all standards. The institutional criteria—qualities demanded of the leader in terms of his role as party spokesman and legislative foreman—depend a great deal on the political context in which he operates. The party's leaders in the Senate will be called on to perform differently if they represent the majority or the minority; this difference will be contingent upon the delicacy of the partisan balance. The party affiliation of the president adds an additional element here, as do such amorphous forces as the spirit of the times.

The private criteria may or may not be consonant with the more general and formal standards. While Lyndon Johnson, for example, drew general praise for his effectiveness in moving legislation, a senator from his own party recalled with great bitterness:

> I know he comes off with high marks for getting things done, but he was repugnant to me. When I dealt with him I always had the feeling that I was standing on a trap door that was waiting to be sprung.

A Republican was even more emphatic in his judgment of Johnson:

> Johnson was a crook. I mean, what else can you say about him? I'm sick and tired of having that side of him passed over by people who feel that his leadership skills excuse everything else he did.

No leader can conform ideally to both the institutional needs as perceived at the time and the highly individualized needs of his ninety-nine fellow members. Both standards, moreover, are an amalgam of political and personal desiderata. The relationship between the two is subtle. What is good for the institution or collectivity must also be of benefit to the individual, especially at a time when individualism in the Senate is so pronounced. In much the same manner that it is impossible in reality to firmly demarcate "political" friendship and "personal" friendship, it is impossible to clearly separate the personal and political components which determine whether a senator as leader will serve to the advantage of both institution and individual.

So while it does seem that rather different criteria enter into the calculations of senators regarding choice of leader and choice of personal friend, and that a potential leader's capacity for the more intimate forms of friendship is considered decisive only as it will either enhance or distort his performance, there is a more modest capacity for friendship, assuming both professional and personal qualities, which does contribute to the estimation of him as a leader. That form of friendship is institutional kinship.

Those elements which go into making up this most basic form of Senate friendship—empathy, integrity, diligence, and restraint—come very near to being an inventory of what is esteemed in a leader. The degree of intimacy, again, is modest but not insignificant. The qualities of empathy, integrity, and restraint are directed to both the institution and the individual. Diligence, while it has important consequences for the individual in terms of conveying accurate and well-interpreted information, also evokes the kind of institutional protection and safeguarding mentioned by several of the senators.

Clearly, the leader or potential leader need not have a wide network of personal friends or even be capable or willing to forge such ties of intimacy; but he must be a good enough "friend," in the senatorial context, to be able to appreciate the individual needs of his colleagues as politicians and people. The good leader will strive to do this, as well as devote himself to the more general and formal roles of party spokesman and legislative strategist, in the recognition that the two are intertwined.

If one accepts that such institutional kinship is indeed a form of friendship, then friendship may be said to influence their choice of leaders very strongly and very directly. These qualities in a colleague are of much greater immediacy and weight as regards leadership than a senator's capacity or incapacity for close personal ties. While most senators felt that certain desirable or undesirable traits might be associated with either acute lonerism or a great aptitude for close personal friendship with fellow members, and were able to provide evidence for this, most felt that either type of senator probably could perform well as a leader. What concerned them more than the advantages or pitfalls associated with either extreme was having a leader who, in addition to the quality of his party spokesmanship and mastery of parliamentary skills, was a person who could be trusted to be alert to their interests and those of the institution, to keep his promises, to understand and sympathize with the detailed problems of their states and the challenges and opportunities they present, and to have sufficient sensitivity and compassion to respect these individual needs and avoid recrimination when they took a senator on a different path from that which the leader might have preferred. It is in this context that senators can unflinchingly call Robert Byrd or Robert Taft as a "friend" as readily as they do Howard Baker or Everett Dirksen.

The response to the question, does friendship affect senators' leadership choices? should be governed by an appreciation of two distinctions: the first relates to the precise meaning of the term "friendship," and the second to the tendency of senators to approach leadership evaluation with mixed motives—those of an individual and an institutional nature. If we define friendship only in terms of its more personal manifestations—social, in the "extramural" sense, or pure—the effect seems quite limited. Given the paucity of such relationships, in selecting a leader a senator cannot limit his range of choice to those with whom he has forged close ties. This definition would be all the more restricting because the personal friend may not meet more comprehensive eligibility requirements such as experience or ideological acceptability. Typically, the senator chooses not from ninety-nine other colleagues but usually from those who have served as whip, conference chairman, or chairman of the party campaign committee. Of course, should one of those colleagues be a personal friend, it may be of considerable benefit to have him as floor leader. Still, the occasion to bring his friendship to bear is not very likely to present itself.

What is more likely—at least at present, when hand-picked successors are not apt to be acceptable—is that personal friendship will not even enter into the calculation. In this situation it appears that the least intimate form of friendship, institutional kinship, figures most prominently in senators' choices. The senators' determinations on leadership seem to coincide quite closely with his characterizations of a colleague in terms of institutional kinship. This is based upon experience, rather than upon such abstractions as whether the colleague approximates the model of the "good senator" or some other ideal which he personally has not had occasion to test.

This brings us to the second distinction—between personally and institutionally relevant criteria, mixed complexly in assessing leadership. A senator wants to be assured that the institution will be well served; despite his own often successful efforts to disassociate himself in the public mind from an institution which often suffers from low public esteem and advance himself as champion of a particular interest or ombudsman to his constituents, at least part of his success is measured by the performance of the collectivity. At the same time, however, he does not measure a potential leader merely by the detached standard of being good for the Senate. He wants very much to be assured that a leader will not only be good for the Senate, but be sensitive and attentive to his needs as an individual member. A senator with a great capacity for friendship and the sensitivity, openness, integrity, solicitude, and aversion to making enemies associated with that capacity may well answer those individual needs, but there are negative qualities senators often equate with these traits—irresoluteness, hesitancy to apply pressure, suggestibility, and an insufficient degree of tough-mindedness in tactical judgments—which may cause serious problems for the institution. What the senator may gain in terms of personal consideration he may have to forgo in terms of firmness of institutional control.

This expectation, indeed desire, on the part of senators that the leader will, all at the same time, master the formal tasks of parliamentarian and spokesman while being attuned to individual needs of both a political and personal nature appears to be related to a more general tendency in formal organizations for members to value a leader who can strike a balance between "instrumental" and "expressive" leadership.[26]

In the search for a balance between interpersonal satisfactions and the institutional requirements of the Senate, a potential leader's capacity for friendship and legislative mastery are weighed in terms of what combination of both qualities will result in the best overall performance. What seems to emerge is a profile of an acceptable leader attentive to individual needs, but not so much so as to shrink from applying the firm hand of direction. Conversely, he should not be so bent on institutional efficiency as to be callous to individual needs. Given a range of choice of candidates—which will probably not include a personal friend—the senator will not discard the standard of friendship entirely, but will apply it in its more attenuated form of institutional kinship. That the person chosen offers little by way of social companionship or emotional sustenance is not really the issue; that can be provided elsewhere, in or out of the Senate. The criterion for leadership, in terms of human friendship, is one of adequacy, not perfection.

---

[26] See Talcott Parsons and Robert F. Bales, *Family, Socialization and Interaction Process* (New York: Free Press, 1955) and Robert F. Bales, *Interaction Process Analysis: A Method for the Study of Small Groups* (Cambridge: Addison-Wesley, 1950). The findings of Parsons and Bales suggest that persons in authority are more valued by the rank and file if they can achieve an equilibrium between task leadership and social leadership. In the nuclear family and in certain experimental groups, it has been found that the burdens of instrumental and expressive leadership are usually borne by two persons; in formal organizations the two traits are often combined in a single individual.

CHAPTER EIGHT

Sources of Senatorial Strife

It was getting close to recess. There weren't many senators on the floor at the time and most of the business was whipping through by unanimous consent. As I came down the aisle I saw X—— studying the chamber very intently. I stopped next to him as he surveyed the empty seats. He turned to me and asked, "Where's Margaret Chase Smith?" "I believe she's up in Maine campaigning," I said [referring to the redoubtable Republican who prided herself on never having missed a roll-call vote in the Senate]. This look of malevolent delight appeared on his face. "I'm going to ask for a roll-call vote on the next piece of business," he said with a wicked grin. I was really shocked, and I said, "You can't do that. Mansfield and Dirksen promised her that there wouldn't be any. It'll ruin her record. She'll have an occlusion!" "Well, I don't guess I will," he said, "but I was sure sorely tempted." He really couldn't stand Maggie Smith for some reason, and I think if I hadn't been there he would have asked for the roll call and ruined her record, but maybe he just couldn't bring himself to do it. As spiteful as he was sometimes, he realized that it would just be too destructive.

If there are inhibitions in the Senate against close personal friendships, there are likewise restraints on unbounded hostility. The formal rules which dictate senatorial decorum serve to some extent to contain spontaneous hostility, but it is really the self-interest of the individual senator who recognizes that his own effectiveness may be impeded by a feud that is the principal safeguard against personal vendettas. "We're both involved in agriculture legislation," said one Midwestern Democrat, commenting upon a Republican from the same region who entered his state to speak against the Democrat's support of the Panama Canal Treaty. "I might need his vote down the line on something that's important to the farmers in [my state], and if I lashed out at him over the canal speech I'd get some temporary satisfaction but I'd sure as hell lose his vote on something I really needed later on."

Edward Kennedy also dwelt on the impermanence of animus in the Senate: "I suppose at different times in the political experience that you have conflicts, and you learn soon that those you oppose one day you are going to work with very closely on another. Otherwise, your effectiveness around here is very limited."[1]

To be sure, there are hatred and feuds in abundance in the Senate which surmount the inhibitory effect of the rules and the remarkable capacity of most senators to separate policy disagreements from personal feelings. In most instances, however, the costs of pressing an attack on a colleague to a point where relationships break down completely are extreme. The exhilaration at humbling an adversary may provide some momentary satisfaction, but in a body as compact and specialized as the Senate, today's vanquished foe may be tomorrow's insuperable barrier to legislative success. Grudges are best harbored in the privacy of a Senator's mind and heart. Sustained, public umbrage can be costly. As one former senator recalled in my interview with him,

> It was all very friendly, you know. There's no getting around it. In my twelve years down there there were only two senators that I actively disliked. One of them was Carl Curtis from Nebraska, and the other one was Russell Long. Now mind you, my relationships on the surface with both of them were quite good. I would have been slitting my own throat if I tangled openly with Long. He was Chairman of Finance, so I smiled sweetly.

The rules which stipulate that senators in debate refrain from questioning a colleague's motives or maligning his state do impose a kind of surface civility. Donald Matthews even went so far as to suggest that this folkway of courtesy, which imposes restraint on the

---

[1] Burton Hersh, "The Survival of Edward Kennedy," *The Washingtonian* (February 1979), p. 91.

venom of debate, may even yield a kind of friendship.[2] Certainly, the Senate is a less meanly partisan place than the House. The very force of these formal deterrents against ad hominem attacks causes Senate enmities to seethe and suppurate rather than detonate. The ultimate result may be beneficial, in the sense that imposed civility is at least arguably better than no civility at all. What occurs, in fact, is that the hostility is vented privately, away from the public gaze; it is exchanged in mordant comments on the floor beyond the bearing of the stenographer, in sarcastic asides in the cloakroom and elevators, and in flurries and sallies where it never enters the record. While there are occasional flashes of incandescent public animosity, enmity in the Senate is more likely to take the form of quiet resentment. Reprisal, when it does occur, is visited more often through denial and hindrance rather than overt aggressiveness.

As the sources of Senate friendships are varied, so are the well-springs of hostility. William S. White's assertion in his *Citadel* that "friction is more commonly ideological—and even personal—than partisan" is true only up to a certain point.[3] A few senators simply consider others ideologically repugnant. They deem a colleague's public position to be so wrongheaded and objectionable that they regard him as their negation of their own values. A liberal Democrat perceived a Western Republican as such an unreconstructed reactionary that he declined even to send him the traditional "dear colleague" letter soliciting co-sponsorship of his bills and amendments. He would send out ninety-eight letters: the only two withheld were to himself and the conservative Republican.

It is the thoroughly dogmatized senator who seems to invite hostility by virtue of an intransigence and single-minded devotion to a cause which makes him resistant to accommodation and prompts him to vest in every issue a matter of principle. At an orientation for new senators in 1978, a moderate Republican freshman took a seat next to a newly elected conservative Republican. Anxious to break the ice with some small-talk, the moderate turned to the other new-

---

[2] Donald R. Matthews, *U.S. Senators and Their World* (New York: Vintage Books, 1960), p. 99.

[3] William S. White, *Citadel* (New York: Harper and Bros., 1956), p. 24.

comer and said, "Tell me, why did you decide to run for the Senate?" The conservative freshman turned to his colleague and asserted firmly, "To save America." It would seem on the face of it that anyone with a prescription for saving America would encounter difficulties with the majority of his colleagues, who essay to achieve more modest goals.

It would be a mistake to conclude that ideological commitment in and of itself invites hostility from colleagues. A number of thoroughgoing conservatives in the Senate in recent years have been among the best-liked of all their colleagues, regardless of political coloration. Certainly, no one is as decisively identified with conservative causes than Barry M. Goldwater (R.–Ariz.), yet Goldwater ranks consistently high in the affections of his colleagues of all philosophical stripes (Goldwater's most notorious public spats on the Senate floor were with Republican colleagues numbered among the party's most consistent liberals). Paul Laxalt (R.–Nev.), who has served as a close advisor to Ronald Reagan in his quest for the Republican nomination, is one of the most popular incumbents. A Democrat who clashed with Laxalt on the Panama Canal Treaty said, "Paul conducted himself in a thoroughly decent fashion. I cannot imagine a more worthy adversary." More conservative even than Laxalt is Jesse Helms (R.–N.C.), who has been identified with the effort to bring to the floor of the Senate a constitutional amendment banning abortions. Of Helms's attempts to make the amendment a matter of pending business, a liberal on the Judiciary Committee, who sought to block Helms, said, "Jesse is a courtly Southern gentleman. He did not try to spring any surprises on the liberals. He tipped us off to what he was going to do and allowed us to marshal our forces." Another liberal Democrat had much the same reaction to the conduct of Jake Garn (R.–Utah). "You know where Garn stands. You may not like what he stands for, but you can deal with him. His colleague from Utah is another case entirely."

The colleague who called forth the aspersion was Orrin Hatch (R.–Utah) whose conservatism is a match for that of Garn, but who has not managed to find much favor in the eyes of liberals. The juxtaposition of these two conservatives from the same state underscores what is truly the wild card in all Senate relationships, both friendly and hostile, and that is the individual personality. The final word on interpersonal relationships in the Senate would, perforce, have to take in account psychological factors which are beyond the purview of this book. It may be sufficient to note here that the effect of personality is certainly apparent with the two senators from Utah, whose political characteristics are virtually identical yet who are perceived in such radically different ways by their colleagues.

The doctrinaire senator, because of the rigidity of his views, is more likely to clash with colleagues on issues in which matters of philosophy are involved. Such issues constitute a minority of all legislation; they are often, however, the most important.[4] The conventional wisdom that the Senate cleaves predictably along partisan and ideological lines, even on the important issues, does not always receive the support of the senators themselves. Republican Ralph Flanders's first advice to freshman Democrat William Benton was, "Bill, I've been in the Senate for four years, and I have never yet seen an important issue decided by the Senate on strictly party lines."[5] Flanders is the author of a maxim related to the necessary flexibility of ideological convictions: "The time comes when you have to forget principle and just vote for what is right."[6]

But if there is a dispute between observers and practitioners about the decisiveness of partisanship and ideology in Senate voting, what of the effect of these political traits on interpersonal relationships? Do party and principle by themselves give rise to hostile feelings among senators? In fact, the tolerance on the part of U.S. senators for colleagues holding contrasting views is, and always has been, one of the strengths of the institution. While outsiders often express amazement that ideological opposites—while they may not attract—do not necessarily repel each other, most senators themselves spurn the notion that divergent principles automatically signify hostility. Not a single senator in the twenty-five who were interviewed argued that a colleague's ideology would necessarily cause him to view him with enmity. So while it appears to be the case that shared principles form

[4] John F. Manley, "The Conservative Coalition in Congress," in Lawrence C. Dodd and John Oppenheimer (eds.), *Congress Reconsidered* (New York: Praeger, 1977), p. 88.

[5] Sidney Hyman, *The Lives of William Benton* (Chicago: University of Chicago Press, 1969), p. 416.

[6] Norris Cotton, *In the Senate* (New York: Dodd, Mead & Co., 1978), p. 17.

an important basis for personal attachment, polarity of philosophy alone does not carry with it the seeds of personal detestation. Differences in party affiliation seem to count even less in the manner in which senators deal with one another as people.

In some earlier periods of Senate history partisanship and principle were more insuperable barriers to personal affection, and they engendered, if not bitterness, certainly a distance and remoteness that were often unseemly. New Hampshire senator William Plumer made the following glum notation in his diary in March, 1806 when most of this fellow Federalists absented themselves from the funeral of a Jeffersonian colleague that month.

> The scene was solemn and rendered peculiarly so by the excellency of the music. There was more than 40 carriages. The day was remarkably unfavorable—The wind N.E. cold and rainy. The masons marched near a mile and then fell off. Not more than 20 carriages reached the grave—There was not I think more than 50 members of Congress—Two federalists only besides myself attended. Cursed be the spirit of the party! Its blind baleful malevolent degrading effects ceases not with the grave—This gross *negligence* to the remains of an honest man roused my indignation.[7]

As a remarkable counterpoint to this harshness of partisan and ideological spirit was the experience, forty-five years later, of the passionate Free-Soil senator Charles Sumner who was greeted grandly by the very slave-state senators whose principles he had been elected to challenge.

> They seemed not to hold his antislavery opinions against him after all, many Northerners made antislavery speeches when running for Congress—but welcomed him with gracious cordiality. Before long Sumner had boasted that Pierre Soulé, the extreme state-rights senator from Louisiana, was his best friend in the Senate: "We deeply sympathize and stand firmly together." Soon he was also on excellent terms with Andrew

---

[7] William Plumer, *William Plumer's Memorandum of Proceedings in the United States Senate, 1803–1807*, Everett Somerville Brown (ed.) (New York: Macmillan Co., 1923), pp. 460–461.

Pickens Butler, whose seat adjoined Sumner's. The good-natured South Carolina senator took a fancy to his new colleague and frequently asked him to verify classical quotations he planned to use in his speeches. In his stiff Boston way Sumner grew fond of the old man, with his genial red face and his long silver-white hair standing on end, as though charged with electricity; he condescended to say that, "if he had been a citizen of New England, [Butler] would have been a scholar, or, at least a well-educated man."[8]

It was Butler, of course, who was the object of Sumner's peroration in his "Rape of Kansas" speech—the ad hominem diatribe that ended with Sumner being assaulted by Preston Brooks. It was the truculent and highly personal nature of Sumner's speech which precipitated the attack. The Southerners had become inured to fiery anti-slavery rhetoric, and it is possible that Sumner might have remained on good terms with them even while continuing to make the welkin ring with abolitionist oratory; but the violence of his denunciation brought about a hostility that divergence of principles by themselves might not have occasioned.

Illinois senator Lyman Trumbull, who yielded to Sumner in his opposition to slavery only in the manner in which his views were expressed, reacted to the attack on Sumner in a very restrained fashion.

He made no speech attacking Brooks and the South but merely expressed his satisfaction when Brooks sent in a meaningless letter of "apology." Trumbull's restraint was undoubtedly motivated by the extremely provocative nature of Sumner's "Rape of Kansas" speech and even more by the fact that he entertained warm feelings of regard and gratitude to Senator Butler of South Carolina, a particular object of Sumner's assault. Butler befriended Trumbull when he entered the Senate and recommended his seating on behalf of the Senate Judiciary Committee.[9]

---

[8] David Donald, *Charles Sumner and the Coming of the Civil War* (New York: Alfred A. Knopf, 1960), p. 209.

[9] Mark M. Krug, *Lyman Trumbull, Conservative Radical* (New York: A. S. Barnes and Co., 1965), p. 126.

Trumbull, a man who shunned demagoguery even in the anti-slavery cause—his feelings on slavery were intense—had developed with Butler an institutional kinship that coexisted with their mutually antagonistic positions on policy. In contrast, Trumbull's relations with his Illinois colleague Stephen A. Douglas—whose principles, although not close to Trumbull's, more nearly resembled his than Butler's—were chronically hostile. When Douglas was defending his seat in 1858 against Abraham Lincoln, Trumbull campaigned vigorously against his colleague, despite efforts made to secure his neutrality. He accused Douglas of "deceit" and "fraud" and Douglas retaliated by branding his colleague as "the miserable craven-hearted wretch [who] would rather have both ears cut off than use that language in my presence where I could call him to account."[10]

If there were any strong association linking partisanship and ideology with personal hostility, it was not in evidence in the relationship between New Hampshire Republican William E. Chandler and Benjamin R. "Pitchfork" Tillman, a South Carolina Democrat, in the post-Civil War years. While not a consistently strong supporter of civil rights for blacks, Chandler's anti-slavery credentials dated back to 1856. Tillman, on the other hand, was identified with the coarsest and most brutal forms of racism. On other issues as well, Chandler and Tillman stood poles apart. Yet the Chandler-Tillman friendship was far more intimate than an institutional kinship. What evolved between the two was an enduring extramural social friendship. The warmth of this friendship between political enemies and the fact that Tillman was more attracted personally to the New Hampshireman than to his own Southern colleagues was expressed in a letter Tillman sent to Chandler when the latter was considering retirement from the Senate. It is a testament to the fact that personal animus need not flow from political or philosophical antagonism between senators and, conversely, that agreement need not be associated with personal amity.

> You have made a fast friend of my wife and she is a firm believer in your integrity of purpose and patriotism. I am very much of her way of thinking, but your backsliding under pres-

[10] Robert W. Johannsen, *Stephen A. Douglas* (New York: Oxford University Press, 1973), p. 675.

sure and your evident purpose to be a Republican, though you repudiate most of the party's recent iniquities, cause me to have serious doubts at times. Anyhow, I like you better than any of my Northern colleagues and you have noticed that, barring Bacon, [Augustus Octavius Bacon, a Georgia Democrat] I have little to do with Southern senators. The Senate improves upon acquaintance and contains many honest and good men, but there is a sad lack of broad, liberal and independent thinkers on both sides. I want you to give up any thought of retiring from the Senate. Strange as it may seem, I would consider it a public calamity to have you do so at this crisis, even to be succeeded by a Democrat. . . . I am becoming sufficiently civilized under your admonitions to allow others to differ with me without quarreling. The Senate is a good school to unlearn dogmatism or rather, extract it out of a man's composition.[11]

The weak association between partisan and ideological differences and personal antagonism makes friendships of the institutional kinship variety a common feature of the Senate. It enabled Sen. Clyde Hoey, a North Carolina Democrat who embodied all of the "Old South" traits, to throw his prestige behind the reelection bid of his earnest, intense, intellectual, and liberal colleague Frank Graham. It enabled Alabama Democrat Lister Hill to cross a regional and philosophical divide to escort the newly elected Hubert Humphrey to be sworn in as a senator when he was shunned by most of his fellow liberals. This kind of thing was not a preeminently Southern gesture; it was Vermont Republican Ralph Flanders who saved Connecticut's liberal Democrat William Benton from the ignominy of having no one assist him in his induction into the Senate, and it permitted Philip Hart to praise James O. Eastland for his fairness in executing the duties of the chairman of the Judiciary Committee. Nor do differences in political characteristics interfere with the establishment of bipartisan or transideological alliances where political collaboration is complemented by warm personal regard. Accordingly, Everett M. Dirksen, the conservative Illinoisan, could support liberal California

[11] Quoted in Leon Burr Richardson, *William E. Chandler, Republican* (New York: Charles Scribner & Sons, 1930), pp. 541–542.

Republican Thomas Kuchel for the post of Minority Whip with the help of one of Joseph McCarthy's old backers, Styles Bridges of New Hampshire, and then defend Kuchel in 1965 when two senators from Dirksen's own region and wing of the party, Mundt of North Dakota and Curtis of Nebraska, attempted to strip him of the post. Whatever pragmatic political value attached to having a liberal spokesman as Deputy Minority Leader, Dirksen actually liked Kuchel, and when he put out the word that an effort by conservatives to unseat the Californian would be intolerable, the challenge was quickly dropped. The Lyndon Johnson-Hubert Humphrey alliance was one that prospered despite substantial political dissimilarities, and was in the deepest sense based upon genuine personal liking.

What may set apart the likeable ideologue from the senator whose intensity of philosophical conviction earns enemies is the manner in which his convictions are expressed, the degree to which he is tolerant of opposing views, and a disposition to conciliate adversaries and distinguish between political disagreement and personal animus. The less dogmatized senator will also avoid making every issue a matter of philosophical gravity. In the 95th Congress Orrin Hatch held up a State Department authorization bill with tactics which caused one colleague to say of him, "He is both arrogant and ignorant." Another colleague was reported to have chided Hatch on this occasion, admonishing him to the effect that "if you want to get anywhere in this place, you've got to stop this sort of nonsense."

What causes the Paul Laxalts, Jake Garns, and Barry Goldwaters to retain their popularity with liberals and the Gaylord Nelsons, Daniel Inouyes, and Charles Mathiases to be held in warm regard by conservatives is the nature of their personalities. Similarly, this factor plays a role in the embittered colleague-relationships suffered by such strong liberals as Mike Gravel (D.–Alaska) and John Durkin (D.–N.H.), on the one hand, and such a strong conservative as Hatch on the other.

While it is true that the doctrinaire senator by the very intensity of his convictions is at greater risk of clashing with colleagues who may not see issues in his stark and contrasting terms, the aspect of personality can either mitigate or exacerbate the asperity of these clashes. But even in cases of senators who do not hold to a more or less consistent ideological position, the effects of individual personality are clearly observable. Indeed, in the case of many Senate moderates, it is their very compulsion to straddle the political middle which often earns them the enmity of colleagues. Time and again in interviews the same names were offered as examples of senators capable of eliciting antagonism from colleagues. A number of these senators who could not be accused of holding consistently strong views were characterized by the adjectives "egotistical," "overbearing," "arrogant," and "inconsiderate." To distinguish oneself with these qualities in so individualistic and competitive a body as the Senate is a badge of distinction.

A Southern senator's staff member supplied an example of ruffled feelings which the behavior of one of these senators tends to produce on a fairly regular basis.

> All the members are up to their eyeballs in work. Committee meetings conflict with other committee meetings and they move from one to the other. Everybody understands that. Mostly, they come in and get a quick briefing from their staff member or from a colleague. They listen for a while and maybe ask a few questions of a witness. Percy [Charles H. Percy, R.–Ill.] comes in like gangbusters.

> One day my boss was chairing a subcommittee meeting and there was a witness from Illinois. Percy marched in, and before he even got to his seat he was demanding recognition and interrupting and saying how busy he was and asking the witness questions about how this proposal would affect Illinois, and then he just breezed out. It made my boss look unimportant, and he really resented it.

A Congressional correspondent for a major metropolitan daily newspaper tried to interpret the ill-feelings often harbored for Massachusetts Republican Edward Brooke.

> He's a trimmer, a sharpshooter. He's always got his finger up to the wind. Not only that, he's insufferably pompous. A lot of his colleagues feel like they're being used as bit players while he takes the starring role.

The twenty-five senators we surveyed were asked to identify those personal traits in a colleague which would be most likely to cause them to clash with him. Their responses indicated five general categories of undesirable personal qualities. Most prominent among these negative personality traits was inconstancy: not keeping one's word, being so vulnerable to opportunism as to back off from pledges, having no fixed set of principles, or habitually holding one's finger up to the political winds—as one Democrat put it, "being as nervous as a Christmas goose on every vote and ready to cave in at the first hint that somebody at home is unhappy with him." Such colleagues are considered unreliable. Their mercurial qualities place in jeopardy those who have reposed faith in them. They are the "trimmers" who cannot be counted on to honor a pledge.

The second most commonly mentioned of the negative personality traits is an arrogant and truculent manner. It was here that many of the senators interviewed entered their denial that ideological differences alone would cause them to regard a colleague as a foe. They argue that the forceful expression of an ideology they do not share causes them no problems, but that the same views asserted bumptiously or dogmatically would cause them to recoil from a colleague. The dissonant opinion is tolerated, even admired on occasion; the bellicose tirade invites both contempt and hostility irrespective of the nature of the views expressed.

The third trait which aroused the ire of the senators interviewed was rigidity. Here again, there was ample allowance for the ideologue, but not for the thoroughly dogmatized senator whose positions allow no room for compromise. He is, in the words of a New England Democrat, "a person who's so fixed in his own point of view that he becomes unrelenting, uncompromising—he thinks he knows it all."

The fourth of the negative qualities which call forth feelings of hostility and resentment is sycophancy, apple-polishing, and ingratiating one's self with the leadership. A staff member to a Republican senator recalled that one of his boss's GOP colleagues had put in an unusual appearance at the Prayer Breakfast; "He never goes over there, but he'd heard that [Minority Leader] Howard Baker was leading the discussion that day and wanted Baker to see that he was one of the boys." A liberal Democrat observed, "There's a certain percentage of people here that try to ingratiate themselves with what they perceive to be the power structure, to apple-shine, or ass-kiss; who'll sell their souls for a trip to Europe or will try to look the part of what they regard as the power-centers."

The fifth undesirable characteristic was self-centeredness and lack of reciprocity—the advancing of one's own needs to the total exclusion of the needs or feelings of colleagues. It was summed up by a Democrat who said, "There are some people around here who never hesitate to run around and expect the institution and the individuals in it to turn themselves inside out to help them with their 'problems,' and then don't recognize that it's a two-way street."

The Senate, of course, is not unique in having in its midst individuals whose personality characteristics invite personal enmity.

> Such persons are to be found in almost every group. Either through a lack of social awareness or selfish desire to dominate, they impose on the tolerance and good nature of their associates until all who know them shun them if possible. Eventually they find that they have forfeited the pleasant social relationships which might have been theirs."[12]

There are sources of interpersonal strife among U.S. senators which cannot be satisfactorily ascribed either to ideology or personality, or to a combination of the two, for in the absence of a triggering mechanism—a structural or situational point of abrasive contact—two senators, irrespective of their ideological differences or incompatible personal qualities, may never have the occasion to clash. To recognize the existence of these institutional sore spots is also to take account of the fact that conflict and enmity can arise between senators whose agreement on principles is virtually perfect and who possess few or none of the negative personal qualities deemed to generate animosity. Grudges and feuds of the most enduring and corrosive intensity can occur among senators who are esteemed for their moderation, disposition to be conciliatory, avoidance of demagoguery, adherence to principle, and possession of an ego not vastly more inflated than that of their colleagues. The opportunist, the arrogant egotist, the toady, and the rigid ideologue may well earn the contempt of their colleagues, but the existence of interpersonal antipathy in the Senate is not restricted to senators who share their peculiarities. The most admirable members of the Senate have

---

[12] Margaret Mary Woods, *Paths of Loneliness* (New York: Columbia University Press, 1953), p. 159.

engaged in feuding. The sources of some bad blood are inherent to the nature of legislative politics; others arise from the structure and organization of the Senate and still others from the needs which inhere in one's conception of what it means to be a U.S. senator. While not dismissing the force of failings of personality, there is a political context in which all senators—noblemen or knaves—are suffered to exist and in which are found sources of conflict affecting all.

In some instances these points of conflict serve to exacerbate preexisting tensions arising from other sources, converting coolness into outright disaffection. In other cases they can overwhelm a formerly friendly association and leave a residue of personal acrimony that future political cooperation may be insufficient to heal. In terms of the classic formulation of the frustration-aggression model as the source of hostility,[13] enmity inheres not necessarily in the characteristics of an individual but in events or conditions which block or threaten the achievement of goals. Aggression is usually directed at an individual, but without a frustrating situation in which aggression is expressed, active hostility may never result.

For all of its specializations, the compartmentalization of the Senate is not always neat. The question of which committee will have jurisdiction over a particular class of legislation is one containing the seeds of great discord between chairmen of standing committees. This is particularly true of "big ticket items": new or important areas of legislative activity. For example, the creation of a new executive branch bureaucracy raises the question of which committee will supervise its activities, hold hearings on the confirmation of its leaders nominated by the President, be responsible for passing its authorization bills on, and overseeing it once it has been established. A new bureaucracy in the domain of a chairman brings with it a built-in external constituency of interest groups capable of mobilization, and legions of civil servants who can be a chairman's footsoldiers within the executive branch. It sets up a special relationship between the chairman and the President and provides an estimable national forum for the chairman's ambitions. The stakes are exceedingly high

---

13 See John Dollard, L. Doob, N. Miller, Q. Mowrer, and R. Sears, *Frustration and Aggression* (New Haven: Yale University Press, 1939).

in such situations, and the uncertainties surrounding them are calculated to produce great anxiety and suspicion among rival claimants. Their personal relationships can be affected for years to come.

In the late 1960s, when concern over environmental problems became acute, Sen. Henry M. Jackson (D.–Wash.), chairman of the Senate Interior Committee, threw his support behind the National Environmental Policy Act. At the same time, Edmund S. Muskie (D.–Me.), chairman of the Subcommittee on Air and Water Pollution of the Public Works Committee had introduced a bill to control water pollution. What was at stake with these two overlapping measures was nothing less than a determination of which of the two committees—or, more pointedly, which of the two chairmen—would have custody over this virgin legislative territory in the future.

When the House passed a somewhat different version of the Jackson's bill, Muskie vowed to block action by the House-Senate conference committee, because he saw in Jackson's bill not only an effort to preempt a legislative area more properly his but a shift of power away from the Eastern-oriented Public Works Committee to the Western-oriented Interior Committee. Jackson's position was that he had pulled no surprises and that Muskie had had ample opportunity to testify against the bill in the Senate and was now acting the role of spoiler at the penultimate legislative stage. Muskie's position was that Jackson was staging a naked power grab. Jackson resolved to play the conciliator, and phoned Muskie in order to head off a crisis in the conference. The two Senate chieftains—the earnest and understated Jackson and the brilliant and tempestuous Muskie—did battle over the phone; Jackson ended by hanging up on Muskie in mid-tirade. Jackson, whose stake in a bill which had already passed both houses was higher than Muskie's—whose tactic was essentially one of denial—pressed the attack by visiting Muskie in the latter's office, and another quarrel ensued. But ultimately a compromise was worked out. The incident left a residue of great ill-will between the two men, which was, if anything, exacerbated by their rivalry for the 1972 Democratic nomination.[14]

---

[14] William W. Prochnau and Richard W. Larsen, *A Certain Democrat: Senator Henry M. Jackson* (Englewood Cliffs, N.J.: Prentice-Hall, 1972), pp. 276–277; see also Theo Lippman, Jr. and Donald C. Hansen, *Muskie* (New York: W. W. Norton & Co., 1971), pp. 151–152.

Muskie had been involved in another jurisdictional battle two years before his affray with Jackson. This situation, in 1967, was the reverse of the battle over the National Environmental Policy Act; here Muskie was depicted as the power-grabber by the amiable Fred Harris (D.–Okla.). Harris at the time chaired the Research Subcommittee of Governmental Operations. Muskie had commissioned a staff report on the possibility of creating a new select committee on environment and technology, and hoped to get the endorsement of the full Governmental Operations Committee. When the committee met to vote on the Muskie proposal it was challenged by Harris on the grounds that the new select committee would infringe on the subject matter of the research subcommittee. Muskie considered Harris's objections to be selfish. A bitter clash ensued, which Harris described as the worst battle between two senators that he had ever witnessed, let alone participated in. In this case, as in the previous one, a compromise was ultimately effected.[15]

Despite efforts over the years to delineate the boundaries of committee jurisdiction, it is at least theoretically possible for virtually any issue, aside from an appropriation, to precipitate a border war. The egos of committee and subcommittee chairmen are tied to the breadth of subject matter which falls within their domains, and the bidding for custody of these issues can be both lively and bitter. Jurisdictional problems, despite the best efforts of those involved to minimize conflict between chairmen and the passage of legislative reorganization acts, have remained one of those areas of uncertainty where savage rivalries still erupt and create hard feelings.

While jurisdictional fights can be viewed as outgrowths of flaws in the rules of the Senate which can at least arguably be remedied by more tightly written regulations, no amount of reform can deal with legislative larceny, the problem of one senator commandeering the pet issue or bill of another. When one senator develops an issue, attempts to become identified with it for its political value, introduces it, and then for a variety of reasons sees it die in committee, perish on the floor, or be deleted in conference, the question arises

---

[15] William W. Prochnau and Richard W. Larsen, op. cit.; Teo Lippman, Jr. and Donald C. Hanson, op. cit.

whether or not the original sponsor has established a proprietary interest in it or whether it is now up for grabs. If the measure is a politically attractive one, its championing by a more effective senator may bring about its passage at a later session. But the prestige and labor invested in the bill by the original sponsor are embodied in the measure, and, although he desires passage, he also wants it to bear his name.

In 1971 Gaylord Nelson introduced a bill to impose stricter control on the manner in which the pharmaceutical industry tests new drugs, advertises them to physicians, and markets them. The bill attracted little notice—a fact made evident when the chief counsel of the Pharmaceutical Manufacturers Association admitted that he had not even taken the time to read it. The indifferent reception accorded Nelson's bill may be attributed to the casual and easygoing manner in which Nelson operates; he is not among the most aggressive headline-grabbers in the Senate. No action was taken on Nelson's bill in the 92nd Congress, but he persisted and introduced it early in the 93rd.

At the time that Nelson reintroduced the drug bill, Edward M. Kennedy was holding hearings, as Chairman of the Health Subcommittee of Labor and Public Welfare, on the subject of the use of human subjects in scientific experiments. The bearings piqued his interest in the procedures used in testing drugs, and he asked a member of the subcommittee staff to prepare a bill. The bill bore an uncanny resemblance to the Nelson bill. One observer characterized Kennedy's actions on the measure thus:

> Kennedy just stole that. Just stole it. Poor Gaylord worked on that for six years, holding the most important drug-industry hearing ever, more informative than the old Kefauver hearings. He wrote his bill and Kennedy just took it as his own, without hardly changing a line, a word, and put his own name on it. He's always doing that, and he always does it to the people he ought to be considerate of—the liberals like Mondale and Cranston and Nelson.[16]

---

[16] Quoted in Theo Lippman, Jr., *Senator Ted Kennedy* (New York: W. W. Norton & Co., 1976), pp. 233–234.

Kennedy's gesture to Nelson was to offer the bill back to him for his cosponsorship. Nelson refused to accept Kennedy's explanation that his actions were in conformity with custom and began to berate the Massachusetts senator, flourishing in his face a copy of a home-state newspaper which had characterized Nelson as ineffective. Nelson argued that he had been on the threshold of success with his own bill and that Kennedy was trying to take his bill away. Kennedy's rejoinder was that he wanted to arrive at a compromise with Nelson. Nelson denied that that was Kennedy's intent at all. Kennedy, his motives being challenged, lost his temper, and the two senators began raging at each other. The subcommittee later held hearings on both bills,[17] but the hurt feelings of both men did not mend easily.

On most issues on which a senator must vote his personal prestige or political survival is not at stake. To make a vote a test of one's own reputation, a risky proposition, is rather unusual. With most voting decisions based upon factors other than the esteem for or popularity of a measure's sponsor, senators are generally free to vote their constituency, their ideology, or the specific merits of the case. Even in those instances in which a senator becomes identified personally with a piece of legislation or a nomination, the senatorial proclivity for segregating personal feelings from political judgements makes it superfluous for any senator to have to explain or defend a vote. From time to time, however, measures are presented which bear the indelible imprint of a particular senator's inspiration or authorship and which are of great political or personal importance to the originator.

At the beginning of this century, Sen. John T. Morgan of Alabama became the personal embodiment of the crusade for a transoceanic canal through Nicaragua, and passionately opposed the Panama route. So identified with the Nicaraguan route was Morgan that many of his colleagues feared for his life when the Panama site was chosen.[18]

---

[17] Ibid.

[18] Shelby M. Cullom, *Fifty Years of Public Service* (Chicago: A. C. McClug & Co., 1911), op. cit., p. 350.

In modern times, Edward Kennedy made the nomination of Francis X. Morrissey to the federal bench a test of personal loyalty to him; this test was administered rigorously to those senators who had voted with him most consistently or were part of his social circle. It is, however, in the interest of individual senators to avoid having issues cast in such starkly personal terms. The author or supporter of a measure will usually prudently refrain from making a vote a personal referendum, for it places his colleagues in the uncomfortable position, in the event that they choose to oppose it, of administering a personal rebuff or of going along with a measure on which they have reservations, in the interests of good relations. When a senator chooses to identify himself so completely with a measure and a friendly colleague finds himself unable to render support, the explanation that support would be unpalatable to constituent groups or hostile to his own state interests is usually sufficient to excuse his negative vote. Similarly, if a senator has been publicly identified with a particular position on an issue, he will be extremely reluctant to retreat from that position even in the face of a personal plea from a colleague to whom he is deeply attached. In such cases it is usually sufficient to argue the force majeure of one's public identification with a position, the needs of the home state, or the pressure of politically important interest groups.

Senators are often willing to entertain pleas for support on matters of personal importance from colleagues to whom they are favorably disposed. If compliance with the appeal would result in political problems for the senator, the supplicant usually accepts the refusal with good grace. This was a situation of a Midwestern Democrat when confronted by an appeal from another Democrat whom he counted among his closest Senate friends:

> I think to a certain extent you try to accommodate someone on a vote if it's very important to them or their state. I think, though, that will usually take you only so far. If you're sensitive to the fact that someone couldn't do it politically, or it involves the violation of a matter of principle, you'd probably never ask him. But certainly one would make a fly-by to tell him that this is important to you, and, whether it's a flood-wall or a dam, he would obviously try to be sensitive to something

that he could help you with. But you've got to qualify that in very important ways.

I know, for example, the case of X——. I've been very interested in the standardization of equipment in the military in Europe, and I've been active in the Senate Armed Services Committee with certain amendments that will further the objective of standardization. Now what this means is that some weapons for the U.S. troops in Europe would have to be purchased from European manufacturers.

Now a couple of years ago there was the question of whether the United States would buy a Belgian machine-gun. Well, it happened that a [U.S.] company wanted the contract and it was important to Senator X——, a man I like and respect a great deal, and the factory was in that state. Well I was allied with the other side and had written letters to the Pentagon urging them to buy the guns in Europe, and it was very difficult when he came to me and I had to turn him down. But he was able to accept that.

Problems of this nature are not always solved so amicably. When personal identification with a bill is high, as when a senator is up for reelection and must demonstrate that he can produce for his state, or when he has invested his personal prestige in the confirmation of a nominee, he may be less disposed to accept with grace the opposition of a colleague.

In 1969 the Senate had voted to support an appropriation to develop the 1,800 mile-per-hour supersonic transport (SST). Throughout much of the following year environmental groups lobbied strenuously to deny further funds for the plane's development, on the grounds that it would be harmful to the upper atmosphere. Many liberals also opposed it on the grounds that its development represented an unwarranted diversion of federal money away from more socially worthy projects. For Washington state's two Democratic senators, Henry Jackson and Warren Magnuson, the SST project promised a major infusion of jobs and money into the Seattle area, where the prime contractor, the Boeing Corporation, was located.

Before the intensive lobbying by environmental groups, a number of Jackson's and Magnuson's liberal allies had supported the SST. By late 1970 the picture had changed drastically, and the liberals—several of whom had presidential ambitions for 1972 and were anxious to develop support among environmental groups—began to shy away from the SST. Others were feeling pressure from minority groups in their states who saw the supersonic plane as a profligate expenditure. Knowing that many liberal votes were slipping away from them, Jackson and Magnuson, through a combination of pleas and threats of blocking certain senators' pet bills, fell back on the position of asking their old allies to at least absent themselves from the SST vote if they could not support it.

Jackson had reportedly secured a promise from Mondale that the Minnesotan would be discreetly absent when the vote came up but a call later to Mondale by Jackson revealed that the deal had been canceled. Jackson then threatened to bottle up a Mondale bill creating a national park in Minnesota; the two senators battled over the phone, and Jackson ended up by hanging up on Mondale. Jackson's relations with cost-conscious liberals like Wisconsin's Proxmire were already in shambles over the latter's leadership of the anti-SST forces, but he had hoped to secure at least the absence of Missouri's Stuart Symington and Edward Kennedy. Jackson had supported Kennedy in his effort to wrest the job of Majority Whip from Russell Long, and saw Kennedy's ultimately negative vote as an act of ingratitude.[19]

The importance of the SST to Jackson and Magnuson and the disappointment they experienced in losing the battle colored their relationships with colleagues for years. Proxmire's zeal in leading the opposition earned him the active enmity of both Washington senators. For the liberal defectors who went on record against the SST there was a great estrangement and resentment. In the case of Kennedy, the vote on the SST cost him the support of both Jackson and Magnuson in his unsuccessful effort to retain the post of whip in 1971. When Kennedy went to Jackson's office early in January 1971 to enlist his support against Byrd, Jackson told him directly that he was supporting Byrd and that the SST vote was the reason.[20]

[19] William W. Pronchnau and Richard W. Larsen, op. cit., p . 123.

[20] Theo Lippman, Jr., op. cit., p. 123.

When a senator takes a leading role in blocking a colleague's cherished measure, the ill-feeling that ensues usually dwarfs the hostility that is associated with a simple denial of a vote or refusal to "take a walk." The prominent role taken by J. William Fulbright (D.–Ark.) in blocking the depressed-areas bill of Paul Douglas (D.–Ill.) in 1957 caused a permanent breach between two senators who had worked closely together to expose corruption in the Reconstruction Finance Corporation. The principles of this particular issue were not even in dispute between the men; Fulbright had long been an advocate of aid to depressed areas. What engendered his opposition was that the measure was directed at small towns rather than rural areas in general. Douglas, who had been shocked by the decline of small towns in southern Illinois, felt that these communities should be the appropriate focus of depressed-area assistance, but modified his bill to include farming counties in the hope of winning the support of the Arkansas Senator (chairman of the Banking and Currency Committee to which Douglas' bill had been referred). This was a bill about which Douglas felt passionately, and he made these changes only with the greatest reluctance, in the hope that they would find favor with Fulbright.

> If I had hoped to win over Fulbright by this tactic, I was grievously mistaken. He continued to be implacable in his opposition, and it was obvious that I would never get the bill out of the subcommittee. I then executed a flanking maneuver. . . . I moved to take the bill from the subcommittee and have it passed on by the committee as a whole. . . . Fulbright tried to rule my motion out of order. Defying him, I got it put to a vote, which we carried. We then moved to have it favorably reported, and this was ultimately done. . . .

> During the discussion, Fulbright and I became very angry with each other, and both of us used rough language. Some reporters said that our epithets were unprecedented. . . . I remember that I called him "a deep freeze artist," while he made scathing references to my origins and beliefs. The encounter colored our relationships ever afterward. From time to time, we would meet, shake hands, and agree to bury the hatchet, but neither of us could forget what had happened,

and our subsequent dealings with each other were governed by wary neutrality.[21]

New Hampshire Republican Norris Cotton, an admirer of Majority Leader Lyndon B. Johnson, ascribed part of Johnson's influence with his colleagues to a principle which, according to Cotton, Johnson adhered to scrupulously.

> Lyndon Johnson loved the Senate and had a soft spot in his heart for every one of his colleagues. As proof of this, he would not go into any state and actively campaign for candidates who were running against any sitting senator with whom he had served, including Republicans. This is a policy he followed as leader of the Senate . . . and no persuasion from the Democratic National Committee or anybody else would move him.[22]

It may be an exercise in hairsplitting to question Cotton's fond recollection of Johnson, but in one violation of this principle—by no means a technical violation—a Johnson incursion left great bitterness in its wake. It occurred during the 1958 general elections in Utah, when Republican incumbent Arthur V. Watkins faced a challenge, not only from Democrat Frank Moss, but from a conservative independent, J. Bracken Lee. Watkins had drawn public praise from Johnson for his conduct of the committee which had reported out censure resolutions against Joseph R. McCarthy, and was using these endorsements in his reelection campaign. Johnson, however, had seen polls indicating that Moss was likely to overtake Watkins and entered the state at the last minute on behalf of the challenger. He praised Moss effusively, and when questioned about his prior testimonials on behalf of Watkins, responded, "The G.O.P. candidate must be desperate to use a letter of recommendation from the Majority Senate Leader as a reason why he should be elected. I am sure that voters will not get the impression that a Majority Democratic Senate Leader wants a Republican returned." Watkins, in defeat, was resentful and

---

[21] Paul H. Douglas, *In the Fullness of Time* (New York: Harcourt Brace Jovanovich, 1972), p. 517.

[22] Norris Cotton, op. cit., pp. 153–154.

puzzled as to how a colleague who had praised him could turn upon him so unexpectedly.[23]

Clearly—Cotton's depiction of the Johnson principle notwithstanding—it was not an inflexible rule. While it is true that Johnson "neglected" to campaign against such Republican allies as Everett M. Dirksen, he perceived Watkins as a loser and was more anxious to build up credits with a likely new colleague than to be consistent on behalf of a man doomed to defeat. But in general, self-interest more than anything else has dictated to many senators over the years that they avoid campaigning against a colleague in his own state. Whatever the value of augmenting the number of one's own partisans in the Senate, a tried and true member of the opposition party is often more useful in terms of achieving legislative goals than an unknown newcomer, even one of the same political persuasion. When pressured between partisan loyalty and pragmatic considerations internal to the Senate, some senators adopt a middle position of putting in a token appearance on behalf of a colleague's challenger of their own party, but make only a pro forma testimonial on his behalf. This usually consists of extolling the virtues of the challenger while making no negative references to the incumbent, or even not mentioning him at all.

The political value of endorsements by outsiders is a matter of debate, but the appearance on behalf of a colleague by a well-known senator is eagerly sought by those who wish to retain a Senate seat. Such endorsements confer stature on the candidate and provide the visitor with important credits that he can draw upon if the incumbent wins. Generally, senators prefer to avoid involvement in primary contests in which a colleague is being challenged, but if they do join in, it is more typically on behalf of the incumbent than the challenger. A ringing endorsement by a senator of a colleague's primary opponent is difficult to excuse by invoking partisan loyalty and comes much closer to a personal rebuff. Floor leaders and members of senatorial campaign committees have generally made it a practice to avoid siding overtly with either incumbent or challenger in a primary struggle, but covert intervention does take place.

[23] Arthur V. Watkins, *Enough Rope* (Englewood Cliffs, N.J.: Prentice-Hall, 1969), pp. 175–177.

Everett M. Dirksen, the Republican Minority Leader, would on occasion, transgress this rule to solidify his own grasp on the Republican leadership. In 1958, Dirksen went to North Dakota to assist incumbent Senator William Langer in a primary election. The primary coincided with a challenge to Dirksen's leadership from a group of liberal Republicans in the Senate led by John Sherman Cooper of Kentucky. Langer fended off the challenge, and when the Republican caucus met early in 1959 to choose its leadership, Langer took a seat next to the Illinois Republican and, with a flourish, wrote on his ballot in capital letters, "Dirksen." Everett Dirksen also had given clandestine support to Sen. J. Glenn Beall, Sr., in a primary contest in Maryland. When the votes for the leadership post were tallied, Beall's ballot was also marked with Dirksen's name.[24]

Intervention on a colleague's behalf in a primary can reap dividends; the conspicuous endorsement of his primary opponent is deemed an unfriendly act. When Democrat Eugene McCarthy came into the state of Washington to endorse Democrat Henry Jackson's primary election opponent, both the fact and the manner of this appearance added a bitter personal dimension to an old political feud. The enmity between McCarthy and Jackson antedated the 1970 campaign, but McCarthy's advocacy of Jackson's primary opponent went beyond the bounds which normally characterize even hostile relationships between two senators differing on policy. Recalling Jackson's opposition to him in the 1968 campaign, McCarthy went on the road vowing to "help the people who went out of their way to help me and . . . hurt the ones who went out of their way to hurt me." In a speech in Seattle, McCarthy chided Jackson for not feeling secure unless "the sky was black with strategic bombers . . . [and] there were so many nuclear submarines in the ocean that they were running into each other."[25]

Although the McCarthy-Jackson feud—which came about as the result of fundamental differences over policy—did not find its first expression in the 1970 campaign, the bitterness was intensified then

---

[24] Neil MacNeil, *Dirksen: Portrait of a Public Man* (New York and Cleveland: World Publishing Co., 1970), pp. 163–164.

[25] Quoted in Albert Eisele, *Almost to the Presidency* (Blue Earth, Minn.: Piper Co., 1972), p. 409.

when McCarthy embarked upon a personal crusade against Jackson, personal in much the same manner that Joseph McCarthy's cultivation of a rival to Margaret Chase Smith in Maine in 1954 was the expression of a personal vendetta. Hostile incursions onto a colleague's home turf are sometimes the product of a prior estrangement and sometimes the triggering mechanism. In the above cases, such hostile incursions constitute the ultimate expression of political disagreement which has spilled over into the sphere of personal relationships, since it is no longer the policies which are under attack but the individual in particular. The manner and style of such raids on a colleague's territory is crucial in terms of its impact on future relations between senators. A formal proclamation of the virtues of a colleague's opponent may not be seen as having irrevocably poisoned the relationship. An ad hominem assault on a colleague in his own bailiwick when he is up for reelection can jeopardize a relationship beyond any chance of reconciliation.

A hostile incursion need not be as obvious or blatant as the invasion of Jackson's turf by McCarthy. The most marginal word of encouragement by a senator to one of the contestants in a primary can often cause resentment on the part of the other candidate. Indiana's Democratic senator Birch Bayh had become acquainted with Arkansas congressman David H. Pryor, who challenged Senate Appropriations Committee chairman John L. McClellan for the seat he had held for more than thirty years. Bayh, a member of the powerful committee, had no intention of antagonizing its chairman by making any endorsement of the challenger, but felt that a cautiously worded note of encouragement to Pryor might give some moral support to the popular congressman. The note that Bayh sent contained no endorsement and no hint of criticism of McClellan.

The note was received, but somehow the contents of the message leaked out to an Arkansas newspaper. Since a similar letter was not sent to McClellan, the interpretation of the note in the state was that Bayh was taking sides against a Senate colleague in a primary election. McClellan went on to defeat Pryor in the primary and was reelected to the Senate. On the day on which the new members and reelected senators were sworn in, Bayh encountered McClellan on the Senate subway on his way to the Capitol to be sworn in. The two men took seats next to each other on the subway car, and McClellan turned to Bayh and in a voice dripping with irony said, "Well, Birch, I guess you're a little surprised to have me back in the Senate." Bayh may have suffered a short-run loss, but his "endorsement" was ultimately vindicated when Pryor succeeded McClellan in 1979.

Remaining aloof from the reelection bid of a colleague from the same side of the aisle can often be as damaging as coming in on the side of his challenger, especially if the incumbent covets your endorsement. This might be termed "hostile non-involvement." A classic example of this was the 1952 senatorial campaign in Massachusetts which pitted incumbent Henry Cabot Lodge, Jr. against Congressman John F. Kennedy. The external asset in this campaign was Joseph R. McCarthy, then at the height of his popularity, especially among Irish voters in the Bay State. Lodge, like McCarthy, was a Republican, and appealed to the Wisconsin senator to speak in Boston on his behalf. McCarthy was at a dinner party at the home of columnist William F. Buckley when the call from Lodge's office arrived. He was apparently torn between an endorsement for Lodge—a fellow Republican who had clashed with him over McCarthy's charges of communist influence in the State Department—and his personal fondness for the Kennedy family (although he was by no means personally hostile to Lodge). Knowing that an important source of Lodge's strength was among Harvard people who detested McCarthy, the Wisconsin senator resolved the dilemma by insisting that Lodge make a public appeal for his support. Willing to benefit from McCarthy's appearance but unwilling to suffer from having made a public solicitation of McCarthy's support, Lodge was forced to campaign without him; his ultimate loss has been attributed to McCarthy's absence.[26]

The manner of endorsement as a source of conflict between senators need not involve a hostile incursion from outside the state. The personal relationships between senators from the same state are also profoundly influenced by this question, whether they be of the same or opposing parties. The relationship between Maine's two senators of opposing parties was harmed irreparably when Margaret Chase Smith took particular umbrage at Edmund Muskie's energetic efforts

[26] Victor Lasky, *Robert F. Kennedy: The Myth and the Man* (New York: Trident Press, 1968), p. 70.

on behalf of her challenger. When senators of the same state are members of the same party, however, potential clashes over endorsement tend to shift from the general election to the primary. A senator will not generally meddle in the primary fights of a colleague from the same state who represents the opposing party; in such a case any potential clash is more likely to involve the general election. However, a senator may find it difficult to remain impartial in an intra-party contest when a colleague is being opposed. In states in which the two senators represent different factions of the same party, the senator not up for reelection may involve himself quite actively. This has often been the case in the one-party states of the South, but it is part of the more general paradox commented upon in Chapter 3 that personal relations between senators of the same party and state are often subject to perils which afflict no other category of Senate relationships.

Mississippi, a state which had adopted the primary election in 1903 and in which a victory in the Democratic canvass led to a pro forma ratification by the Democratic legislature (this was before the constitutional provision for direct election of senators was established), saw a particularly bitter example of two colleagues of the same party battling each other. James K. Vardaman and John Sharp Williams were two old political collaborators whose esteem for each other had diminished by the time Vardaman's term was coming to an end in 1918. In the Democratic primary that year, Williams sided openly with Vardaman's challenger, Pat Harrison. Policy differences over the war in Europe divided the two senators, but Williams's two weeks of speeches on Harrison's behalf were thinly veiled philippics against his colleague.

Williams accused Vardaman of being "disloyal," "willful," and "egotistical," and worked behind the scenes as well to insure Harrison's victory. He urged President Woodrow Wilson to fire Vardaman's patronage nominees, and sent Wilson a copy of a local newspaper article in which Vardaman was quoted as having said that Wilson led the country into war at the behest of Wall Street bankers and munitions makers. In the August primary, Vardaman was defeated by Harrison. After his retirement from the Senate Vardaman continued a barrage of criticism of the man who had defeated him, but

> Vardaman reserved his most vicious attacks for John Sharp Williams whom he accused of having sided with the conserv-

ative Republicans throughout his years in Congress and having wrecked himself by excessive drinking: "He is like an old worn-out race horse—you have to use a lot of cocaine and ginger to make him step up."[27]

Occasionally, the hostile incursion in a colleague's own state does not involve campaigning against him, but rather the holding of politically embarrassing hearings in his state when he is running for reelection. This occurred in 1950 when no less a person than the Majority Leader of the Senate was made vulnerable by the decision of a colleague to hold hearings in his state. Estes Kefauver (D.–Tenn.) had resolved to pursue his investigation of political corruption by holding hearings in Chicago, where, he announced, there was evidence of official wrongdoing. The Majority Leader and senator from Illinois, Scott Lucas, saw the hearings, which would occur on the eve of the election, as a threat to his chances of being returned to the Senate. Personally, Lucas had nothing to fear, but it was clear that Kefauver's target was the Cook County Democratic Organization, and any evidence of corruption by Democratic officeholders would be damaging to a Democratic candidate.

Lucas begged Kefauver to postpone the hearings until after the election, but Kefauver refused. Lucas then turned to Clinton Anderson of New Mexico, then chairman of the Democratic campaign committee, and urged him to use his influence to get Kefauver to defer the hearings, but Anderson's intervention failed to sway him. Kefauver held his hearings, incriminated a number of Cook County politicians, and reduced the Democratic majorities in the county which Lucas had counted on for reelection. Lucas went down to defeat at Everett M. Dirksen's hands.[28]

In the case of Lucas, many things led to his defeat by Everett Dirksen: the opposition of the powerful *Chicago Tribune*, reactions to the Korean War, disclosures by the Kefauver Commit-

[27] William F. Holmes, *The White Chief: James Kimble Vardaman* (Baton Rouge: Louisiana State University Press, 1970), pp. 347, 371.

[28] Clinton P. Anderson, *Outsider in the Senate* (New York: World Publishing Co., 1970), p. 107.

tee about corruption in the Democratic stronghold of Chicago. Lucas himself laid his defeat principally to Kefauver.[29]

Lucas never forgave Kefauver for his ill-timed incursion into Illinois. There had been bad blood for some time between President Truman and Kefauver, and Lucas was on the president's side in these controversies, so the potential for strife between Lucas and Kefauver was already great. Kefauver's refusal to reschedule the hearings in Chicago brought the conflict down to a level where political division was converted into personal animosity. Although the political characteristics of Kefauver and Lucas were similar, the former was a maverick and the latter a consistent supporter of the Truman administration. Lucas, moreover, was a social friend of the president's and part of his poker-playing group. Kefauver had determined by 1950 to oppose Truman in the 1952 primaries; when the Tennessean began to enter primaries in 1952, Lucas determined to thwart his presidential hopes by encouraging Connecticut's Democratic senator Brien McMahon to enter the Illinois primary against Kefauver.

The question of colleague endorsements is one which has always bedeviled the interpersonal relationships of U.S. senators. Unless there are overwhelming reasons against it, a modern senator will try to accommodate a colleague who comes to enlist his help in securing reelection. Such a request represents an exchange of assets: the candidate receives the public support of a colleague whose endorsement he sees as useful, and the endorser is able to amass credits which can be applied to both his legislation and campaigns for reelection.

When an endorsement involves less than a visit to the state of the colleague who is up for reelection, there are even fewer obstacles to compliance and thus more resentment when a senator declines to render assistance. Clinton Anderson was enraged at his Democratic colleague John Pastore of Rhode Island when the latter declined to write a letter to Italian-Americans in Anderson's state of New Mexico. According to Anderson, "[Pastore] didn't seem to care too much about anyone but himself. Though he had no real opposition at

---

[29] Sidney Hyman, op. cit., p. 447.

home, I know of no time when he went out of his state to campaign for anyone else.[30]

The changes in campaign finance laws have made the campaign fundraiser a new test of interpersonal relationships among senators. Very often an appearance at such a function need not even involve travel outside of the District of Columbia. Appearing at a colleague's fundraiser is sometimes a test of one senator's personal commitment to another, as well as an opportunity to expand political credits or attract contributors. In the wake of his clash with Charles Percy during the Bert Lance hearings, Thomas Eagleton was said to have sent invitations to some fellow senators inviting them to a Washington fundraiser on his behalf and urging them to come to demonstrate, in effect, that, "Chuck Percy to the contrary, I do have some friends in the Senate."

Donald R. Matthews argued in *U.S. Senators and Their World*[31] that one of the forces which influences a senator's nonconformity to Senate folkways is higher political ambition. "His legislative duties," Matthews wrote, "are likely to be neglected in the ceaseless quest for publicity and personal advancement."[32] Without resuming the argument set forth in Chapter 2 about the putative force or fragility of Senate norms and folkways, the behavior of senators vis-à-vis their colleagues is altered, often for the worse, when visions of the White House come into view. The above-mentioned hostile incursion of Estes Kefauver into Scott Lucas's domain was prompted in large measure by the visibility and recognition that he would achieve by spotlighting the questionable activities of Illinois Democrats. Less spectacularly, the determination to seek the nomination often generates deeply felt resentments no less important for the fact that they never explode into print as public donnybrooks.

Even scholars who uphold the existence of strong norms and folkways in the Senate concede that standards of interpersonal courtesy diminish or disappear altogether when a presidential quest beckons.

[30] Clinton P. Anderson, op. cit., p. 289.

[31] Donald R. Matthews, op. cit., pp. 109–110.

[32] Ibid.

Thus, from 1970–1972, Senator George McGovern of South Dakota, then a contender for the Democratic presidential nomination, and Senator Robert Dole of Kansas, the chairman of the Republican National Committee, engaged in a series of vitriolic remarks on the Senate floor over policy in Vietnam (most of which were expunged before they appeared in the *Congressional Record*).[33]

In the Senate, which has spawned so many presidential aspirants in recent years, conflicts of ambition need not cross party lines. Indeed, at the nominating stage, enormous pressures are often applied by aspirants to the nomination on those colleagues of their own party who represent important primary-election states. There are pressures of endorsement; failing that, there are pressures for help behind the scenes; in the event that that degree of support cannot be attained, there are pressures for a colleague to simply remain neutral. It would not be difficult to imagine the appeals made to New Hampshire's Democratic senator Thomas McIntyre prior to his state's crucial primary election in 1976, when his social friend and neighbor Birch Bayh and his Armed Services Committee colleague Henry Jackson were preparing themselves for campaigns in the early primaries. While it is unusual for an aspirant to get tough with a colleague who declines to offer assistance in a presidential primary in his state, there is a tendency to "call in the chips" and be resentful when they are not forthcoming.

When Minnesota's Hubert Humphrey resolved to enter the Democratic presidential primaries in 1960, he formulated his strategy around the contest in his neighboring state of Wisconsin. Humphrey had worked hard to build a base in Wisconsin. In 1957 he had gone into the state to campaign on behalf of William Proxmire, who was running in a special election to fill the Senate seat left vacant by the death of Joseph McCarthy. When Proxmire came to the Senate, Humphrey intervened on his behalf with Majority Leader Lyndon Johnson to secure favorable assignments for the freshman. Johnson

---

[33] Robert L. Peabody, Norman J. Ornstein, and David W. Rohde, "The United States Senate as a Presidential Incubator: Many Are Called but Few Are Chosen," *Political Science Quarterly*, vol. 91, no. 2 (Summer, 1976), p. 255.

was suspicious of Proxmire, but Humphrey prodded his ally to accommodate the new senator. Three years later, when Humphrey was fighting an uphill battle for the Democratic presidential nomination against John F. Kennedy in the Wisconsin primary, "Proxmire was nowhere to be seen." As Humphrey recollected with bitterness, "He could have given us the kind of help and influence we needed to combat the Kennedy campaign."[34]

Beyond the walls of the Senate chamber—where some rules of civilized debate prevail—senators in competition for the nomination are less constrained from making remarks that cut their rivals close to the bone. In the same Wisconsin primary in 1960, Humphrey, in an exasperated reply to the accusation that the Kennedy campaign was better organized than his, told a Jewish audience in Milwaukee "The most organized thing that ever happened almost destroyed civilization."[35] Making an analogy between the efficiency of the Kennedy campaign and the efficiency of Nazi Germany to a Jewish audience was not the sort of parallel that Humphrey would have drawn had he and Kennedy been in the Senate chamber and not in the heat of Presidential battle.

As the presidential plans of a senator begin to develop, he begins to marshal the resources at his disposal in the Senate and essay a more expanded role for himself. If he is a committee chairman, he may attempt to extract attractive issues from his subcommittees and deal with them at the full committee level. This, of course, is at the expense of subcommittee chairmen. He may even scan the horizon for measures which he can pirate from his colleagues. He becomes acutely aware of the necessity to have his name listed as the sponsor of legislation, and may attempt to broaden the jurisdiction of a committee or subcommittee of which he is chairman. The external attention and approval that he may garner as the result of aggressiveness in pursuit of the presidency may cost him dearly in terms of his per-

---

[34] Hubert H. Humphrey, *The Education of a Public Man* (Garden City, N.Y.: Doubleday & Co., 1976), p. 472n.

[35] Arthur M. Schlesinger, Jr., *Robert Kennedy and His Times* (Boston: Houghton Mifflin Co., 1978), p. 197.

sonal relationships with colleagues—both those who are comfortably senatorial and those who harbor their own presidential ambitions.

In the early days of the 96th Congress, the presidential plans of Sen. Edward M. Kennedy were unclear, but as he took charge of the Judiciary Committee as chairman he began to survey the activities of its subcommittees and to arrogate to the full committee a number of issues which had hitherto been in the province of the subcommittee chairmen. His predecessor, Mississippi's James O. Eastland, had granted the subcommittees considerable latitude and earned from those chairmen—several of whom were liberals—great affection which a more authoritarian chairman would not have gained. Kennedy, in the early days of 1979, was already coming in for criticism in his home-state press and within the Democratic caucus for attempting to usurp the jurisdiction of such subcommittee chairmen as Dennis DeConcini (D.–Ariz.) and Howard Metzenbaum (D.–Ohio).[36]

Squabbling over sponsorship and parentage of certain popular bills is another peril to senatorial amity which presidential ambition tends to ignite. The disputed paternity of a tax-reform bill in 1974 produced a rancorous battle between a number of former, present, and future presidential hopefuls from the ranks of Senate liberals. Early in 1974, Walter F. Mondale declared his intention to introduce legislation to substitute a $200 tax credit in lieu of the personal exemption on the federal income tax. The previous week Kennedy had proposed an amendment to the tax bill to increase the personal exemption. Mondale, who was well along in his testing of the presidential waters, decided to combine his reform efforts with those of Kennedy to produce a compromise amendment suitable to both. A problem quickly emerged over whether the compromise amendment bill would be sponsored by Kennedy or Mondale. Additional ambitious liberals became involved when the Kennedy-Mondale (or Mondale-Kennedy) bill was merged with a more complex measure developed by Birch Bayh, Hubert Humphrey, Edmund Muskie, Philip Hart, and Dick Clark of Iowa; the struggle over authorship became more intense

---

[36] Adam Clymer, "Kennedy Gives Priority to Antitrust Policy and the Criminal Code, " *New York Times*, January 5, 1979.

And civil war broke out over who would put his name on this bill. The usual arguments were advanced: one would work hardest, one would provide most staff, one had done the most work so far—one needed the publicity.[37]

Of the principals involved in the dispute over authorship, only Hart and perhaps Clark were totally innocent of any presidential ambitions. Bayh, who was up for reelection in Indiana and facing a spirited challenge, was given the honor of sponsorship, but parentage ultimately devolved on Humphrey when the rigors of campaigning diverted Bayh's energies.[38]

When Lloyd Bentsen began to explore the possibilities of seeking the Democratic presidential nomination after the 1972 elections, be perceived the need to establish for himself a reputation as someone familiar with urban problems. His claim on expertise in the area of highways was a solid one by virtue of his chairmanship of the Public Works Transportation Subcommittee. Urban mass transit matters, however, had been vested in the Banking Subcommittee on Housing and Urban Affairs, chaired by Harrison A. Williams, Jr., (D.–N.J.) who was at work at the time developing mass transit legislation. Bentsen held a series of hearings in urban areas, and proposed a substitute mass transit bill which encroached substantially on Williams's urban domain.

Whatever conflicts may arise from ambition within the chamber itself, ambition for higher office adds a degree of urgency to a senator's empire-building and can jeopardize long-term relationships should the presidential quest prove unfruitful and the aspirant return to being just another senator.

No Senate practice, with the possible exception of the filibuster, has come in for as much criticism over the years as the seniority system. The more or less mechanistic process whereby chairmanships, ranking minority status, and memberships on the most desirable committees are accorded to senators on the basis of their simply having held their seats longer than others has been depicted as one of the most serious flaws in the institution, although even its most ardent

---

[37] Theo Lippman, Jr., op. cit., pp. 151–152.

[38] Ibid.

detractors concede that one reason it has endured is the lack of any workable alternative.[39] One seldom-cited virtue of the seniority system is the fact that its very automatic nature eliminates struggles for chairmanships, with the ensuing hard feelings that would almost necessarily erupt if such choice positions were the subjects of competition. While interpersonal harmony is not a raison d'être of the Senate, the clashes which would erupt over elective chairmanships would create serious problems at the commencement of each session; the Senate could arguably suffer from a net loss of efficiency as these struggles preoccupy members.

The rancor which often attends the filling of those positions which are elective, such as majority and minority leader, whip, and secretary of the conferences, hints at some of the perils in democratizing the selection process for leadership posts. Senators find themselves involved in what is in effect a personal referendum on a colleague. It is far easier for a senator to discriminate between the merits of a bill introduced by a colleague and his feeling for its sponsor as an individual than it is to separate the role of the leader from the individual qualities of the candidate. A senator approached by a colleague to support a bill he has originated can decline to give his vote by invoking any number of legitimate and well-sanctioned excuses. But when solicited by a claimant for a leadership post, what is at issue is the colleague himself. The candidate leaves himself open for personal rebuff, and the senator whose support is being enlisted finds himself in the position of having to administer that rebuff. It is certainly true that any senator so thin-skinned as to harbor a grudge against a colleague for failure to support him in a leadership contest would probably make a poor leader. Senators who seek these posts usually have a fairly accurate picture of which of their colleagues are and are not likely to lend support. At the early stages of a leadership campaign, moreover, the candidate may not ask for a "yes" or "no" answer but

[39] Joseph S. Clark, Democratic senator from Pennsylvania, was one of the most articulate and tireless Senate reformers. He argued for elective chairmanships, but conceded that if elections did take place there was a strong likelihood that the most senior members of the majority party would be named chairman anyway. See Joseph S. Clark (ed.), *Congressional Reform: Problems and Prospects* (New York: Thomas Y. Crowell Co., 1965), pp. 352–353.

rather for what might be called "contingent support"—a promise that a vote will be delivered in the event that a colleague's first choice for leader has been eliminated from the running. The tentative approach to a colleague may even be as indirect as a request to a fellow member for his advice on the wisdom of seeking the post.[40]

There is another difference in terms of interpersonal contact between solicitation for legislative support and for commitments on leadership votes, and that is that the latter is carried out without staff mediation. On legislative matters there is usually a considerable amount of preliminary negotiation between the staff members of senators before the deal is actually clinched by the principals themselves. In leadership contests it is senator-on-senator.[41]

The subtlety and delicacy of solicitations for support are especially notable when approaches are made to colleagues known to favor another candidate. In the early stages of the 1971 battle over the post of Majority Whip, Robert Byrd, the eventual victor, called a liberal Democrat in the Netherlands, where he was attending a NATO parliamentarians' meeting. Byrd had good reason to believe that the liberal had made another commitment, but pressed his case with flexibility and finesse. As the liberal recalled his impressions of the incident,

> Bobby knew that he wasn't my first choice. He had in my view, a bad history. He was once a Ku Kluxer. I told him I wouldn't support him. As a matter of fact I told him there was no point in challenging Ted [Kennedy]. "Ted's the incumbent," I told him. He said, "Give me a chance to talk to you before you make your decision, you can't say no to that very well." I told him that I was for Fritz Hollings. He came right back and said that he didn't think Fritz had enough support, and if Hollings dropped out would I consider giving him the support? You see, he came to me knowing full well that he wasn't my first choice, but he was all ready with a fall-back position and would have been happy if I'd accept him as my second.

---

[40] Robert L. Peabody, *Leadership in Congress*, (Boston: Little, Brown & Co., 1976), p. 373.

[41] Ibid.

What surrounds these negotiations is an air of uncertainty. A promise can be extracted, but given the human tendency to prefer to believe what is pleasing, a pledge of support may be heard in a manner far more positive than that in which it is uttered. Given the secrecy of the ballot, no one ever knows for certain how the vote actually goes, and educated guesses are subject to a substantial margin of error. Senators who go back on their pledges are unlikely to admit to political infidelity. Even in the case of the most skillful head-counter, some slippage is bound to occur between pledges and actual votes. The gap between perception and reality afflicts senators especially when their colleagues are passing personal judgment on them.

Leadership fights bring to the surface not only new tensions, but also have the capacity to reawaken old enmities. Bad blood has existed between Edward Kennedy and Robert Byrd since the 1960 Democratic presidential primary in West Virginia when Byrd acted as a conduit for aid to Hubert Humphrey from Lyndon Johnson in that contest in which Edward Kennedy's brother had emerged victorious. Their unhappy relationship continued during the period in which Kennedy was whip. Byrd felt that he had been doing all of the diligent work on the floor, while Kennedy had garnered most of the credit. The challenge to Kennedy on Byrd's part was both political and personal.

Similar recriminations were in the air after the 1965 battle for the same post—the struggle which saw Russell Long prevail over John O. Pastore of Rhode Island. Pastore had believed that he would receive important help from Majority Leader Mike Mansfield; when the help was not forthcoming, Pastore blamed Mansfield for his defeat. Robert Griffin, who was ousted from the post of Minority Whip by Howard Baker, was said to have received pledged support from Charles H. Percy of Illinois and Edward Brooke of Massachusetts. In the end, Percy and Brooke allegedly gave their support to Baker, and Griffin was reported to have felt abandoned by these two colleagues on whom he had counted for support.

Despite the rules and conventions which dictate that floor speeches be free of personal venom and acrimony, the history of "the world's greatest deliberative body" is replete with examples of rhetorical overkill and the threat and actuality of physical abuse. When senators clash bitterly in floor debate it is usually the product of some preexisting difference. But a particularly violent outburst on the floor of a legislative chamber has the effect of making personal differences a matter of public record. Vitriolic floor debate, then, can be both a source and symptom of enmity. Bitter public disputation can also have the effect of formalizing interpersonal conflicts and making reconciliation more difficult. While it has often been the case that senators who have clashed bitterly on the floor or in committee hearings later repair to the senators' dining room for lunch—in the manner of trial lawyers (which many of them are) who, having crossed swords in the courtroom, then go off arm-in-arm for a drink—the strident public debate can often be a symptom of underlying tension or hostility. Interpersonal problems may become exacerbated by bringing these resentments to the surface and committing the combatants to a future course of antagonism, especially if one of the belligerents is caused to lose face.

There was little evidence of any initial affection between Maine congressman James G. Blaine and New York congressman Roscoe Conkling when the two Republicans first encountered each other in the House in 1863. From then until 1866, the two maintained a guarded but correct relationship. In 1866, however, Conkling found himself opposed to an appropriations bill that Blaine favored, and attacked not only the measure but the man as well. Undaunted by the withering tirades of Conkling, Blaine lashed out,

> As for the gentleman's cruel sarcasm I hope he will not be too severe. The contempt of that large minded gentleman is so wilting, his haughty disdain, his grandiloquent swell, his majestic, super-eminent, overpowering turkey-gobbler strut has been so crushing to myself and other that I know it was an act of the greatest temerity for me to venture upon a controversy with him.[42]

Blaine's use of the term "turkey-gobbler strut" was to serve as a caricature for Conkling all the days of his political life. In the cruel cartoons of the day, the man who was to serve with Blaine in the Senate would often be depicted festooned with feathers and wattles and

---

[42] Quoted in Henry L. Stoddard, *As I Knew Them* (New York: Harper & Bros., 1927), p. 96.

puffed-up like the barnyard fowl. What might have remained a bitter but decorous private grudge or estrangement became, with Blaine's derisive sally, a public and notorious vendetta.

Feelings between Texas Democrat Tom Connally and Montana Democrat Burton Wheeler were uncordial from the earliest days of the New Deal, when Wheeler's closeness to President Franklin D. Roosevelt had caused Connally to call Wheeler a "teacher's pet." However, when world conditions worsened, Connally became a reliable spokesman in the Senate for Roosevelt's foreign policy while Wheeler became a committed isolationist. Although no one would ever have mistaken them for friends, their occasional jousts on the floor had been more pointed than bitter. One day, however, the restraint broke down with Wheeler calling a Connally amendment a "stump speech." Connally replied by calling Wheeler a coward and a hypocrite, and hurling a book across the chamber in Wheeler's direction. After that incident, all semblance of civility disappeared. They went to great lengths to avoid each other even in the collegial environment of the senators' dining room.

Restraint as entailed in institutional kinship operates, with those senators for whom this understanding is applicable, to mitigate the rancor of floor debate and segregate it from personal feelings. Those who have established even this most basic form of Senate friendship are less apt to personalize attacks. Even if an attack is particularly severe, there is an expectation that personal relationships will not be jeopardized in the long run. Senators are not so thin-skinned, nor are their friendships so fragile, as to deny the possibility that a colleague may lose his temper in the heat of debate and lash out against a friend. (The rule which allows senators to correct their statements in the *Congressional Record* recognizes that spontaneous excesses may occur and that devices be made available to expunge these lapses of civility and restraint.) The late Wayne Morse would often be as harsh on friends in floor debate as on those he disliked. "No one," recalled Paul Douglas of Illinois, "was more denunciatory of his fellow liberals than he. Indeed, he would turn on long-term friends and allies with searing denunciations and do it all in the name of high principle. But though I often felt the whiplash of his tongue, I always believed that he was a valuable force."[43]

---

[43] Paul H. Douglas, op. cit., pp. 232–233.

Floor debate can grow quite heated—at late hours or on the eve of adjournment even testy and petulant—but few enduring grudges emerge from these skirmishes, unless the seeds of hostility are already germinating in the relationship between senators. If there is preexisting hostility from some other source, a savage denunciation of another senator is capable of poisoning relationships beyond redemption. If ridicule, scorn, and contempt are employed by a senator in his debate with a colleague it is generally symptomatic of some more deep-seated conflict. The vituperative floor debate will only rarely be the original source of senatorial hostility; but going public for the purposes of berating a colleague can give finality to a conflict by giving it formality. No more dramatic example of this could be found than Republican whip Ted Stevens's arraignment of his Alaska colleague Democrat Mike Gravel over the Alaska Land Bill in 1978. With a relationship already known to be one of the worst in the Senate, Stevens and Gravel clashed head-to-head on a major piece of legislation affecting both their states. Chiding Gravel for allegedly reneging on an agreement, Stevens said of his colleague, in terms that formalized their feud,

> This is the second time the senator has done this to me, and he is not going to do it again. It is on record now and cannot be erased. The senator is not going to let the people back home or here in this town believe that he would agree to a bill that would sell his State down the river. That is what my colleague is implying and now he faces a big battle from me because it is not going to happen again.[44]

If a senator feels that he has been the victim of foul play by a colleague, what courses of action are open to him? How does the member betrayed by a colleague's pledge of support, whose issues have been stolen, whose committee jurisdiction has been infringed upon, who has been the victim of a hostile incursion into his home state, or who has been the victim of inconsiderate treatment by a colleague retaliate? What are the devices that can be used to punish the senator who makes personal attacks on colleagues, who tramples on the

---

[44] *Congressional Record*, 95th Congress, 2nd session, October 14, 1978, p. S19140.

needs of others to further his own goals, or who is simply treacherous in his interpersonal relationships?

In answering these questions it is necessary to observe at the outset that only the greatest transgressions have occasioned outright censure or reprimand. Most of these have involved blatant illegality, as in the case of Sen. Thomas Dodd of Connecticut, censured in 1967 for misuse of campaign funds. It is a mark of the tolerance of the Senate for even the most egregiously churlish behavior that it has not expelled a member since 1862 and has censured but seven. But what is at issue here is not censurable behavior or activities which would court expulsion, not violations of criminal codes or even expressions of institutional contempt, but rather breaches of interpersonal comity. These actions fall well below the level at which the institution itself takes cognizance of a breach, but are rather those to which individuals or small groups of senators might respond. How, in short, does one settle a score in the U.S. Senate?

The weapons of senatorial reprisal are not impressively large. As a senator will not give a vote to a friend on an important issue simply out of friendship if that vote would conflict with his political needs, so he will not refuse to support a major bill simply because it is sponsored by someone who has wronged him. One of the most thoughtful younger members of the Senate explained it this way:

> You don't have to like anybody at all in order to vote with him. Your motivation for voting on an issue is reached independently. You decide that it's the right thing to do and then you hold your nose. Now I have known cases where people on matters that weren't all that consequential have voted against someone just because they were irritated, even though it's against their interests—just out of irritation and as a demonstration of their own frustration with the other person's attitude. I've seen that. Sort of a shot across his bow.

In 1949, when the government of the Netherlands was fighting to reestablish its colonial control of Indonesia in defiance of the United Nations, an effort was begun in the Senate by Sen. Owen Brewster, a Maine Republican, to deny Marshall Plan aid to Holland in the amount that the Dutch were spending to suppress the insurrection in Indonesia. Brewster had earned an unsavory reputation for his dealings on behalf of the Franco government in Spain. He was also said to be receiving money from a major airline to sponsor legislation favorable to the company.[45] Thus, liberals in the Senate who regarded Brewster with distaste found themselves in a quandary; they were loath to support anything with Brewster's name on it, but were equally in favor of punishing the Dutch for their efforts to reimpose colonial rule. Irving Ives (R.–N.Y.), a liberal stalwart, had planned to vote against the Brewster amendment because of his distaste for the Maine senator, but after the background of the measure was explained to him, he changed his mind and went along with such fellow liberals as J. William Fulbright, Claude Pepper (D.–Fla.), and John Sparkman (D.–Ala.).

Reprisal at the voting stage, then, is limited, especially on important measures. But there are other conceivable modes of reprisal short of possibly self-defeating opposition on tabulated votes. Social psychologists have found that one's ability to mete out punishment and reward is related to one's power and status in the group.[46] It would seem natural, then, that senators of high status and power, such as party leaders or chairmen of key committees, would be able to effect reprisals more readily than others. There is evidence to suggest that a clash with a chairman may indeed invite retribution, especially if the chairman has the wherewithal to respond credibly. But even here the modern chairman's capacity to inflict punishment is limited.

Sen. Edward Kennedy was said to have been on the receiving end of a reprisal as the result of a usurpation of jurisdiction. The retribution grew out of a series of hearings that Kennedy held as chairman of the Subcommittee on Administrative Practices and Procedures. The hearings involved a particularly attractive issue—that of airline deregulation. The colleague upon whose jurisdiction Kennedy was encroaching was Howard Cannon (D.–Nev.), chairman of the Aviation Subcommittee of the Commerce, Science, and Transportation Committee. Cannon might have protested in vain at this infringe-

---

[45] See Drew Pearson, *Diaries, 1949–1959*, Tyler Abell (ed.) (New York: Holt, Rinehart, and Winston, 1974), *passim*; and Drew Pearson and Jack Anderson, *The Case against Congress* (New York: Simon and Schuster, 1968), pp. 358–361.

[46] See Norman Miller, Donald C. Butler, and James A. McMartin, "The Ineffectiveness of Punishment Power in Group Interaction," *Sociometry*, vol. 32 (1969), pp. 24–42.

ment of jurisdiction, but he had more at his disposal than wrath; he was also chairman of the Rules and Administration Committee, which has jurisdiction over such matters as staff and office space. Cannon retaliated by being extremely uncooperative when the Massachusetts senator wished to increase the size of his staff. Cannon ultimately provided the staff, but not without prolonged dilatory tactics.

Sometimes repayment in kind is the preferred method of retribution. Stuart Symington (D.–Mo.) became one of the most popular members of the Senate at least in part because of his refusal to ever enter another colleague's state to campaign against him. In adhering to this principle, Symington may have believed that others would honor the principle with equal consistency. In 1970, however, Robert Dole invaded Missouri to call for Symington's defeat. Relinquishing his long-held principle, Symington struck back at Dole on his own turf. This type of reprisal applied to an equal is very effective at making a point.

Some reprisals are made on behalf of others. An injured senator who is in no position to strike back may have a friend better-situated to retaliate deliver the blow by proxy. An example of this occurred in the aftermath of the Florida Senate primary in 1950 when Congressman George A. Smathers defeated incumbent Senator Claude Pepper in a campaign which textbook writers delight in citing as a classic example of the use of innuendo. Smathers had been a protégé of Pepper, and his cleverly demagogic attacks on his onetime patron did not go unnoticed outside Florida. Particularly offended, not only by the manner of Smather's denunciation of Pepper, but by his apparent ingratitude as well, was House Speaker Sam Rayburn. Rayburn could not punish Smathers directly nor could he do it immediately, but he bided his time and used as an instrument of retribution his ally and protégé Lyndon B. Johnson, who, ironically, was personally fond of Smathers. By 1953, when Johnson was gathering support to become the Democrat's floor leader, he began searching for a whip who would serve him loyally; he settled on Smathers. One of Johnson's lieutenants was well along in securing pledges of support for Smathers, when a call arrived from Johnson telling him to suspend his activities on Smathers's behalf. Pressed for an explanation later as to why Smathers was dropped, Johnson said that Rayburn had become furious when he heard that the Florida senator was in line for the post. According to Johnson, Rayburn had expostulated,

Once a son-of-a-bitch always a son-of-a-bitch. . . . When Claude Pepper was in the Senate, he made George Smathers an Assistant U.S. Attorney in Florida. The next thing you know, Smathers turned around and ran against him and defeated him. He's an ingrate and he's not to be trusted. He'll cut your throat as quick as he cut Claude Pepper's.[47]

It is worthy of note that even in that Golden Age of powerful senators, the chastisement of a putative ingrate was not unduly harsh. Smathers was elected as Secretary of the Democratic Conference in a subsequent move.

The infirmity of norms in the contemporary Senate has produced a situation in which there are no real outcasts in the upper chamber. While there are individual senators whose dealings with colleagues have been thoughtless and inconsiderate on a chronic basis, manifestations of collective disapproval of a colleague to the extent of making him a social isolate are rare. Occasionally, there are manifestations of mass disrespect for a colleague who has exhibited some undesirable personality traits. One senator recalled an instance in which the session had extended into the early evening and Mike Gravel of Alaska arose to make a floor speech. "At that point," the senator recollected, "forty senators decided that it was time to have dinner." Not long thereafter, Gravel, who had urged the creation of a commission to survey transportation needs in his home state, went to the organization meeting of the commission in anticipation of being elected chairman and was passed over by his colleagues in favor of another.

Despite these examples of legislative retribution, the settling of scores is not a preoccupation of most senators, nor is the harboring of grudges to a point where all contact is foreclosed. Deep and abiding enmities in the Senate are as rare as deep and intimate personal friendships. While considerable coolness does exist between many senators, estrangement rarely takes the form of planned, active expression of aggression. Senators do not generally lie in wait for a disliked colleague with the intention of ambushing him. A number of factors militate against that type of strategic reprisal.

---

[47] Bobby Baker, with Larry L. King, *Wheeling and Dealing* (New York: W. W. Norton & Co., 1978), p. 62.

Most prominent among the inhibitions to revenge or the harboring of long-term grudges in the Senate is that this is simply inefficient and self-defeating. It takes time and energy to attempt to structure a situation in which the desire for vengeance may be satisfied. This is not to say that if an occasion opportunely presents itself, such as one in which a senator can deny a discretionary vote to a person who has wronged him, he will not take advantage of it. But as has been pointed out in the case of the Brewster amendment in 1949, a popular measure supported by an antagonist is not the occasion to register displeasure.

Retribution, when it occurs, is a strategy of denial rather than of active aggression, and falls within a narrow range of action. It was said of Congresswoman Bella Abzug, when she was in the House, that her name on a bill would automatically cost it some percentage of support. This may have been true for measures affecting her district or specialized matters of little concern to her colleagues' constituents. It may also have occurred on controversial measures which her detractors were unlikely to support in any event. However, if Mrs. Abzug, or any other legislator whose views or personality antagonized colleagues, were to propose a measure giving relief to middle-income taxpayers, it would require an unusually self-destructive frame of mind to oppose such a bill because of its authorship.

A certain amount of voting does take place on the sole basis of authorship, but the pitfalls in this type of voting-cue are obvious. One particularly embarrassing example of voting by name cue was described by a conservative Republican.

> Often someone will rush in and they'll be told, "This is a Mondale amendment or a Buckley amendment," and if there isn't time for a briefing a lot of people will automatically vote for or against just on the basis of authorship. I recall one case where Tom McIntyre of New Hampshire rushed in late, and it happened to be a Buckley amendment, and I guess he thought that the authorship condemned it, so he voted "no." It was then pointed out to him that the amendment was passing unanimously. I think he was really mortified.

This embarrassing episode took place because of the political characteristics of the measure's author, not his personal qualities. Voting blindly on the basis of personal likes and dislikes could produce even more damaging results.

Clearly, the capacity to mete out punishment is superior in the case of those senators whose leadership positions provide them with the instruments of reprisal. The refusal to hold hearings on a bill of someone personally distasteful, blocking it from being reported out, or denying resources such as staff or office space are theoretically within the province of these senators, even in a Senate where the pyramid of hierarchy has been flattened. But in fact little of this is done. Colleagues can be made to sweat, but little outright obstruction or denial of resources can be documented. Most of the senators interviewed were of the opinion that bestowing rewards on colleagues was a far more effective device for modifying behavior than doling out punishment. The behavior of leaders and chairmen in practice more nearly resembles the model of "exchange" put forth by George C. Homans in which those endowed with strong power to reward are more likely to obtain satisfactory behavior than those with strong power to punish, who are apt to elicit only hostility and resistance.[48]

Pushing personal animus to the point of open warfare simply makes little sense in a body as compact as the Senate. There are few places to hide there, and the satisfaction of habitually baiting a personal adversary can have negative political repercussions. The principal political support for a senator is external, and his downfall can usually be insured only through rejection by his constituents, not by anything a fellow member can do by way of attempting to reduce his effectiveness. The ability of a single senator to so incapacitate a colleague within the Senate itself is so limited that efforts at obstruction or willful acts of retribution merely add to a vicious cycle which impedes the work of both antagonists. In the final analysis, what enmity implies in the Senate is a disinclination to accommodate, where accommodation is discretionary, rather than the consistent use of overt gestures of malice.

Perhaps the most pragmatic limitation on the impulse to punish is that staging a reprisal is simply a poor use of one's time and energy.

---

[48] See George C. Homans, "Social Behavior as Exchange," *American Journal of Sociology*, vol. 63 (May 1958), pp. 597–606.

"I suppose," said one Senate veteran, "that there is every reason in the world to strip Harry Byrd (Independent–Va.) of his perquisites. A lot of people around here think he's a silly old fart. But you simply don't go out of your way to pick fights with your colleagues, whatever you may think of them personally."

CHAPTER NINE

LOVE AND HOSTILITY IN THE U.S. SENATE

Human relationships in the U.S. Senate operate within a narrow range. There is little real love and no great evidence of unbounded hostility. Friendly relationships, which are the product of both professional regard and personal affinity, typically take the modest form of institutional kinship or intramural social friendship. Enmities, likewise a result of judgments of both a political and personal nature, are also usually restrained and muted. As the threshold is approached between those friendships in which political and professional liking predominate and those in which emotional attachments are more prominent, fewer relationships are found.

The effect of shared political values appears to be a very important ingredient of the more personal forms of friendship among senators, but as necessary as this ideological harmony may be in the forging of extramural social friendships, mentor-protégé relationships, and pure friendships, it is insufficient by itself as a precondition for the most intimate ties. The existence of a large number of bitter rivalries among those whose political characteristics are identical suggests strongly that the sharing of these objective traits moves senators only a part of the way towards personal affection. The addition of significant shared experiences and spiritual and social similarities seems to account for some of the most intimate friendships in the Senate, but, laden as they are with so many preconditions, such friendships are not common. Apart from these criteria, allowance must be made for those senators who simply "take to" each other without any apparent political, ideological, situational, social or spiritual similarities. Individual personality does indeed have an independent influence in both friendship and enmity. The most profound effect of personality, however, seems to operate in conjunction with the political and philosophical characteristics of the individual senators and the situations in which they find themselves.

The combination of significant shared experiences with compatibility of personality and ideology figured very prominently in a Midwestern Democrat's evaluation of his own personal friendships with colleagues.

> You can have countless acquaintances here and any number of people you're fond of, but friendship in the real sense—where you're prepared to make considerable sacrifices on their behalf, and they're prepared to make considerable sacrifices on your's, and you genuinely feel that the presence of that individual makes a real difference in terms of your own personal happiness in life and gives meaning to your life in a rich sense—those are very rare. I know that the people that I'm closest to here are people whose relationships with me antedate this place. Your best and closest friends are oldest friends—friendships, you know, which have endured for a long time. You have shared experiences with them that are mutually meaningful. Now here, for example, in the Senate, my best friend is X——. . . . We became good friends because we came into the House of Representatives at the same time fourteen years ago, and our friendship developed there because of a lot of things we had in common and a lot of fights where we found ourselves on the same side. We'd also gone to the same college, we'd gone to the same law school, and our personalities were compatible. In this instance, philosophically, part of that friendship was based on the fact that intellectually and emotionally we were very compatible on the issues. We never served on committees together, but on some tough issues we were lined up together. We were together when a vote came against the flag-burning bill and a number of other highly emotional political issues. It's very comforting to find that someone whom you like and respect independently arrives at the same position and has the convictions to vote that way.

It appears to apply to hostile relationships as well that senators may simply take an instinctive dislike to each other, but there is usually some very concrete policy difference or philosophical disagreement involved. If these differences are expressed in a particularly contentious and nettlesome fashion, a relationship of abiding hostility can develop. There are also areas of institutional sensitivity which can produce conflict between senators irrespective of their partisan or philosophical traits. Structural tensions between senators of the same state and party were examined above in Chapter 3. Sources of senatorial conflict which affect senators more generally were enumerated in Chapter 8. These built-in tension points can be either exacerbated or mitigated by the influence of individual personalities, but they seem to be inherent in the nature of the institution and the senatorial role rather than principally the product of personal idiosyncrasies.

Individual personal qualities do of course play a major role in the choice of leaders. The personality of the potential leader in terms of his capacity for real intimacy or sociability with colleagues is evaluated somewhat obliquely by senators. The ability to form the closest personal ties with colleagues or the strict avoidance of such intimacy is determined by them in terms of how these traits would influence the leader in his performance of his formal tasks. Of greater immediacy is the senator's desire for a whip or floor leader who pursues his formal tasks with a decent sensitivity to the individual personal and political needs of the members. While the instrumental aspects of leadership are probably paramount, expressive qualities are also important, at least insofar as they mitigate detachment. Gestures of personal thoughtfulness on the part of a leader can win him the loyalty of his colleagues, and his ability to confer protection may even cause him to be seen as a friend in the institutional-kinship sense of the term.

Insofar as leaders are capable of doing "friendly" things for members, they are regarded as friends. Just what is it that a leader does to call forth such feelings of friendship from the rank-and-file? In the Senate, at least, he must possess the ability to confer protection on individual members, to be attuned to their problems and vulnerabilities, and to respond to those needs in a way consistent with his formal obligations to the institution. There is reason to believe that this ability in a leader would be seen as an expression of friendship in a state legislature as well. Having attained leadership status, then, the leader is seen as someone who, by dint of his power to help members, may be perceived as a friend. As Albert Pepitone has noted, status and security are powerful determinants of attraction and hostility. . . . Research evidence shows that the attractiveness of others varies with their capacity to satisfy security or status motivations.[1]

Intramural social friendship is facilitated by the many facilities in the Senate which provide for informal personal contact. The cloakrooms, dining rooms, and various recreational facilities and watering-holes provide settings in which relationships of a strictly business nature can be softened and humanized. They also allow the exposure of a less public side of members, enabling senators who know their colleagues only as the embodiments of certain regional or ideological viewpoints to deal with them in an environment in which these characteristics are less ostentatiously on display. Senators can let down their hair, establish personal rapport, and even lay groundwork for compromise and cooperation, all of which may not be possible in the more sunlit arenas of the floor and committee rooms.

For those senators who participate in the Prayer Breakfast, these socio-spiritual encounters are valuable in enabling them to gain a measure of insight into their colleagues. Despite the nonpartisan, nondenominational, and nonideological nature of the breakfasts, the bulk of the regular members tend to be the more conservative Southern and Midwestern senators who are communicants of the more conservative churches. Those few liberals who are consistent attenders are usually also drawn from these denominations. The Roman Catholics, Episcopalians, and Unitarians who were interviewed expressed feelings about the breakfasts which, on the whole, ranged from indifference to acute discomfort. The single Catholic senator who attends regularly is a strong conservative. There was little evidence that any of the Jewish senators participate with any regularity (nor is there an unusual degree of personal closeness among senators of the Jewish faith, although they tend to be allied on questions affecting the Middle East).

The Prayer Breakfasts do appear to function as a reception area for senators experiencing personal problems and as a device to recruit

---

[1] Albert Pepitone, *Attraction and Hostility* (New York: Atherton Press, 1964), p. 16.

members for smaller and more intense cliques of senators who seek a less public and more heightened religious experience. These senators, whose ideological orientations are roughly comparable, are deeply involved in each other's personal and spiritual lives. For them, the Prayer Breakfast has been a springboard for pure friendship where spiritual and ideological agreement operate upon each other to produce not only great intimacy but also a level of political cooperation and accommodation that occurs nowhere else in the Senate with such consistency or force.

The extramural social friendships of U.S. senators are fewer in number than the intramural ones. The threshold between the intramural and extramural social relationships constitutes a formidable barrier. Senators who are regular luncheon companions or chat informally over drinks do not necessarily extend to each other the hospitality of their homes or draw each other into the intimacy of the family circle. While the social demands on a senator are considerable and most do indeed lead an active social life, these activities can be said to be "outside" the Senate only in the most technical spatial sense. Senators see a good deal of each other at banquets, White House functions, fund-raisers, and some regular gala events, but circumstance rather than choice seems to dictate these contacts. More intimate gatherings of senators and their families based upon attraction rather than obligation occur with much less regularity. The explanations offered by senators to explain this infrequency of informal contact vary. Most cite the lack of time and the related fear of intruding upon a busy colleague. Others simply do not wish to spend social time with those with whom they share so much professional time; they look elsewhere for social friends.

In the social and recreational life of senators, there appear to be a number of "activity friendships." Card-playing, once the sport of politicians, has now taken on certain unsavory connotations; moreover, it seems to be held in low regard in terms of its value for human betterment or physical well-being. Golf is time-consuming and tends to be played principally by older members. Tennis, handball, and racquet-ball, while not team sports, are the principal forms of activity nowadays which involve a senator with his colleagues. The even more individualistic sports of jogging, swimming, and calisthenics, answer both the need for vigorous good health and the apparent desire on the part of senators for individual achievement and competition with oneself. Individuality in recreation, then, seems to be an accurate reflection of individuality in behavior in the workplace. The individualistic sports, moreover, primarily entail tasks and challenges; they are pragmatic and utilitarian rather than simply fun. Perhaps it is the case that fun has simply been redefined to comport with a public view of political life which holds that politicians who are too obviously enjoying themselves are flouting the solemnity required of officeholders in perilous times.

Senators do not flock together outside the chamber. There are no salons, no cafés, no eating places or clubs where senators congregate. Their choices of places to live are dictated by taste, finances, convenience, or family needs. The Washington of the legislative quarter or the boarding-house is a relic of the distant past; senatorial neighbors there are, but this seems to occur by chance, given the relatively few places where people with their income and formal social status might choose to reside. The concentrations of senators' homes which do occur are the product of no political, regional, or ideological calculations. Even within the Senate office building little significance can be read into the propinquity of offices. The relationship between personal attraction and seating patterns in the chamber is no longer as clear as it was formerly. Some locations are chosen for reasons of convenience; others for reasons of sentiment stemming from the identity of the previous occupants. Some choices of seats are undoubtedly influenced by a desire to be with friends, but it is by no means clear whether liking has proceeded from proximity or vice versa. One thing is clear, however, and that is that senators will try to avoid being seat mates with colleagues for whom they harbor an active dislike.

Friendships of all varieties do not seem to be impeded by party lines, but the partisan spatial organization of the Senate chamber does mean that Democrats tend to be thrown together with other Democrats and Republicans with their fellow partisans. Senators may form friendships of the more personal sorts across party lines, but usually these are with those of the opposite party most like them in ideological terms. Deep personal friendships between strong liberals and strong conservatives are unusual; institutional-kinship relationships, however, are not. While partisanship by itself may not be associated with any attributes that would make a colleague ineligible for close personal friendship, a senator simply sees more of those colleagues who share the same caucus and partisan space. While the committee structure which reflects functional, as opposed to partisan, organization, attenuates this to a considerable degree, senators' designations of their closest personal friends reflect not simply ideological compatibility but, to a great degree, partisanship as well. This came out in a conversation with a liberal Republican who was asked to designate those members with whom he was on closest personal terms in his Senate career:

> I felt very close to John Cooper, for instance. Any time I wanted to talk to him about anything at all, even private matters, I would have. Jack Javits, Mac Mathias, Jim Pearson. It's more a matter of the quality of the person than anything else. I know they felt the same about me.

When I pointed out that he had nominated only those who shared his own liberal Republican characteristics, he responded,

> Well, it just happened to be. You are thrown in with your own party people a little bit more than in just an ordinary way. We were all members of the Wednesday Club, which had neither Democrats nor conservatives of our own party.

When senators do cross party lines for their personal friends, they generally do so only if ideological compatibility awaits them on the other side.

The general tendency on the part of senators to hold themselves open to institutional-kinship relationships with ideological opposites and members of the other party, while at the same time maintaining their closest personal ties with members who resemble them most closely in a political and philosophical sense, was expressed with great clarity by a Western Democrat.

> I think it's inevitable that you'd reserve your most personal friendships for people who share your political principles. You can have all the amenities with the others, but you really don't feel close to a fellow that you just have to be butting heads with all the time on ideological issues, and obviously a person who subjectively thinks his view is the right view and is so stubborn that he can't even imagine how you take the positions you do is really going to cause you trouble. I do feel, though, that it's rarely carried to the extreme.

As a general proposition, though, you just can't feel as close and warm, and you don't mingle quite as much with those who had the other view. Of course, the Senate tends to promote that a little bit by its organization—the Republicans sit on one side and the Democrats sit on the other, and there's the business of the separate cloakrooms and lunch tables, but even among Democrats there are some pretty imposing differences of ideology. I could be friendly with Jim Allen and others that I almost never voted with when votes were cast. Oh, I could be friendly with them—quite generally friendly, I think—but I never feel fully relaxed and totally comfortable, as I do with others whose political philosophy I share and whose personal friendship with me is helped along by our agreement on basics. . . .

I haven't noticed that ideological disagreement actually drove people away so that they no longer had any social connection, but it's an impediment all right, because, as I say, you just don't relax as much. It's hard to joke along and be open and never concerned about what it is that's being said in private conversation, if you're with a person of a strong ideological difference. You just know, or feel, that that's going to come through in some way.

As a general proposition the political payoffs of friendship with a colleague do not, after a certain point, increase in direct relationship to the degree of intimacy. A senator can approach a social companion more readily than someone tied to him only by institutional kinship, and he will usually be able to secure a greater degree of consideration and attentiveness, but the benefits associated with pure friendship relate more to emotional support and the availability of someone to lean on in times of stress or doubt than to any superior political advantage. Pure friendships which unite politicians are not embarked upon with the expectation that they will yield concrete political gains of a high order. To seek out a colleague to whom one can turn for personal advice and make revelations of a private nature does not presuppose favored professional treatment. There is an additional reason why the payoffs do not increase in proportion to intimacy, and that is that the structure of payoffs is limited. There is only a very slight difference in terms of value and significance in the favors that a senator can confer on an institutional-kinship friend and a more personal friend. The importance of these favors is circumscribed by the limits on a senator's discretion and how accommodating he can be without causing trouble for himself.

In the normal course of events in the Senate, institutional-kinship relations are all that a senator really needs in terms of personal consideration. With these relationships the senator is able to profit from fair-minded treatment, good intelligence and evaluation, understanding and sympathy for his individual problems, and a dependable work-partner. A greater expectation of political support will flow from an alliance, but since there is general agreement on fundamentals among alliance partners, support tends to flow more from similarity of positions than from personal accommodation. There does, however, seem to be a more personal obligation to forewarn of defection and avoid breaking ranks without notice on matters contributing to the cohesion of the alliance. This signaling of imminent defection is also said to prevail among "friends" in a state legislature.

> If a member cannot support a friend's bill, he is expected to tell his friend why he cannot "go along" before he votes against the bill, and to explain why he must vote as he does. Otherwise, his friend will most likely automatically "count" on him, and an unwarned adverse vote may sever the friendship relationship. Since members tend to select persons of like mind as their friends, this problem does not create serious difficulty. A member will be most frequently "forgiven" for voting against his friend if his reason is based on the nature of his district, that is, if he cannot "go along" because of district pressure.[2]

In personal terms, it is probably in the intramural social friendship that a senator, without venturing too deeply into the personal life of a colleague, is privileged to take his measure as a person and establish an idiom of communication less dependent upon formal structures. This type of relationship helps break down the barriers of stereotyping. Senators who enjoy it are able to discard the more visi-

---

[2] Samuel C. Patterson, "Patterns of Interpersonal Relations in a State Legislative Group: The Wisconsin Assembly," in Samuel A. Kirkpatrick and Lawrence K. Pettit (eds.), *The Social Psychology of Political Life* (Belmont, Calif.: Duxbury Press, 1972), pp. 81–86.

ble trappings of their public selves and establish an association in which flexibility and personal accommodation are more likely.

In extramural social friendship, companionability begins to transcend the political factor as the defining characteristic of the association. Brought together because they in large measure share the same political values, these senators come to like each other and look forward to social contact for the personal satisfaction it brings. The addition of an important personal dimension to what is most typically preexisting political agreement bids senators to go out of their way to help a friend if that entails no serious political risk. Pure friendship and its component, the mentor-protégé relationship, signify an even more personal stake in another senator's life. The significance of this stake might cause a senator to do a favor for another for no other reason than to assure his political survival so that the association can endure within the institution. But what a senator could do to further this objective is really not appreciably greater than what he could do for a social friend, and he will not jeopardize his own career. There was a suggestion in the case of the evangelicals that there is a high degree of persuadability and even evidence that minds are changed on occasion, but even the most intimate friendship is limited in its political payoffs by the very practical factors of the constraints of constituencies, ideologies, and public identification with particular policy positions.

What, then, are the political benefits that accrue to personal friends generally in terms of what they can expect from each other and what in fact they are able to deliver?

A Midwestern Democrat placed the influence of friendship in its proper Senate context in a very straightforward manner.

> I think you'd see personal friendship operating in the kind of situation where a vote meant a great deal to one friend but didn't mean a great deal to the other.

Somewhat more emphatically, a New England Democrat expressed the same view.

> The idea that if I know you like a brother that I'll go along with you because you're my friend and end up hurting myself — that's unimaginable. Now I may go along with you out of friendship on a procedural thing—a motion to adjourn, a

motion to bring a bill up, or a motion to report a bill out of committee—but the idea that because you're a personal friend of mine I'll stand up on a thing that might be damaging to me and to my state, well that just never happens. Senators are selfish people; they try to protect themselves at all times. I'd be a fool to go along with somebody just out of friendship because he's a dear heart and I want to give him a helping hand and by doing so injure myself. Never! Never!

The view of this senator carries the strong implication that the degree of importance attached by the supplicant to a particular issue will be insignificant in the mind of the senator whose help is being enlisted compared to the possible dangers associated with compliance, and that personal friendship yields political support only on matters of little consequence.[3]

Both the marginality of the favors rendered to a Senate friend and the assumption that repayment will be forthcoming were touched on by a Midwestern Republican who spoke of the political dividends that friendship produces.

If it's something major, nobody's going to change his mind. He's not going to compromise his own principles, but if he has no big stake in it one way or the other he'll probably help you out. If it's for the Tombigbee waterway in Tennessee and you have little interest in it one way or the other, you might vote for it because your buddy will benefit. By the same token, you kind of assume that when the appropriation for the eradication of Lamprey eels in Lake Michigan comes up, he'll help to vote funds for it.

There is then an undisguised drift in the testimony of these senators that a friend granting a favor is expected to be indemnified. This expectation, however, is not generally so crass as the little black book of favors rendered which Lyndon Johnson was said to have carried in his back pocket or the scorecard of dispensation of the quid pro quo kept by Oklahoma senator Robert Kerr.

---

[3] John C. Wahlke, Heinz Eulau, William Buchanan, and LeRoy C. Ferguson, *The Legislative System* (New York: John Wiley & Sons, 1962), p. 91.

It is important to note here that no senator admitted to arrant vote trading or even recalled having witnessed any. Vote trading involves giving another member a vote and extracting a promissory note for his support on a future measure. Having thus helped a colleague in the past entitles a senator to "call in his chips," but that practice is quite distinct from rendering favors for specific future considerations.

This raises a related question of considerable significance: Will a request from just any colleague for a vote be honored, or is this a privilege extended only to a friend? Donald Matthews, in using "logrolling" as an indicator of the norm of reciprocity, quoted a senator's administrative assistant as saying,

> My boss will—if it doesn't mean anything to him—do a favor for another senator. It doesn't matter who he is. It's not a matter of friendship, it's a matter of I won't be an S.O.B. if you won't be one.[4]

On the whole, it appeared from the interviews that senators will try to pick up support wherever they can find it, and that logrolling is not just restricted to friends. Reciprocity is neither an institutional norm nor evidence of friendship; it is rather a constant in human relationships. There do, however, appear to be different etiquettes governing such overtures for friends and for more casual associates. As a liberal Democrat from an Eastern state described it,

> With acquaintances, as distinguished from friends, there's a certain amount of "you scratch my back and I'll scratch yours"—quite a lot of it. "Remember, Joe, I gave you a vote on such and such, how about paying me back on this one." With friends there's still that expectation of repayment, but the accounting system is much more subtle.

The expectation of repayment or the calling in of chips is more manifest and undisguised in the case of less-intimate Senate friendships, and the justification for help put forth with greater bluntness. More intimate friends, not surprisingly, are more aware of each other's

---

4 Donald R. Matthews, *U.S. Senators and Their World* (New York: Vintage Books, 1960), p. 100.

needs and require less by way of explanation. Another liberal Democrat, this time from the Midwest, put it this way:

> If the guy's your friend, you know pretty well how important it is just by the nature of your relationship. I mean, knowing enough about him to be his friend, you know what's important to him.

In a peculiar way, it may be easier in the Senate to swap favors when there are no close personal ties. Among such colleagues who are approachable there need be no great personal closeness. Logrolling then can take place with mercantile briskness: profit and loss are weighed, the transaction is very straightforward, and the bookkeeping more overt. There may be gratitude or disappointment, but the fate of a close human relationship does not ride on the outcome. Personal friendship does not figure prominently in these transactions.

With personal friendships the etiquette of the good turn can be more complicated. If a senator cares very much for the supplicant, he knows that denial may impair a relationship of great personal value to him. And the expectations of the supplicant may be higher when he appeals to a personal friend. He may accept a rebuff from a non-friend with more grace and understanding than a refusal from a friend. But close friends in the Senate, armed as they are with greater insight and more complete knowledge of their comrades, may also hold back from making an appeal that they might have made to a more casual acquaintance. Close friendship thus may be a deterrent to an overture for a favor, as it creates inhibitions based upon intimate knowledge of a colleague, his problems, and vulnerabilities. Such approaches may be seen as placing a strain on a relationship which may be too important to jeopardize even for a crucial vote. In a relationship where a person is valued highly for personal qualities a request for a favor—especially a risky one—may be bypassed to avoid impairing it. A Midwesterner described the operation of this inhibition as it affected his closest Senate friend, who he knew needed his vote, a vote which the Midwesterner could not deliver without great political peril.

> He never pushed me on it. He understood my position because we're that good as friends, and one of the reasons that we're friends is that we've both recognized in each other matters of

principle. And while I certainly understand his interest and motivation in respect to his view, I know that if the situation were reversed I'd have understood too. That's one of the reasons our friendship is so strong. We don't ask each other to do things that would compromise principles and be unacceptable. He knew it would be too big a wrench for me, that it would create conflict.

Getting close to a colleague personally may not result in a higher order of political benefits, but may even create problems for a senator. A close friend in the Senate can be a political liability; he can reduce a senator's freedom of action by subjecting him to cross-pressures and forcing him to choose between personal loyalty and the pursuit of his political obligations and opportunities. His ability to apply pressure on a friend is likewise similarly limited; it is difficult to lean remorselessly on a friend. What serves also to reduce the attraction of an intimate friendship with a colleague is that other, more limited varieties of friendship may be all that are required to produce satisfying collegial relationships. There is little by way of increased effectiveness in the Senate which cannot be achieved by the respect and trust found in the institutional kinship. There is little in terms of coalition-building that any relationship more intimate than the alliance can yield. And there is nothing in excess of social friendship that is required to break down the barriers of a purely professional relationship and provide politically useful social contacts and companionship. In purely political terms, then, there is a point in interpersonal relationships where the law of diminishing returns begins to operate, where the political benefits of a relationship begin to be canceled out by the demands of a deeply intimate form of friendship.

In stark political terms, accordingly, a pure friendship may not even be a rational choice, because of the constraints it imposes, the expectations it sets up, and the marginal political dividends—over and above those of less intimate associations—that it provides. Moreover, if a senator needs the emotional support of a very close friend, he may well seek such friendship outside the Senate. Involvement with other colleagues in the less emotionally taxing forms of friendship that stop short of pure friendship or even extramural social friendship may provide a senator with an optimal degree of institutional acceptability and respect (as in the institutional kinship), reliable sources of coalitional support (as in the alliance), or satisfying intramural social interaction with colleagues. To have gained the respect and trust of colleagues is a sufficient accomplishment for most senators; to have reliable allies is a political bonus; and to be sought out by colleagues for informal or extra-institutional associations may solidify political relationships and yield sufficient additional dividends of companionship and personal contact. Confidences, problems, and secrets will then be shared only with those outside the Senate; the result of such a structure can be a senator both popular and effective. Without reliance on the emotional sustenance of a colleague, a senator may yet have a completely serviceable set of interpersonal relationships.

There are few tangible political incentives for a senator to develop close personal ties with a colleague, for the benefits in the Senate of the higher orders of personal friendship are more emotional than professional. There is likewise little political value in engaging in an enduring feud with another member; self-vindication at the expense of another member can be emotionally satisfying, but it is usually politically costly. It must be a "cheap shot" only in the sense of little cost; if a senator's willingness to help a friend is influenced in large measure by a calculation of the risks involved to himself, his disposition to punish a foe is similarly measured.

> You could have a strong personal distaste or dislike for some-one, but if the reason for supporting him is overpowering and it's the right thing to do, you're only spiting yourself by being petulant. I've seen it done, of course, but it usually is on something that the aggrieved party couldn't care less about. Joe Blow may be a *schmuck*, but you don't hold his feet to the fire and burn yourself in the process.

With the complexity of the Senate and the multiplicity of issues, senators often find that today's antagonist may be the very person whose support is indispensable on a crucial matter tomorrow.

> You can really have a knock-down, drag-out on the issues, and there are times when people are personally unpleasant. You have to be constitutionally made up in a way that you can accept that and carry on, because you've got to work with these people day in and day out—and tomorrow's another ball game

with new interests and new issues—and not succumb to that pressure to lash out, even though some people really ask for it.

The pragmatic reckoning of political profit and loss ensuing from manifestations of friendship or antipathy means that extravagant gestures of bonhomie may be less natural than they appear and gestures of contempt less spontaneous. Commenting on Thomas Eagleton's broadside at Charles Percy during the Bert Lance hearings in 1977, a friend of Eagleton's ventured the interpretation, "It may have been the case that Tom knew exactly what he was doing and did it calculatedly." One draws inferences about the nature of interpersonal relations from observations of public behavior in the Senate at one's own peril. This is perhaps more true of friendship relations than hostile ones; the ritualized civility of the Senate produces an atmosphere in which there is little manifest hostility and much overt, hearty hobnobbing. This superficial cordiality, in which the Senate abounds, should not be discounted; it well serves both the institution and the individual senator. The underlying reality of interpersonal relationships is equally functional, but infinitely more complex.

Forty years ago, a social scientist posted himself in the gallery of the Illinois senate and concluded, from the frequent contacts among members of the Democratic majority and also across party lines, that these informal conferences mitigated "the conflict of interests that collide in the legislative halls" and were the "ingredients of the social cement which bound the divergent factions of the Senate together into a functioning whole."[5]

The observer did not attempt to infer anything about the substantive nature of the interpersonal relationships of the state senators he observed. He did make an assumption that contacts across party lines were of a positive nature, since he saw in them the ingredients of institutional cohesion. Floor behavior, however, may be highly deceptive; legislators engaged in conversation may be exchanging neither pleasantries nor information, but rather may be laying into a colleague. Certainly the hail-fellow-well-met gesture of an arm around a colleague can belie a conversation of a very different nature. Take,

[5] Garland C. Routt, "Interpersonal Relationships and the Legislative Process," *Annals of the American Academy of Political and Social Sciences*, vol. 195 (January 1938), pp. 131, 135.

for example, the exchange which took place when New Hampshire Republican Norris Cotton approached Virginia Democrat Harry Byrd, Sr., chairman of the Finance Committee, to ask him to hold hearings on a matter of personal concern to Cotton:

He greeted me cordially, even affectionately, for I was one of a stalwart band of senators who voted with him, constantly, against what we thought were unnecessary expenditures. He had a habit of slapping a friend on the back and laughing, as if they were both enjoying a good joke. I asked him for the hearing. He continued to pat me on the shoulder and to laugh, but he said, "Sorry, boy, you can't have a hearing on it. This committee hasn't time to act on every minor flaw in the tax laws. We're constantly engaged in major revisions." I then asked if he could not assign a couple of members of the committee as a subcommittee, just to hear the story. He said, "This committee never acts through subcommittees, but only as a whole." "But," said I, "it's embarrassing for me to notify a leading lawyer in New Hampshire, who is settling the estate of a former governor, that I can't get him even a hearing before a committee of which I am a member." He continued to pat my shoulder and laugh. "Sorry, boy, if we gave you a hearing, we would be holding hearings every day on tax complaints." Then, with a final hearty laugh and a slap on the back, he ushered me out.[6]

Exchanges which might be interpreted from the gallery as evidence of friendly contact are sometimes even less cordial and substantive than the Byrd-Cotton exchange.

[Wayne] Morse could no longer sit on the Republican side of the aisle because Republican senators were treating him to a continuing barrage of scurrilous, personal attacks. Herman Welker of Idaho and Irving Ives of New York, for instance, constituted themselves a two-man whispering insult squad whenever Morse denounced President Eisenhower. While Morse spoke, a typical Ives whisper told him, "You silly jackass. Why don't you shut your silly mouth and go out and drop dead?". . .

[6] Norris Cotton, *In the Senate* (New York: Dodd, Mead & Co., 1978), p. 165.

Welker's specialty was to walk up and down the aisle while Morse spoke, and as he passed him, he spat out in a whisper, "You stupid ass. Everybody knows you're a dope."[7]

This paradox of "hostile proximity" illustrates Erving Goffman's distinction between two types of activity: "front region" activity of a more formal and public character and "backstage activity" of a more relaxed and informal nature. Observable gestures of consultation or even gregariousness tell us little about whether we are witnessing the more guarded and formal relationships or the more intimate ones— or, indeed, the interaction of enemies who have adopted conventions of civility in their essentially adversary relationship.

> In saying that performers act in a relatively informal, familiar, relaxed way while backstage and are on their guard when giving a performance, it should not be assumed that the pleasant, interpersonal things of life—courtesy, warmth, generosity, and pleasure in the company of others—are always reserved for those backstage and that suspiciousness, snobbishness, and a show of authority are reserved for front region activity. Often it seems that whatever enthusiasm and lively interest we have at our disposal we reserve for those before whom we are putting on a show and that the surest sign of backstage solidarity is to feel that it is safe to lapse into an asocial mood of sullen, silent irritability.[8]

The Senate is not a heartless place in which the word friendship rings hollow, but it is a place where friendship has some very specialized meanings. In its most common form it is more of the head than of the heart; a friendship which must coexist with sober political calculations. It may be tinged with emotion, but emotion must never be allowed to dominate it. The few friendships of a higher emotional order which have existed in the Senate provided their own justification in human terms; generally, emotional bonds must confront the overriding dictates of political necessity. The political value

---

[7] Alfred Steinberg, *Sam Johnson's Boy* (New York: Macmillan Co., 1968, pp. 397–392.

[8] Erving Goffman, *The Presentation of Self in Everyday Life* (Garden City, NY: Doubleday Books, 1959), p. 132.

of Senate friendship most generally can be summed up in a formulation favored by economists: If the marginal benefits of helping a friend exceed the marginal costs, you will help a friend; if the costs exceed the benefits, you will refuse. In his refusal, however, the senator will be supported by his colleagues, who will interpret his refusal not as treachery to a comrade but as a sensible appreciation of his own political survival needs—a human emotion well-understood in the U.S. Senate.

How good a friend must you be with a Senate colleague to "call in the chips"? Must the friendship be of a particularly warm and intimate variety to be the basis for a claim? The answer is no; to be a trustworthy reliable, reciprocal, and empathetic colleague is sufficient in most cases. In the political marketplace of senatorial friendship a shilling is usually as good as a pound.

If there is considerable imprecision on the part of outsiders in applying the label "friends" to Senate members, senators themselves understand only too well that beneath a superficially straightforward term there lurks great complexity. While using the terms themselves to describe associations ranging from the routine—where it is no more than an expression of civility—to the most intimate, few harbor any illusions that, for all the extravagance with which the term is used, friendship of any variety is the dominant feature of interpersonal relationships in the Senate.

Some senators look upon the often indiscriminate bestowing of the term on colleagues—however limited their capacity for human warmth—with amused skepticism. In an early interview with a very wise and well-liked senior Democrat—this took place at a time when I was still grappling with what friendship meant in the Senate context—I expressed amazement at the number of senators who eulogized John McClellan in the language of friendship and confessed that in my brief association with the Senate I had never detected the depth of feeling toward the man that was so apparent in these tributes. A sly grin played out across the face of the senator, and he said to me,

> Did you ever hear the story of the old curmudgeon who died and was laid out in a coffin in front of the pulpit, and the whole family was there while the preacher went on at great length about his virtues and what a noble life he led, and the

wife leans over to the son and says, "Son, run up there and look in the casket and see if he's talking about our Daddy."

Ironically enough, it was Solon, the lawgiver, who admonished us to say nothing but good of the dead. But whatever excesses were involved in extolling the human virtues of McClellan, it was clear that in his professional dealings with colleagues he stood high enough in their estimation to be unhypocritically described as a friend. In a world in which love does not abound, such a designation is not without meaning or sincerity.

Senators do not expect fond friendships to flower with their colleagues, and expect little by way of special treatment from those they do deem to be friends. They are too realistic to think otherwise. They know the world in which they move and are, on the whole, captives of no fantasies about the nature of personal friendship therein, its effects, or even the need for it.

Competitiveness is always beneath the surface, at least among the more ambitious senators—and as a class senators are rather an ambitious group of people. The thing that fosters friendship in the Senate are the common undertakings, the alliances that are formed, and the help that senators will give to one another, supporting their friends and their political allies. The social contact that senators have with each other also causes a more personal friendship to develop. You just can't be a part of so small a group and spend so much time together without developing friendships which—if not intimate—are nonetheless real.

When that roll was called I could tell you, man for man, the way they would vote even before they voted. You learn that after a while in the Senate. Now I'm not saying that in an isolated case where your relationship back home is not at stake as to how you vote, that you might not be accommodating to a certain individual in the hope that one day if the same circumstances apply he might be accommodating to you, but those circumstances are isolated and rare. This idea that much of what goes on in the Senate comes out of the fact that I like you as an individual and I met your wife and she's a lovely person and she has tea with my wife and that because of that I'm going to vote the way that you do . . . no . . . that's not the way it works.

I don't think you have to be friends with your colleagues to get things done. I think that you can have personal friends—I mean, I think that personal friendships are wonderful and I'm all for them, but I don't think they're necessary in the U.S. Senate. I think that a willingness to compromise and a willingness to do your part of the job, to inspire trust and be dependable, all do more than actual close friendships.

The membership of the Senate does not, of course, delimit the friendship networks of most senators; most do not rely on the ninety-nine other people in the upper chamber to provide them with counsel, companionship, or solicitude. In the manner of most Americans, they cast a broader net which encompasses neighbors (both from Washington, D.C. and their home state), army buddies, former law partners, campaign aides and contributors, or simply people to whom they have been attracted in the course of plying the political trade, a trade that brings them into contact with a broader range of humankind than those encountered in most other walks of life.

In these extra-Senate friendships, senators behave in a manner not markedly different from ordinary men and women. Fairly typical of senators' extra-Senate friendships are those with people who are no less cherished for being so seldom seen. Most people have found in the course of their lives a man or woman so winning and inviting that absence poses no barrier to intimacy—a person who, when the press of business slackens, is the first one we think of, who is a long-distance call away and with whom, when the conversation begins, the old fires of friendship are immediately rekindled. Most senators to whom I spoke had such friends. A Republican commented that such friendships

> reflect a universal experience and not just a Senate question. I know myself that I have a law partner in New York, two or three years older than I am—very much the senior partner. I see him every four or five years when I have something I want very much to talk about. I go to him, but we go for years without seeing each other. The frequency of contact just doesn't matter.

Eleven of the twenty-five senators and former senators I interviewed had had prior service in the House. They were fairly uniform in their characterizations of the differences in interpersonal relationships that prevail between the two chambers. An Eastern Republican who spent ten years in the House before coming to the Senate summed up the feelings of most House alumni in the Senate on this subject.

I think it's very difficult to form close friendships in the Senate. I would distinguish it in this respect from the House. There's less rivalry between two House members than there is between two senators. Senators are very independent and tend to be on the arrogant side and are always trying to get themselves out front. There's a whole different context in the House; it's a closer knit group. A senator, by contrast, is much more important as an individual; he has a variety of privileges that they don't have in the House. In the House, no matter what position you occupy—chairman, Majority Leader, or Speaker—there's a definite limit to your powers. In fact, I think that the rules of the House are *too* strict.

In the Senate all you really have to do in most cases to prevent a vote on a day is tell the Majority Leader you don't want the vote and give him some credible reason for it. He won't always go along with you if you get near the end of the session or if there are scheduling problems or that kind of thing, but there's always a disposition to accommodate you if there's a reasonable basis for your request. And there's senatorial courtesy on a whole variety of things. They are almost always cordial, but it's hard for me to remember any close friendships among senators. The Senate is more cordial than the House, but it is harder to make close friends there than in the House.

A freshman Senator in the 95th Congress who previously had served three terms in the House reflected upon these differences after having spent less than a year in the Senate.

The House is a very different place. It's more free-wheeling. I think I mean the numbers—the difference in number is bound to have that kind of impact on interpersonal relations. I think that the pressures are not as great in the House. In the Senate every minute is being grabbed at by something or other. In the

House you'd sit there on the floor sometimes for an hour or so, talking with people, and following a debate, and so forth. Much less of that happens in the Senate. The Senate is, you know, under so much pressure to do so many things that they tend to move, as I said, much more separately than in the House. There was more getting together in the course of the day; I mean you'd spend time on the House floor together. Oh, some of that goes on here, but, you know, if a senator's in committee, the next thing you know he's jumping up because he's got some other committee meeting. House members spend more time in a single committee, and your principal committee assignment brings you together on a more continuous basis than here; at least that's my impression.

The relationship of senators and congressmen to the committees, particularly the greater focus in the House on the work of a single committee, was indicated as a major source of differences in interpersonal contact by most of the former congressmen who ended up in the Senate. A Republican ex-senator from a small state emphasized this difference.

In the House you may serve on two committees, but you have one primary committee because you're working with those subcommittee members day in and day out. You very quickly get to be on a first-name basis with them, even though you may never have known them before you got to the House. You all get involved in a single set of issues that you're working on. In the Senate you are on at least two and sometimes three committees and then you're on a half-dozen subcommittees, and you spread yourself thin. You are usually cordial, but you just don't have time for the closer friendships with a few people. You're just too busy doing too many different things.

This same senator also put forth the idea that the physical arrangement of the Senate chamber and the practice of holding assigned seats was an inhibition to social contact.

In the Senate you've got your own seat and you sit next to Hiram Fong or Carl Curtis or Chuck Percy and you talk to them a lot because they're right there. In the House you can just plunk yourself down practically anywhere.

The arrangement of physical space in the congressional office buildings has been indicated as a factor affecting informal contacts among staff. There are differences among the three House buildings and Senate office buildings.

> Within Longworth [a House office building], the geography of the building throws Congressmen from diverse backgrounds together [due to the fact that Longworth is considered "less desirable" and tends to be where freshmen are placed], many in offices which are vastly overcrowded. Aides to Congressmen in Longworth pointed to the "warmth" of LHOB, in contrast to [the Rayburn House office building], and said, "There's a lot of socializing." One LA [Legislative Assistant] to a Southern Democrat specifically mentioned exchange with staff of a West Coast Republican Congressman because, "Our workrooms . . . are next to each other. . . . There's much jollying back and forth." The same aide talked about "block parties" (that is, corridor parties), and thus indicated that there is at time a "corridor feeling" which enhances solidarity and communication too. . . .

> Senate office buildings do not appear to be so clearly differentiated. . . . Senate personal offices appear to be more isolated and apparently more self-contained than those of the House; in a smaller membership group office geography seems to be less important to the communication process among offices."[9]

Among senators there appears to be, on the whole, much less interoffice visiting than among congressmen. The proximity of office suites has little to do with the growth of familiarity among senators. Such fundamental forces as a heavier and more diffuse workload, the self-perception of the senator as more of an individual and free agent than his House counterpart, and other factors that inhere in the role of senator militate—more than any physical factors—against the kind of associations which appear to be far more common in the House.

It is certainly the case that there are few parallels in the Senate to the sociopolitical groups that abound in the House. The tendency,

[9] Harrison W. Fox, Jr., and Susan Webb Hammond, *Congressional Staffs* (New York: Free Press, 1977), pp. 110–112.

especially among House Republicans, to hive off into small groups has only the faintest parallel with the Senate's Wednesday Club of liberal Republicans and the Senate Steering Committee of conservative Republicans.[10] The same observation would apply to the congressional "class groups" of members elected in the same year. Class solidarity, once a significant bond in the Senate, has gone into decline. A Western Democrat said that his class "banded together rather strongly—certainly more than any other entering class that came later—and that continued for a long time, and I made lasting friendships with senators like Ed Muskie, Gale McGee, and Pete Williams from our class of '58." There was, however, an observable closeness among the young Senate Democrats of the class of '64:

> [Robert] Kennedy's daily chums were the three freshmen with whom he shared a new fifth row, installed in the back of the chamber to accommodate Democratic gains in the Goldwater election—Walter Mondale of Minnesota, Fred Harris of Oklahoma, Joseph Tydings of Maryland. Young, liberal and irreverent, the four vastly entertained themselves by sotto voce comments on the scene before them.[11]

Despite the periodic emergence of a cohesive class group, there is nothing in the Senate as powerful as the House class phenomenon.

> The House freshmen in the 94th Congress (1975–1976) organized early and cohesively and were instrumental in many of the 1975 reforms. Some observers maintain that this class has been dysfunctionally cohesive and never fully assimilated. Although class communication lessens as members develop other ties and commitments, ease of communication among class members continues to be important.[12]

There was a strong feeling among the former House members who "graduated" to the Senate that the conditions for developing

---

[10] See John Elliott, "Communications and Small Groups in Congress: The Case of Republicans in the House of Representatives," unpublished docoral dissertation, The Johns Hopkins University, 1974.

[11] Arthur M. Schlesinger, Jr., *Robert Kennedy and His Times* (Boston: Houghton Mifflin Co., 1978), p. 681.

[12] Harrison W. Fox, Jr., and Susan Webb Hammond, op. cit., p. 109.

personal friendship were more favorable in the House than in the Senate. Individual House members are cast less in the mold of the celebrity, partly because there are more of them; it is more difficult, after all, to stand out and be recognized in a body of 435 than in one of 100 members. There are more informal groups there which have political as well as personal value. An individual congressman can magnify his voice through such a sociopolitical group; a solitary Senator speaks with the resonance of an Aeolian harp. Committees in the House more nearly resemble cohesive work-groups; senators' committees, where responsibilities are more segmented, resemble drop-in centers. Individualism and competitiveness in the Senate are carried to an extreme rarely reached in the House. Despite the brevity of their terms, congressmen are in some ways more secure than senators; the low turnover rate among congressmen and their inheritance of the mantle of political "boss" in their districts contrast with the recent relatively high turnover rate among senators and the fact that their high-prestige jobs are coveted so enviously and invite challenge so frequently. The latter phenomena accentuate in senators a selfishness born of self-preservation.

One very simple explanation for the apparently greater ease with which personal ties are forged among House members may lie in the simple fact that House members are generally younger than senators and arrive in the House at a younger age. This is not only the product of the minimum age requirements of the Constitution—twenty-five for congressmen and thirty for senators—but what Joseph A. Schlesinger refers to as "the politician's life-cycle," which holds that the best period of opportunity for the prospective congressman is between thirty-five and fifty and for senators between forty-five and sixty.[13]

The decline of the political party and the rise of individualized campaigning now permits the younger individual who has not undergone an exhaustive period of party tutelage to gain a seat in Congress. In fact, the average age of the newly arrived Congressman is down to forty years from forty-four years of age a decade ago;

[13] Joseph A. Schlesinger, *Ambition and Politics* (Chicago: Rand McNally Co., 1966).

freshman senators in the 96th Congress averaged slightly over forty-four years of age.[14] While there is no firm evidence to suggest that intimate friendships develop more readily among younger people than their elders,

> diffidence, the emotional cost of potential rebuff, or fear of failure in establishing friendships may all operate to inhibit the making of new friendships and favor the retention of those no longer representing trials of self. It would seem that these potential costs of new friendships would rise with age, since with each year an individual has that much more added to his own idea of who and what he is, to his "presenting self."[15]

Among the older senators, especially, there was the feeling that

> the more mature you get the fewer close friendships you develop, especially, for example, if you have a happy marriage. This takes the place of most kinds of close associations that develop at a younger age—you know, great pals or buddies, an undying friendship.

> I don't know of any pair of senators who were buddy-buddy the way, for example, certain members of the House were when I was there.

Having concluded this study of interpersonal relationships in the U.S. Senate with a brief comparative excursion into the House, it is apropos to pause and consider the question, how different are senators from ordinary Americans in their capacity for forming close personal friendships? Is the Senate, or indeed the entirety of political life, so anomalous in the relatively scant evidence of deep personal ties it offers? Is what is deficient in the elite abundant in the mass? Is one of the costs incurred in taking up a political life the forfeiture of the warmth and intimacy that only those in private life can enjoy? With

[14] Alan Ehrenhalt, "Congress Is Getting Younger All the Time," *Congressional Quarterly Weekly Report*, vol. 37, no. 4 (January 27, 1979), p. 154.

[15] Beth Hess, "Friendship," in Matilda White Riley, Marilyn Johnson, and Anne Foner, *Aging and Society*, 3 vols. (New York: Russell Sage Foundation, 1972), vol. 3, p. 379.

the entry into the world of conflicting interests, the battleground of partisanship and ideologies, is the field necessarily abandoned to self-interest, with true affection the privilege only of those far from the scene of the battle?

In one of the most widely respected recent books on the subject of man's passage through the stages of his life, *The Seasons of a Man's Life*, there occurs a brief passage on the subject of friendship.

> In our interviews, friendship was largely noticeable by its absence. As a tentative generalization we would say that close friendship with a man or a women is rarely experienced by American men. This is not something that can be adequately determined by a questionnaire or a mass survey. The distinction between friend and acquaintance is often blurred. A man may have a wide social network in which he has amicable, "friendly" relationships with many men and perhaps a few women. In general, however, most men do not have an intimate male friend of the kind that they recall fondly from boyhood or youth. . . . We need to understand why friendship is so rare, and what consequences this deprivation has for adult life.[16]

A more popular study of the life of the adult American male reports much the same conclusion.

> As adult males in our culture the phenomenon of being without even a single buddy or good friend is a common one—so widespread in fact, that it is not seen as unusual nor is it even spoken about. Rather, it is taken for granted. Many men I interviewed admitted to not having one intimate male friend whom they totally trusted and confided in. However, most of them seemed to accept this as being a normal and acceptable condition.[17]

---

[16] Daniel J. Levinson, with Charlotte N. Darrow, Edward B. Klein, Maria H. Levinson and Braxton McKee, *The Seasons of a Man's Life* (New York: Alfred A. Knopf, 1978), p. 335.

[17] Herb Goldberg, *The Hazards of Being Male* (New York: New American Library/Signet Books, 1977), p. 127.

Lamentations about the absence of close personal friendships among Americans have become commonplace. The argument that our lives are enriched by intimacy with others and that the failure or inability to develop intimate ties constitutes a pathology is heard extensively. From a popular commentator we hear,

> Our relations [with friends and neighbors] must be so trusting that we can express our feelings to them freely and without self-consciousness. And they must be people to whom we have "ready access." If we are in Indiana, they can't be down in Texas. . . Such relationships serve the vital function of providing us with our need for "*intimacy* for want of a better term." Without such intimate relationships we experience a sense of "emotional isolation" better known to us as loneliness."[18]

From an academician and clinician we hear,

> America is populated with millions of people who seek always to *seem* in a certain expedient way, and who experience all of their being that departs from the image as dreadful. As they conceal their truth from others, they succeed in concealing it from themselves. The toll of physical breakdown from stress and dispiritation, and the frequency of the so-called nervous breakdown is to me evidence that such an "all-American" way is unlivable, or it is not worth the price.[19]

Intimacy and self-revelation are seen as necessary ingredients in counteracting the maladies which accompany the dislocations, mobility, and superficiality of life in modern society. We need to have others close to us, to whom we can pour out our aspirations and apprehensions, in order to make life livable. The statement and restatement of the dreary etiology of the transience and imperma-

---

[18] Vance Packard, *A Nation of Strangers* (New York: David McKay Co., 1972), p. 207. Packard takes the terms "intimacy" and "emotional isolation" from a report prepared by Robert S. Weiss and associates of the Harvard University Medical School's Department of Psychiatry based on studies of individuals who have been uprooted by divorce, retirement, or relocation for business reasons.

[19] Sidney M. Jourard, *Self-Disclosure: An Experimental Analysis of the Transparent Self* (New York: Wiley-Interscience, 1971), p. 183.

nence in modern interpersonal relationships giving rise to feelings of detachment and alienation and yielding up in the aggregate a breakdown in the sense of community have summoned in reaction an articulate expression of the opposing point of view, which holds that intimacy can be suffocating and oppressive and that people have the right not to be saddled with the personal problems of others.

> To speak of incivility is to speak of reversed terms. It is burdening others with oneself; it is the decrease in sociability with others this burden of personality creates. We can all easily call to mind individuals who are uncivilized on these terms: they are those "friends" who need others to enter into the daily traumas of their own lives, who evince little interest in others save as ears into which confessions are poured. . . .

> Intimacy is a field of vision and an expectation of human relations. It is the localizing of human experience, so that what is close to the immediate circumstances of life is paramount. The more this localizing rules, the more people seek out or put pressure on each other to strip away the barriers of custom, manners, and gesture which stand in the way of frankness and mutual openness. The expectation is that when relations are close, they are warm; it is an intense kind of sociability which people seek out in attempting to remove the barriers to intimate contact, but this expectation is defeated by the act. The closer people come, the less sociable, the more painful, the more fratricidal their relations.[20]

Political life, with its cordial superficiality, may offer a refuge from what Richard Sennett calls, the "tyranny of intimacy." One Washington journalist has even postulated what she calls an "escape hatch" theory of political careers as a sanctuary from deep emotional involvement, especially from one's family.[21] This flight from intimacy brings people into a world in which love is wholesaled, not

---

[20] Richard Sennett, *The Fall of Public Man* (New York: Random House/Vintage Books, 1978), pp. 265, 338.

[21] Myra MacPherson, *The Power Lovers* (New York: G. P. Putnam's Sons, 1975), p. 24.

retailed, and where adoration is expressed by the multitudes but rarely by individuals, or if expressed by individuals it need imply no deep emotional attachments.

One can only speculate whether there is something intrinsic to political life that precludes intimacy or whether that deficiency—which seems to be a characteristic of public careers—is a product of the combined force of so many individuals seeking surrogate relationships which make no emotional demand on them. But that a person can hold himself aloof from intimate attachments with colleagues and perform effectively, even admirably, seems inescapably true, especially in the U.S. Senate. From a normative point of view, can this be said to be an undesirable state of affairs? Is the Senate as an institution weakened by this insufficiency of close friendships among its members?

From a political and institutional perspective, it seems a good thing. It is the job of senators to be spokesmen for their states' interests and to give voice to, and action on, other national concerns. The Senate is not an extended family or an affinity group, nor should it be. A Senate based upon friendship cliques would be an oppressive and suffocating institution which would induce the most stifling forms of conformity. Cohesion based on personal attachment and carried to an extreme would cause every issue to be decided on the basis of like and dislike, every vote to turn on personality and ego and every outcome on favoritism or aversion.

From the point of view of the individual senator, the effect would be equally disastrous. A senator hoping to cultivate a following with a national interest group would have little hope for their support if he failed to protect their interests out of consideration for a treasured friend. Constituents would be justly enraged by their senator's failing to pursue a course of action beneficial to them out of fear of alienating a comrade in the chamber. The obligations which attach to the function of representation would be wholly at odds with a Senate in which an individual member was forced to pass muster with colleagues judging him by his endearing qualities or his aptitude for being "one of the boys."

What can realistically be asked of senators by way of friendship with their colleagues is trust, integrity, hard work, and a decent tolerance for those with whom one differs. This is what friendship means, instinctively, to most senators. It is a standard of friendship that could well be emulated by people in other walks of life.

This form of friendship, which has been referred to here as institutional kinship, is more than simply a good business relationship or a "political friendship." It is a more complicated form of human association, which for many senators comes to define the meaning of their experiences in the Senate. Rather than pointing to a single legislative accomplishment, a particularly hard-fought and dearly won battle, or an interest staunchly defended, senators often look back on their careers and evaluate them in terms of this kind of friendship.

Shortly before the 96th Congress convened in January 1979, CBS congressional correspondent Phil Jones visited one of the senators for whom the 95th Congress was the last. For the first time in forty years, Mississippi Democrat James O. Eastland was not taking the congressional oath. Eastland had always been perceived with a curious dualism by political liberals, depending upon whether they were inside or outside the Senate: For outsiders, he was the dogged and inflexible opponent of social progress who only in recent years had come to terms with the inevitability of change—implacable at worst, paternalistic at best. However, the James Eastland seen by his liberal colleagues was a man who, despite his energetic and tenacious efforts to thwart progressive measures, exemplified in his relations with them the best traits of even-handedness, considerateness, and fair play.

In their interview, Jones asked Eastland to look back on his thirty-six years in the Senate and recall his fondest memories. It was not filibusters or voting rights bills bottled up in his Judiciary Committee that the senator mentioned; nor was it the memory of legislative triumphs, of deft parliamentary maneuvers unhorsing liberal antagonists. Eastland paused after Jones's question and lighted his cigar: "Friendship," he said. "I like to be with my friends."

INDEX